POLITICS
IN THE
STREETS

The origins of the civil rights movement
in Northern Ireland

Bob Purdie

THE
BLACKSTAFF
PRESS

BELFAST

First published in 1990 by
The Blackstaff Press Limited
3 Galway Park, Dundonald, Belfast BT16 0AN, Northern Ireland

This book has received financial assistance under the
Cultural Traditions Programme which aims to encourage acceptance and
understanding of cultural diversity.

Printed by The Guernsey Press Company Limited

British Library Cataloguing in Publication Data

Purdie, Bob
Politics in the streets : the origins of the civil rights movement
in Northern Ireland.
1. Northern Ireland. Civil rights movements, history
1. Title
323.09416
ISBN 0–85640–437–3

Bob Purdie was born in Edinburgh in 1940. He graduated from the University of Warwick with a BA in history in 1979; he was awarded an M.Sc. in politics in 1980 and a Ph.D. in 1989 by the University of Strathclyde. He spent over seven years in Belfast, researching and lecturing in politics. At various times he has also worked as an engineering worker, a political organiser and a journalist. He is now a politics tutor at Ruskin College, Oxford. His previous publications include *Ireland: Divided Nation, Divided Class* (1980), joint editor with Austen Morgan, and numerous articles for Scottish and Irish political and historical journals.

ACKNOWLEDGEMENTS

Material in the Public Record Office of Northern Ireland is reproduced by permission of the Deputy Keeper of the Records. Permission to use material from particular PRONI collections is also acknowledged: Professor Kevin Boyle for permission to quote from the Kevin Boyle Papers; Patrick Byrne Esq. for permission to quote from the CDU Papers; F.J. Gogarty Esq. for permission to quote from the Gogarty Papers; Dr Conn and Mrs Patricia McCluskey for permission to quote from the CSJ Papers; and Mrs Janet McElroy for permission to quote from the McElroy Papers.

Grateful acknowledgement is also made to: M. Allen and Emerald Music for permission to quote from 'Gerry's Walls' by James Young; Blackstaff Press Limited and the estate of John Hewitt for permission to quote from 'The coasters' (*The Selected John Hewitt*, 1981); and Thomas Kinsella for permission to quote from 'Butcher's Dozen: a lesson for the octave of Widgery' (Pepper-canister 1, Dolmen Press, 1972).

*in memory of
my mother and father*

CONTENTS

FOREWORD

Bob Purdie's account of the origins of the civil rights movement in Northern Ireland is warmly welcomed by those of us who knew about his researches and were looking forward to seeing his analysis of that crucial period. Bob may speak with an Edinburgh accent, but we count him as one of us. He has been able to get closer to the events and the personalities involved than many earlier writers, who in some cases obscured the real truth of the civil rights movement. The story needed to be told; Bob was the right person to tell it, and he has done a fine job.

At the outset the movement was supported by every shade of political colour, including some individual members of the Unionist Party. In the end the campaign was hijacked by the gunmen who created a new and even greater need for basic civil rights in Northern Ireland. Bob investigates the background and the various components that made civil rights such an issue in Northern Ireland. Sensitive to the misconduct of the Unionist government and incisive in his interpretation of each incident, he analyses the movement's failure to achieve adequate reform. The tragedy is that it was almost our last hope for change by the ballot box. This depended on parliamentary responses in the debating chamber at Stormont: street politics should have been complementary to a parliamentary interface.

But that was not to be, and *Politics in the Streets* explains why. However late this story is, there are still lessons to be learned. Bob has helped us to understand our problems better.

PADDY DEVLIN
BELFAST
1990

LIST OF ABBREVIATIONS

AOH	Ancient Order of Hibernians
APL	Anti-Partition League
AUEWTASS	Amalgamated Union of Engineering Workers
	Technical and Administrative Staffs Section
BBC	British Broadcasting Corporation
CDU	Campaign for Democracy in Ulster
CPNI	Communist Party of Northern Ireland
CSJ	Campaign for Social Justice in Northern Ireland
DCAC	Derry Citizens' Action Committee
DHAC	Derry Housing Action Committee
DUAC	Derry Unemployed Action Committee
DUP	Democratic Unionist Party
EEC	European Economic Community
GAA	Gaelic Athletic Association
HCL	Homeless Citizens' League
ICTU	Irish Congress of Trade Unions
IRA	Irish Republican Army
ITGWU	Irish Transport and General Workers' Union
IWG	Irish Workers' Group
MP	Member of Parliament
NCCL	National Council for Civil Liberties
NDP	National Democratic Party
NICCL	Northern Ireland Council for Civil Liberties
NICRA	Northern Ireland Civil Rights Association
NIHT	Northern Ireland Housing Trust
NILP	Northern Ireland Labour Party
PD	People's Democracy
QUB	Queen's University Belfast
RLP	Republican Labour Party
RSSF	Revolutionary Socialist Students' Federation
RUC	Royal Ulster Constabulary
SDLP	Social Democratic and Labour Party
SRC	Student Representative Council

TD	Teachta Dála (member of the Dáil)
UVF	Ulster Volunteer Force
YSA	Young Socialist Alliance

INTRODUCTION

'The Proper Place for Politics is in the Streets'
Slogan carried in Derry on 5 October 1968

Northern Ireland became world famous during the 1970s as a battle front. For most commentators, the events preceding the outbreak of the Provisional Irish Republican Army's military campaign in 1970 have been relevant mainly as an explanation for the violence of the last two decades. The civil rights movement, therefore, has been seen as a prelude to the violence. But during most of its history Northern Ireland was at peace; even now, for most of the time, the vast majority of Northern Ireland people live together in amity and with a warmth of neighbourliness not to be found in many other places. Northern Ireland is gripped by an unresolved conflict which has its origins further back in history than the creation of the state; but it is wrong to ignore everything in that history except the conflict. The civil rights movement marked the transition from a period of peace to a renewal of the conflict and it has to be seen in the light of the events of the 1970s and 1980s. But it also has to be seen as a consequence of the 1960s and as a product of events that took place during a time of rapid, but peaceful, change. To revisit Northern Ireland in the 1960s is to enter a lost world in which most of the political landmarks are different and different assumptions and aspirations underpin politics. In the 1990s we can see why the society was liable to be torn apart in the 1970s, but the 1960s lacked that foreknowledge and peace seemed secure enough for new departures and new experiments. The civil rights movement was one of these new departures.

The movement began as a new way of conceptualising an old problem. Complaints about discrimination against Catholics in Northern Ireland were older than the state itself; they deserve to be assessed in their own right, but it has to be noted that they were always closely linked to nationalist politics and arose in part from perceptions that were deeply rooted in nationalist ideology. Until

1

the 1960s nationalism supplied the grammar with which to discuss possible solutions. Before 1918 the favoured solution was Home Rule; after World War I a minority of northern nationalists went along with the majority of southerners in supporting an independent republic. After 1921 hopes were pinned on a revision of the border which would eventually make the northern state unviable and immediately deliver large numbers of nationalists from Belfast rule. During the 1930s and 1940s, and reaching a crescendo in the 1950s, the demand was for the British government to transfer the six counties of Northern Ireland to the jurisdiction of the Dublin government. Attempts to pursue this objective through diplomatic and political channels failed, giving rise to the 1956–62 Irish Republican Army's border campaign, and when this failed it opened the way for a fresh approach.

The new strategy was inspired by the Black civil rights movement in the United States. The term 'civil rights' had not been used to define the aspirations of the minority community in Northern Ireland before the 1960s and it had never before adopted a strategy that was both militant and constitutional. Either it had focused narrowly on electoral activity and parliamentary pressure or it had rejected constitutional politics altogether. Both approaches proved equally unproductive. The Black civil rights movement militantly expressed the passion of Southern Blacks and their demand for the rights their citizenship should have given them. At the same time their aspirations were moderate; they simply demanded that the United States apply the letter of its constitution. This idea of fighting for existing constitutional rights was a new one for Northern Ireland nationalists. They had often made the propaganda point that Catholics in Northern Ireland were denied equal rights as citizens of the United Kingdom, but this had never been more than a means of exposing the Unionists in front of British public opinion; the solution was still seen as a united Ireland. The civil rights movement was innovatory precisely because it *did* restrict itself to demanding legal and constitutional rights within the United Kingdom. Most, if not all, of the movement's supporters continued to aspire, ultimately, to Irish unity. Unionists pointed out the inconsistency in their position and questioned their sincerity; but the moral force of the movement came from its deliberate moderation.

But the civil rights strategy was not an easy one to pursue. The civil rights movements in the United States and in Northern Ireland both utilised the tensions produced by the threat that violence might rise from their activities, either because they had lost control of some of their supporters or because they had provoked their opponents. For such tactics to achieve success the state must respond by using inappropriate force while the movement exercises restraint, thus augmenting support for the movement and increasing pressure for the state to make concessions. If the state responds with further inappropriate force, the spiral will be given another twist. But if generalised violence breaks out, the tension is released. The key to success is for the movement to exercise effective control of its own supporters, but this is a very difficult strategy to pursue, especially for a largely spontaneous and amorphous movement. The best way to combine tactical freedom for the leadership with trust on the part of the followers is through charismatic leadership, such as that exercised by the Reverend Martin Luther King, Jr, but the Northern Ireland civil rights movement had no leaders with this degree of moral authority.

The Northern Ireland civil rights movement was already on its way to failure at the moment of its greatest success. The baton charge by the Royal Ulster Constabulary in Derry on 5 October 1968 helped to create a mass movement, but it was united more by anger than by strategic and tactical agreement. At first everyone agreed on peaceful, non-violent protest, but for some it was a matter of principle, for others a temporary tactic. When the Northern Ireland government offered some concessions towards the end of 1968, the unanimity broke down. The movement, inexorably, became involved in communal tensions and more and more of its time was spent trying to damp down sectarian outbreaks as the old fracture lines between Catholics and Protestants began to reappear and as the mobilisation of one community evoked a hostile response from the other.

The resulting violence led to the intervention of British troops in August 1969. During the next year the emergent Provisional Irish Republican Army began to shift the focus, for many of the civil rights movement's supporters, from a campaign against discrimination by the Unionist government at Stormont to a war against

3

the British Army and the Westminster government. When members of the Parachute Regiment opened fire on demonstrators in Derry on 30 January 1972, they became the execution squad for the civil rights movement. The subsequent mass demonstration in Newry to commemorate the thirteen victims was both the last great civil rights march and the movement's funeral procession. The Derry march had been one of a number called by the Northern Ireland Civil Rights Association in an attempt to reassert the place of peaceful protest in the fight against internment, as an alternative to the tactics of the Provisional Irish Republican Army. The deaths in Derry led the Northern Ireland Civil Rights Association to abandon street protests once and for all.

What happened after 5 October 1968 was not a chapter of accidents – it is readily explained by the effects of protest activity on Northern Ireland's divided society. The mobilisation of large numbers of Catholics in street demonstrations opened up a fault line that had always been there. What has to be explained is not the consequences of the events in Derry on 5 October 1968, but how the demonstrators came to be there in the first place.

Accounts of the civil rights movement which begin with 5 October 1968 or later dates are inadequate. After that date we are dealing with a movement that was slithering rapidly to the crisis of August 1969, and by the time members of this non-violent movement were priming petrol bombs in Derry or slipping over the border for arms training, it had become far too late to understand what brought them to such a pass. In October 1968 and August 1969 they were responding not just to single events but to a series of experiences which had profoundly altered their attitude to society in Northern Ireland and to political activity. Those experiences have to be traced through in more detail than has yet been done in order to understand what brought them to Duke Street in Derry on 5 October 1968.

The history of a movement is more difficult to chronicle than that of a political party. A party is an institution with a continuous life and a bureaucratic structure; its history can be written from the documents preserved by its officials and from the public record of its actions. The history of a movement is never filed away so tidily; it has to be followed through a patchwork of events, most of which only become significant in the light of later developments. It

4

is recorded in the scattered evidence left behind by the groups and individuals who met it at some point and who helped to transform it and were transformed by it. This book draws on newspapers and documents of the time, as well as contemporary literature and reminiscences published later. It is not an oral history, but each chapter was submitted to at least one person who had been involved in the events described. Their comments helped to fill in gaps and to give the analysis greater depth. Responsibility for the finished work, however, is mine alone.

The structure of the book is not chronological. Each chapter focuses on a different aspect of the civil rights movement and follows the time sequence which seemed most appropriate for explaining that aspect, but because of the way in which the main components of the civil rights movement emerged, there is a broad chronological sequence throughout the work.

The first two chapters set out the political background to the emergence of the civil rights movement. Chapter 1 discusses the O'Neill years, showing how the modernising face of Northern Ireland in the early and mid-1960s concealed a society still profoundly divided over sectarian issues. Chapter 2 looks at the various parties and groups offering an alternative to unionism and shows how significant it was that the 1965 Stormont general election closed the door on the option of a change of government through the ballot box. The remaining chapters examine different strands of the civil rights movement, tracing them back to their origins and analysing their contributions to political events. Chapter 3 looks at the Dungannon-based Campaign for Social Justice in Northern Ireland and the London-based Campaign for Democracy in Ulster. Chapter 4 deals with the most important civil rights organisation, the Northern Ireland Civil Rights Association. Chapter 5 is concerned with the city of Derry and its various action committees, ranging from the moderate and respectable University for Derry Action Committee and the Derry Citizens' Action Committee, to the radical Derry Unemployed Action Committee and the Derry Housing Action Committee. Chapter 6 examines the Queen's University-based People's Democracy and its background in student protest and left-wing Marxism in the early and mid-1960s. The Conclusion ties the threads together and discusses the significance of contemporary government initiatives to eliminate religious discrimination in Northern Ireland.

This book is based on my Ph.D. thesis, which was submitted to the University of Strathclyde in September 1988, and much of the research was supported by the Social Sciences Research Council. I am grateful to my supervisor, Professor Richard Rose, for his advice, support and encouragement during the research and writing of the thesis.

I am grateful to Anthony Barnett, Michael Farrell, Conor Gilligan, Brian Gregory, Fred Heatley and Eamonn McCann, who gave valuable interviews. Fred Heatley also made useful comments and provided additional information during the drafting of the thesis. Others who supplied information, made comments or gave me permission to consult papers were: Cecil Allen, Jack Barkley, Kevin Boyle, Paddy Byrne, Anthony Coughlan, Terry Cradden, Madge Davison, Paddy Devlin, Andrew Finlay, Mrs Frank Gogarty, Ann Hope, Gery Lawless, Rayner Lysaght, Conn McCluskey, Patricia McCluskey, Mrs Albert McElroy, Kevin McNamara, Austen Morgan, Ken Pringle, Briad Rowan, Peter Rowan, Edwina Stewart and James Stewart.

I am indebted to the staffs of the following libraries and institutions: the Andersonian Library, University of Strathclyde, Glasgow; the Archives Department, Library, University College Dublin; Belfast Central Library; the Bodleian Library,Oxford; the British Library of Political and Economic Science, London; the Library, Nuffield College, Oxford; the Library, Ruskin College, Oxford; the Library, University of Ulster, Magee College, Derry; the Library, University of Ulster at Jordanstown; the Linen Hall Library, Belfast; the Main Library, Queen's University Belfast; the Mitchell Library, Glasgow; the National Library of Ireland, Dublin; the National Library of Scotland, Edinburgh; and the Director of the Public Record Office of Northern Ireland, Belfast.

I am grateful for opportunities to test out and clarify the ideas in the book at fora provided by: the Institute of Irish Studies, Queen's University Belfast; the Irish Labour History Group, Ruskin College, Oxford; the Irish Labour History Society; the Irish Political Studies Association; the Lipman Seminars on

Ireland; the Politics Society, Queen's University Belfast; and the Workers' Educational Association.

Jackie Cameron, tutorial secretary at Ruskin College, Oxford, typed the original manuscript; other typing was done by June Riddle, Nicola Purdie and Maureen Purdie.

BOB PURDIE

OXFORD

1990

I

THE O'NEILL YEARS
1962–1968

You coasted along.
And all the time, though you never noticed,
the old lies festered;
the ignorant became more thoroughly infected;
there were gains, of course;
you never saw any go barefoot.

The government permanent, sustained
by the regular plebiscites of loyalty . . .
Faces changed on the posters, names too, often,
but the same families, the same class of people.
A Minister once called you by your first name.
You coasted along
and the sores suppurated and spread.

Now the fever is high and raging;
who would have guessed it, coasting along?
The ignorant-sick thresh about in delirium
and tear at the scabs with dirty finger-nails.
The cloud of infection hangs over the city,
a quick change of wind and it
might spill over the leafy suburbs.
You coasted too long.

from 'The coasters' by John Hewitt

The period from 1962 to 1968 saw the last year of Lord Brooke-borough's premiership of Northern Ireland and his succession by Captain Terence O'Neill. Under the new leadership it was widely believed that decisive changes were taking place and that Northern Ireland was being 'modernised'. By this term, technocratic politicians, media commentators and middle-class intellectuals meant that, in their opinion, Northern Ireland was ceasing to be obsessed by sectarian symbols and was beginning to share the pre-occupations of the rest of the Western world with economic growth and consumer satisfaction. Challenges to this outlook, especially those which were motivated by sectarian suspicions and old political antagonisms, were seen as a final atavistic spasm. This was an illusion which helped to weaken the O'Neill government, to disarm moderate opposition to it, and to prevent fundamental problems from being addressed. In 1964 and 1966 serious outbreaks of communal violence in Belfast warned that less had changed than surface appearances might indicate. But almost nobody was looking below the surface.

The Ulster Unionist Party went into the May 1962 Stormont general election still seeming supremely confident that it could keep its traditional base of support together. At the press conference to announce the date of the election, Brookeborough was asked if the party would make history by not presenting the border as an issue. In answer, Minister of Home Affairs Brian Faulkner pointed to a poster bearing the slogan 'this we will maintain'. When asked whether Catholics were free to join the Unionist Party, Brookeborough would give no definite answer, saying that it was a matter for local Unionist associations. In fact the election campaign proved to be much less concerned with sectarian issues than with economic ones and it resulted in a major increase in the vote for the Northern Ireland Labour Party (NILP), from a total of 37,000 in 1958 to 77,000. In Belfast, Labour emerged from the election as a major threat to the position of the Unionist Party; although it did not win more than its existing four out of sixteen seats, its overall vote and its majorities were substantially increased.

These unpleasant facts for unionism were put aside in September 1962 to celebrate the fiftieth anniversary of the Ulster Covenant of 1912, the major landmark in the history of Ulster Unionist resistance to Home Rule for Ireland. The celebrations, however, were carried out in seeming unconsciousness of the fact that the 'Ulster people' would not be unanimous in welcoming them. Prime Minister Lord Brookeborough's message for Covenant Day stressed the unchanging nature of the Unionist heritage and its determination to remain part of the United Kingdom and the Commonwealth, and the commemoration blurred the lines between the Government, the parliament, the Unionist Party and the Orange Order. The event was organised by the Belfast County Grand

Orange Lodge, with helpers seconded from the Unionist Party. Among the speakers were Brookeborough, Sir Norman Stronge, the Speaker of the Northern Ireland House of Commons, and the lord mayor of Belfast. There was a protest by the British Labour Member of Parliament (MP) Marcus Lipton in the Westminster House of Commons at the presence of the banner of LOL 1688, 'Friends of Ulster', which showed the portcullis symbol of the House and bore the legend 'House of Commons Westminster'. [1]

Exactly a month after the red-white-and-blue bunting had been taken down, Brookeborough was at the dispatch box facing the unhappy task of presenting to parliament the Hall Report on the Northern Ireland economy. A series of lay-offs in shipbuilding and linen had emphasised the serious decline in Northern Ireland's traditional industries. Unemployment had gone up from 6.7 per cent in 1960 to 7.5 per cent in 1962, sparking off trade-union demonstrations and protests. The Government had promised that the Hall Report would provide a strategy for overcoming these problems, but the prime minister had to tell the House that the central plank of the Government's strategy had failed to win unanimous support from the Hall Committee and had been vetoed by the Westminster government. This was for a subsidy of 10 shillings (50 pence) per week for all employees in productive industry. The Westminster government's reponse, contained in a letter from Home Secretary Henry Brooke, was that such a subsidy would 'have the opposite effect to that intended by impeding the flow of labour from contracting industries to those which are growing'.

Vivian Simpson, NILP MP for Oldpark in Belfast, tore into the Government; the situation, he claimed, was 'a major economic problem, if not a crisis, for which the Hall Committee has failed to find adequate remedies' and for which the Stormont government had 'failed to find remedies which the Westminster Government could accept'. The proposed subsidy 'would have covered less than half the insured worker population' and was 'ill-conceived', since 'public funds would be paid out to efficient and inefficient alike'. The NILP's answer was the immediate creation of a Regional Economic Planning Unit, under the National Economic Development Council of the United Kingdom: 'The British Government have come to believe in national planning and we have the right to demand . . . similar measures suited to our own Province.' The major stumbling block to such a strategy, however, was the Government's attitude to the trade unions. Official recognition was withheld from the Northern Ireland Committee of the Irish Congress of Trade Unions (ICTU), because the congress had its headquarters in Dublin. The Government did recognise individual trade unions and the Confederation of Shipbuilding and Engineering Unions, which was separate from the ICTU; but the organisation that represented the overwhelming majority of Northern Ireland trade-unionists was excluded. Simpson put the issue squarely:

> Until the Government of Northern Ireland recognise and are willing to work with the official trade-union body, progress on productivity and long-term planning can only be limited in its effectiveness. This very afternoon the Prime Minister said that trade-union co-operation is vital. Can he not see the need to get reality into this idea of the recognition of the trade unions? How can the trade unions give of their best if the Government refuses to recognise them?

When heckled by Unionist MPs, Simpson challenged them to show that the Northern Ireland Committee of the ICTU had ever displayed 'one iota of disloyalty to this country' or that it was 'anything but ready to help in the development of the Northern Ireland economy'.[2]

The debate on the Hall Report showed clearly that the only coherent proposals which were being advanced for dealing with the economic situation involved planning and the enlistment of both sides of industry in developing the economy. But Unionist hostility to the ICTU was an obstacle to winning the support of the trade unions in Northern Ireland. There was a rumour in November 1962 that the Government was to reverse its position, but later that month Brookeborough announced that there would be no change until the Northern Ireland Committee separated itself from the ICTU. A Unionist MP, Edmond Warnock, rubbed salt in the wound by claiming that the ICTU was a 'Republican-loaded body' and that the Northern Ireland Committee was a 'daughter in its mother's house'.

Nothing illustrated better the unyielding nature of Brookeborough's last years and it was inevitable that his administration

d give way to something different. The Government was
er pressure from two different groups within the ranks of its
supporters: one which reflected the 'modernising' values
d at that point where the British political parties had most in
mon and which has been called 'Butskellism'; the other from
populist' wing of the party,[3] which was anxious to preserve its
with plebeian Protestantism and which combined sectarianism with demands for measures that would benefit the less
privileged. An example of the populist group was Desmond Boal,
the only Unionist MP to vote against the Government on the
unemployment issue. In 1971 he joined Ian Paisley in the Democratic Unionist Party (DUP). Some of the strongest criticism from a
modernising standpoint came from the ranks of the Young
Unionists. In February 1962 Bob Cooper, treasurer of the Young
Unionist Council, was critical of the Government, not so much
because of its economic policies, which he described as 'courageous' and 'successful', but because of the party's 'image':

> The man at the bench, the man at the office, the man in the
> University, have an image of a party which will brook no criticism
> from its members and a government of ageing tired men who cannot
> look forward with hope and who are forced to look back with
> nostalgia; who prefer to celebrate an event of fifty years ago [the
> Ulster Covenant] rather than to plan for the next fifty years.[4]

When O'Neill took over the premiership in March 1963 he set
about changing this image. After twenty years of Brookeborough,
he was a vigorous new broom; under his leadership the operations
of government were streamlined and modernised. The Northern
Ireland Committee of the ICTU was recognised and the trade unions
were incorporated into economic planning and industrial training,
but only after an attempt to involve individual unions, without the
Northern Ireland Committee, had failed. The Government set out
to attract new industries and outside investment to replace the
worn-out engineering and textile factories and the declining
shipbuilding industry. The landscape was strewn with new roads,
hospitals, office blocks, housing estates and factories. Much of the
groundwork for this was laid under his predecessor, and although
as finance minister for seven years O'Neill had made a major
contribution, the significance of his premiership was not so much

the physical results of this burst of activity as a style and rhetoric which made it appear as if Northern Ireland was in the rapids of change and that this change would bring improved material prosperity and communal reconciliation.

O'Neill was strong on gestures and bold statements. His meetings with Taoiseachs Sean Lemass and Jack Lynch have gone down in history, as has his attempt to bring President John F. Kennedy to the north, and his visit to a Catholic school which resulted in his being photographed in front of a crucifix and chatting amiably with nuns. There were smaller but equally significant gestures: he crossed the floor of Stormont to congratulate veteran Nationalist MP Cahir Healy on the eighty-seventh birthday of a man who had once been regarded as so dangerous that he was banned from visiting part of his own constituency; and he showed equal solicitude for Nationalist MP Patrick Gormley when he was injured in a car crash. O'Neill's vision was summed up in a speech in 1965: 'We want to build an opportunity state in which no man will be imprisoned by his environment and in which every citizen will have the chance to realise his full potential.'[5] He painted a roseate picture of a regenerated 'Ulster', with Craigavon, its new city with a population of one hundred thousand, contrasting with the 'haphazard development elsewhere in the Province'.[6] 'Our symbol,' he said, 'is the modern factory not the dole queue.'[7] This vision of progress was linked to his attempt to improve community relations. Pressure from the British treasury pronounced the doom of traditional industries and O'Neill knew how much Northern Ireland was dependent on subsidies from Westminster. Economic realities demanded that Northern Ireland move closer to the mainstream of policy, society and culture within the United Kingdom.

O'Neill's economic policies were already well established by the time he came to office; they had been tested by his department when he was minister of finance and, in any case, were derived from British experience. He believed firmly that Northern Ireland's economic future was tied to the relationship with Britain and that this more or less dictated the line to be taken on economic matters. The innovative aspect of O'Neill's premiership was his 'style', which consisted of making liberal and modernist statements and gestures, while using extreme caution in nudging his party towards changes in its traditional outlook. The immediate impact of this was an upsurge of hope for significant and rapid change in Northern Ireland. In March 1965 the authoritative current affairs periodical, the *Round Table,* hailed O'Neill for

> thinking even more internationally. This is to say that in building up a better impression of Northern Ireland, chiefly in the interests of its industrial development, he has been anxious to show the world that it is not skulking in the backwoods . . . It is in keeping with his conduct as Prime Minister that he should show a power of decision, an independence of the old restraints and an ambition to prove himself master of the Northern Irish situation.

Desmond Rea, a Methodist, an economist and a liberal Unionist, saw O'Neill's successes in the 1965 Stormont general election as proof of a fundamental shift in Northern Ireland politics, which were now

> about pragmatic and not about doctrinaire policies. Mr Sam Napier [secretary of the NILP] is said to have said that the Unionist Party stole his clothes and in a sense he is right . . . The Labour men . . . have prodded Ulster politics in a healthier direction . . . but . . . in a direction that Captain O'Neill was not only prepared to follow but . . . to lead . . . Captain O'Neill presented to the people an attractive Unionism, non-doctrinaire and pragmatically based . . . His appeal was – from reason to reasonable men – a welcome change in Northern Ireland politics.[8]

On the nationalist side in 1965 *New Ireland,* the magazine of the New Ireland Society of Queen's University Belfast (QUB), noted the enthusiasm with which the O'Neill–Lemass meeting had been greeted:

> Men and women of every political allegiance, of every denomination, and of all classes welcomed the meeting . . . and in their almost universal welcome revealed the fanatics for what they were – a divided and meaningless rabble of inconsequential men whose apparent power was founded only on the silence of the majority.

In the same magazine a year later, J. Conor Bradley summed up the progress that had been made:

> At elections North and South, the issue of participation was largely removed from political campaigning, and Britain and Ireland signed

a trade agreement which brought about a greater measure of integration between the two countries than has existed since pre-independence days. The Nationalist Parliamentary Party assumed the role of official opposition . . . and set about taking some faltering steps towards establishing itself as a serious political party. A general liberalisation of attitudes towards the Northern problem proceeded apace in the Republic, while all parties in Stormont echoed the feelings of the majority of people in welcoming the various exercises in cross-border co-operation . . . Despite the suspicions of a vocal minority of old-guard Unionists, practical results of the new policies are already beginning to be visible in the field of tourism, and 1966 should see many more achievements in other fields.

The point about the Irish Republic was important; changes taking place under the Lemass administration provided the counterpoint to what was happening in the north. As Robin Bailie, a liberal Unionist, put it:

The Republic having rejected the notion of a Sinn Fein economy and a Sinn Fein culture, now seems prepared to cast aside the last remnants of Sinn Fein Political Philosophy and take its place in the world, in co-operation with the rest of Western Europe.[9]

In September 1966 the *Round Table* saw a

wind of change . . . blowing across the [Southern] Irish scene. Old Feuds are dying out, old politicians are retiring, old resentments and loyalties are fading away. Younger leaders are taking over, and new issues taking shape . . . Poverty, not partition, is now the problem to be solved, prosperity, not separation from Britain, the goal to be won . . . age and changing circumstances have now at last caught up with the politicians and they must now face retirement or reality.

These responses demonstrated a series of assumptions: first, a belief in the primacy of economic factors; second, a conviction that there was a single, easily ascertainable set of policies that would achieve economic progress and that all 'sensible' people could recognise and agree upon what was necessary; and third, a linked assumption that politics was the art of efficient administration and that loyalist or republican ideologies were an outdated encumbrance. It was summed up in the very 'sixties' term used by Bob

Cooper in February 1962 about the 'image' of the Unionist Party, as if the essential reality of Northern Ireland society could be changed by altering the impression that unionism made on the senses. The liberals, modernisers and reformists had a clearly defined ideological position but they tended not to recognise it as such and underestimated the influence of ideology on the minds of others. They did not give enough weight to the fact that their own aspirations were based, as one young Catholic writer put it, on

> a deep anguish in the conviction of our present divisions and limitations and weariness of the resultant cacophony. A growing number of people want to see an end to closed circles that may not touch each other. They want to see instead mutual agreement and mutual integration. Realising that in the modern world it is disastrous not to be united, they believe in this we absolutely must succeed.[10]

Recognising the expectations of the reformers as aspirations, not realities, we can examine Northern Ireland society in the 1960s for evidence for and against their optimistic prognosis. One development that roused hopes of change was a series of discussions in 1962 between the leaders of the Ancient Order of Hibernians (AOH) and the Grand Orange Lodge of Ireland, known as the 'Orange–Green talks'. These arose from a proposal made at an AOH rally in Omagh, County Tyrone, on 24 August 1962, by Senator James G. Lennon, national vice-president of the AOH. Lennon spoke of the threat posed by 'international Communism directed from Moscow' and of the example given by Western European unity. Was it too much to hope for, he asked, that a way could be found to remove the 'bitterness and discrimination' which disgraced the public life of Northern Ireland?

There was an initial meeting between Lennon and Senator Sir George Clarke, Grand Master of the Orange Order, on 17 October 1962. On 12 December, Sir George announced that the Grand Lodge had set up a committee to discuss with Senator Lennon and his colleagues, but there was a catch – 'recognition of Ulster's constitutional position within the UK by the Nationalists would be our choice for first discussion'. Prospects of success were further diminished by a cool response from the Nationalist MPs and senators; they welcomed the talks but stressed that they were 'not on behalf of the Nationalist Party'. The two senators were damned with faint praise; while the Nationalists wished 'success to their efforts . . . the full value of such talks will best be judged by results'. In the event the difference over the issue of recognising the constitution proved unbridgeable and the talks petered out early in 1963, having made no progress.

A more important factor working for better community relations was the ecumenical movement. One indication of this was an editorial on 3 June 1963 in the strongly Unionist Belfast daily, the *News Letter*. Commenting on the impending death of Pope John XXIII, it said that he had 'appeared to elevate his high office' and spoke warmly of the pope's 'simplicity, sincerity and courage'. The death of the pontiff drew messages of sympathy from Prime Minister O'Neill, the Speaker at Stormont and the Northern Ireland government. In an unprecedented gesture, the flag over Belfast City Hall was lowered to half mast.

A survey of young people in the churches seemed to justify optimism. As David Bleakley, NILP MP for Victoria in Belfast and a leading Church of Ireland layman, put it:

> It is evident . . . that Young Ulster, growing up in a world very different from that of our forefathers, is inclined to be more tolerant than those who went before him. The young man who, when asked to name a great Christian, could say: 'Well I've been brought up a good Ulster Presbyterian, but I still think Pope John was a very good Christian', was speaking a language quite new to older ears, but by no means foreign to his contemporaries. His comment was matched in generosity by the young Roman Catholic who wanted to see '*All* branches of the Christian Church' growing in strength in these materialistic days.[11]

The Catholic Primate of England, Archbishop John Heenan, visiting Northern Ireland in August 1962 to lay the foundation stone of a new Cistercian monastery, spoke of the 'new and precious friendship between Protestants and Catholics' and regretted the 'almost geographical' division of Christians in Ireland. At his enthronement in September 1962, the Catholic Bishop of Down and Connor, Dr William Philbin, said: 'Many evidences are showing today that a new spirit of reasonableness is asserting itself.' Shortly afterwards Dr Philbin was welcomed to Belfast City Hall for an informal meeting with the lord mayor.

In January 1963 there was what the nationalist daily newspaper, the *Irish News*, described as 'a unique meeting in the history of the relations between the various churches in Northern Ireland'. The Catholic Bishop of Down and Connor, two Church of Ireland bishops and the Presbyterian Moderator dined together before attending a lecture at Queen's. In another lecture at QUB a Catholic priest spoke about 'the [Vatican] Council and Unity'. Religion and politics, he said, were inextricably mixed in Ireland, but now Catholics were learning that 'our Protestant neighbours are Christians too and that we have more in common than is apparent at first sight'. As a result of the Vatican Council, 'Catholics were coming to have a broader, saner outlook'. Presbyterians were also influenced by the council; at their 1966 General Assembly a former Moderator, the Reverend J. C. Breaky, referred to those who believed that 'Rome had never changed and never would'. He accepted that there had been no doctrinal change but he had no doubts that the attitude of the Catholic Church was changing. Fears and suspicions that the ecumenical movement might 'sell the pass [were] unworthy of the spiritual heirs of Calvin and Knox'.

In February 1964 the journal of the Irish Methodists urged its readers to take a stand against bigotry and in January 1965 the prominent Methodist clergyman, the Reverend Eric Gallagher of Belfast Central Mission, called for opposition to 'Protestant Fascism', which was threatening religious liberty. In June that year the Presbyterian General Assembly passed a resolution asking Catholics to forgive them for 'attitudes and actions . . . unworthy of our calling as followers of Jesus Christ'. They decided to investigate the problem of religious discrimination in Ireland and this was welcomed by the Church of Ireland magazine, the *Church of Ireland Gazette*. There were many joint services. In June the Moderator of the Ballymena and Coleraine presbytery expressed disappointment at the poor turnout for a Mass to mark Antrim Town's Civic Week. (The Ballymena Urban District Council had rescinded its decision to attend, after protests from the Reverend Kyle Paisley, Ian Paisley's father.) However, at a service attended by all sections of the Ballymena community, including Catholics, in St Patrick's Church of Ireland Church, Canon C. H. B. Craig said that 'one of the qualities of a good community was tolerance'. They had to respect other people and give them credit for being sincere in their opinions.

In pursuing ecumenism, leaders of the Protestant churches stood up to the Orange Order. In July 1966 the Presbyterian Church issued a statement refuting the charge, made in the Twelfth of July resolutions, that its 'advocacy of peace and good-will towards our Roman Catholic fellow-countrymen' represented a 'Romeward trend'. In February 1967 the Church of Ireland Bishop of Down and Dromore expressed 'disappointment' at the fact that the Belfast County Grand Orange Lodge had called for services to 'reaffirm their Protestant faith and determination'. He would assume personal responsibility for any of his clergymen who refused requests to hold such services. In September that year the *Church of Ireland Gazette* supported a Yorkshire-born curate who had brought the wrath of the Sandy Row district of the Orange Order down on his head by taking a party of boys to see a new Catholic church. The Church, it said, 'neither needs nor desires the gratuitous assistance of any organisations in ordering its affairs'. The demand that the curate apologise was 'so preposterous that there is a case for ignoring it completely'.

The political and religious leaders of the Catholic community were more optimistic about ecumenism than their Protestant counterparts. This was understandable since they had most to gain from a breaking down of religious barriers and because they were more united than the leaders of the majority. However, it should be stressed that groups in both communities were influenced by ecumenism and by its values of tolerance, reconciliation and rationality.

The hopes raised by ecumenism were not realised. Almost everywhere else, the movement led to closer relations between Christian denominations and to an erosion of old distrusts and hostilities, but in Northern Ireland significant minorities put up vigorous resistance. And just as the proponents of ecumenism saw a connection between increased religious tolerance and a breakdown of political barriers, many Protestants feared that what was on the agenda was what they interpreted as 'surrender'. Such fears were expressed by the Grand Master of the Independent Orange Order, W. J. McClure, quoted in the *Irish Weekly*, the *Irish News*'s weekend publication, of 21 July 1962: 'Rome is therefore unchanged and carries in her the same spirit of evil as in the days of her greater power to torment the saints. Others may compromise and shake hands with this Hellish institution, but we of the Independent Orange Order will never bow the knee.'

At the 1963 Presbyterian General Assembly, the Moderator's tribute to Pope John XXIII was challenged by a minister from County Cavan. He was rebuked for his 'churlishness' and the minutes containing the tribute were passed without dissent. However, following the assembly, six ministers, among them W. Martin Smyth, later to become Grand Master of the Orange Order and Unionist MP for South Belfast, sent a letter to the Belfast newspapers opposing any compromise with 'the Church of Rome'. They could not accept that the Catholic Church was Christian in the full New Testament sense nor as understood by the Reformers. 'The hand stretched out to us' from Rome, they claimed, was the 'hand of absorption' and to grasp it would mean dishonesty or compromise: 'There is a difference between being charitable and being gullible.' A less reputable form of anti-ecumenical pressure was experienced by the minister of Fisherwick Presbyterian Church in Belfast. He complained of 'persecution by the Protestant underworld' after he had invited a Catholic priest to speak to his church in June 1964. A similar incident occurred in January 1967 when the Church of England Bishop of Ripon, John Richard Humpidge-Moorman, was invited to speak in St Anne's Church of Ireland Cathedral in Belfast. The combined pressure of the Orange Order and one or two smaller Protestant groups, including Paisley's Free Presbyterian Church, resulted in the cancellation of the invitation to the bishop, whom they denounced as a 'Romaniser'. Unionist politicians were also subjected to pressure. Phelim O'Neill, Stormont MP for North Antrim, was expelled from the Orange Order for having attended a community week service in a Catholic church in Ballymoney in June 1966. Nat Minford, Stormont MP for Antrim, escaped the same fate when he explained to a meeting of the Antrim County Grand Lodge that he had attended a Catholic service only as part of the opening ceremony for a new school. In Larne, Jack McAuley, a former mayor, was less fortunate – he was expelled from his lodge in July 1967 for attending the wedding of a Catholic friend. Its members did not object to his attending the reception, but to the fact that he had gone to the wedding Mass as well.

The Orange Order's strong opposition to ecumenism seriously

undermined the official leaders of the Protestant churches. The order had many more opportunities for getting its message across to rank-and-file Protestants. The brochure brought out by the Belfast County Grand Lodge for the 1968 Twelfth of July demonstration, for example, claimed that those who advocated church unity

> would deny us our fathers' faith – gloriously battle-won at Derry, Aughrim, Enniskillen and the Boyne – in order to have one united church having the Pope at its head. [They] should cherish no malice or bitterness toward our Roman Catholic neighbour [but] in maintaining our Protestant position we cannot condone error and be true to God and to the faith of our fathers once delivered to the saints.

The leadership of the Orange Order was less openly hostile to the new direction taken by the Unionist Party under O'Neill. The Orange belief that Unionists should remain united, and a traditional deference to the office of prime minister, worked for a time in O'Neill's favour. But the ideology of Orangeism was strongly resistant to the message of tolerance and reconciliation that O'Neill's approach implied. Orangeism considered Catholicism to be a threat not only to Protestant religious principles but to their political liberties as well. Little, if any, distinction was made between fostering goodwill among church people and opening the gates to their political enemies.

In 1962 Protestants celebrated the Twelfth of July with their usual enthusiasm, but the *Irish News* claimed to have detected a change: 'It was not the same hysterical drum-beating flag waving political demonstration that we have been used to in the past, but had more of a carnival atmosphere on Continental lines, with the teenagers not waving so many Union Jacks but wearing sun-glasses and crazy-coloured hats.' Some Orange leaders supported such a change. In Ballymena, Dr Robert Simpson MP said that there was a growing feeling in mid-Antrim that the Twelfth should be regarded as a religious pageant rather than as a political rally. Over the border in Rossnowlagh, County Donegal, Brian McRoberts, the defeated Unionist candidate for South Armagh in the 1962 Stormont general election, commented on the presence of Cahir Healy. The veteran Nationalist MP was, he said, 'a man of integrity and charm'. As Father of the House at Stormont, he had the 'respect of all Orangemen'. The Grand Master, Senator Sir George Clarke, made a plea for a 'calmer political climate'. It was their duty as citizens to strive to 'ensure a better understanding of each other's problems'. While he commended the 'will and determination' of those who signed the Covenant, he wanted to see such qualities being used to enable the nations to 'live together in harmony and in peace, trading and assisting each other in great social undertakings and education'. In Castledawson, Major C. B. Clarke, Grand Master of the County Londonderry Grand Lodge, spoke out in favour of the Orange–Green talks and said that he was sure they would have the support of a majority on both sides.

Orange demonstrations, however, provided an opportunity for rank-and-file discontent to be expressed. In 1965 Sir George Clarke was heckled at the Field at Finaghy, near Belfast, by Orangemen shouting 'Lundy' and singing 'The Sash'. A Protestant Unionist councillor, wearing a collarette, distributed leaflets which denounced Sir George, O'Neill, the Church of Ireland Bishop of Connor and various other O'Neillite Unionists. The situation became extremely fraught and a fight broke out between two bowler-hatted Orangemen. In 1986, Brian Faulkner and Brian McConnell, Stormont government ministers, were heckled at Black Institution rallies, and in 1967, at the Twelfth rally in Coagh, County Tyrone, George Forrest, the Westminster Unionist MP for Mid-Ulster, was hauled off the platform and kicked unconscious. In June 1988, Norman Porter, president of the Evangelical Protestant Society, speaking at the opening of a new Orange hall in Dungiven, County Derry, said that the order still had 'some Phelim O'Neills in it and they would have to go'. The moderate wing of the Unionist Party, he warned, thought that it could do without the support of the Orange Order but it would need to 'think again and keep on thinking'. This turbulence caused the leaders of the Orange Order a great deal of concern. A leading officer was quoted in 1966 as fearing a 'civil war or a split'. He said this at a meeting of the central committee of the Grand Lodge of Ireland, which was called to discuss the wearing of Orange regalia on Paisleyite demonstrations. He claimed that a majority of Orangemen objected to this and to a Paisleyite demonstration being advertised as leaving from a west Belfast Orange hall.

In its 1968 Twelfth brochure the Belfast County Grand Lodge

ruminated on 'the image of Orangeism'. Most Orangemen were decent, neighbourly and industrious, but it had to be admitted that 'there have been things which the institution cannot recall with pride'. There was strength in numbers but 'the Institution has lost out because its very size has made the percentage of bad members larger and therefore more noticeable. It has sometimes been poor in discipline.' The contradictions of Orangeism in these years were exemplified by an incident at the Field at Magheragall, County Antrim, in 1964. After a resolution 'welcoming friendship with our Roman Catholic fellow-countrymen' had been passed, a Catholic ice-cream salesman was expelled by a hostile crowd.

Among opponents of unionism, the popular image of the Orange Order was of a powerful, secretive organisation that manipulated Unionist political leaders from behind the scenes. During the O'Neill years, however, the uncertainties and divisions of the movement were more important. All previous Unionist prime ministers had enjoyed the support of this mass popular organisation. It had given the party multiple links and contacts with its political base and had facilitated a two-way flow of information and influence. Its highly respectable leadership had sheltered Unionist leaders from extreme loyalist pressure and had ensured discipline in the ranks. But during the O'Neill years the order gave out contradictory signals and failed to prevent the growth of a strong, extreme, minority loyalist opposition.

The indecisiveness of the Orange Order contrasted with the vigorous, unshakeable leadership given to his followers by Ian Paisley. The emergence of the ecumenical movement, combined with O'Neill's premiership, transformed him from a leader of fundamentalist Protestantism into a politician. He responded quickly to the Orange–Green talks; his Ulster Protestant Action issued a manifesto on 17 October 1962 denouncing them as 'a complete betrayal of Orangeism'. This was one of his earliest challenges to the established leaders of Orangeism and unionism. Paisley's roots were in Ulster's long tradition of turbulent street preachers. During the O'Neill years he was still very much part of that tradition and was as prominent in protests over religious issues as over politics. In October 1962 he received widespread publicity for his trip to Rome to demonstrate against the attendance of Protestant church leaders at the Vatican Council. In June 1963 he led a demonstration to Belfast City Hall to protest at the tributes being paid to Pope John XXIII. This event showed how skilfully he could use the techniques he had learned as a street preacher for political purposes. The demonstration was technically illegal, and upon being summonsed, he led another march to Musgrave Street police station. Further demonstrations took place at the hearing and the appeal. When he was saved from imprisonment because his £10 fine had been paid anonymously, he sent a telegram to O'Neill congratulating the Government for having paid it.

Unionist leaders saw Paisley as a nuisance. Minister of Commerce Brian Faulkner denounced him for 'rowdyism' after his demonstration outside the Presbyterian Assembly Buildings in Belfast in June 1966, at which the Governor of Northern Ireland, Lord Erskine, and Lady Erskine were subjected to abuse. William Stratton Mills, the Westminster MP for North Belfast, accused Paisley's followers of an anti-Semitic campaign against a Unionist candidate in a municipal by-election. A 'high source' was alleged to have warned members of the Paisleyite Ulster Constitution Defence Committee at QUB that it would be inadvisable to continue with their plans. Paisley called off a march to the governor's residence at Hillsborough, County Down, after the councils of Holywood, County Down, and Ballyclare, County Antrim, refused him the use of local halls. He was also refused the use of Lisburn Orange hall and the King's Hall at Balmoral in Belfast. On the other hand, after a bitterly fought battle in the Belfast City Council's Estates and Markets Committee, an attempt to bar him from the historic Ulster Hall was defeated, and the Minister of Home Affairs rejected demands to prohibit Paisley's outdoor meetings and demonstrations. Most Unionist leaders disliked the stench of violence that hung about Paisley. His protests had a habit of breaking into rowdyism, abuse and intimidation. There were constant rumours about his associations with shadowy organisations like the Ulster Volunteer Force (UVF). In June 1966, for example, Gerry Fitt, the Republican Labour Party (RLP) Stormont MP for Belfast, Dock, and Westminster MP for West Belfast, claimed that he had been approached in Stormont by two men who had been signed in by John McQuade, a Unionist MP who was sympathetic to Paisley. The men were from an unnamed Protestant 'action group', and they told him that MPs must realise that

Paisley 'must not be stopped' and that they were prepared to 'deal' with Lundys in the Unionist Party.

Various attempts have been made to establish a link between Paisley and the illegal UVF, and it seems that there was an overlap in membership between the UVF and Paisley's Ulster Protestant Volunteers. But no direct connection between Paisley and illegal paramilitary activities has been proven. Indeed the UVF members convicted of murder and conspiracy in 1966 had closer connections with the Unionist Party than with Paisley.[12] It ought also to be said that the aura of violence resulted as much from the opposition Paisley provoked as from the actions of his followers. In September 1967 his wife Eileen was subjected to abuse and missiles when she visited a development in a Catholic part of Belfast's Docks area. Only appeals by Gerry Fitt and an escort of RLP councillors got her out of the area safely. Some of the worst violence with which Paisley was associated was the rioting in Cromac Square in Belfast in June 1966. This broke out when he led a march from east Belfast to the city centre and chose a route that lay through the Catholic Markets area. The Royal Ulster Constabulary (RUC) succeeded in keeping the two sides apart, but there was extensive damage to property. The affair highlighted Paisley's talent for posing the authorities with a dilemma. There was a tacit understanding that Orange and loyalist processions were excluded from Cromac Square, but if they had re-routed Paisley's demonstration, they would have left themselves open to charges of capitulation to republicanism. In the event the authorities got the worst of both worlds: they were blamed for creating the circumstances in which the riot became possible, and as a result of his behaviour Paisley was prosecuted and was able to claim his martyr's crown.

Paisleyism gave leadership and direction to a section of the Protestant population whose antagonism to the Catholic Church and distrust of Catholics made it ready to respond to his message. There was a sectarian culture in Northern Ireland that helped to shape its view of the world, but which generally appeared in more aimless and violent forms. During the 1960s there was a constant trickle of court cases involving sectarian violence or provocation. In October 1962 the Belfast RUC was reported to be determined to stamp out sectarian disturbances following the prosecution of three supporters of Linfield Football Club, a team which has an exclusively Protestant following. The defendants were alleged to have been part of a group of youths which had tried to march through a Catholic street, singing sectarian songs. In November six Protestant youths were given prison sentences for assaulting a nineteen-year-old Catholic who had been visiting his Protestant girlfriend: 'Every night they have been "running me" because of my religion,' he said. Not all of these cases involved direct violence, and the most typical involved youths who were drunk, such as the group that was arrested for singing 'We will follow Linfield' while walking through Chapel Lane, Belfast, the site of a well-known Catholic church and grotto. Another example of the role of drink was the case of a thirty-year-old publican in Tandragee, County Armagh, who was convicted of an arson attack on a local Catholic church in January 1966. This incident reveals something of the arbitrariness of much of the violence. He had been drinking until the early hours of the morning and suddenly 'took a notion'. He ran over to the church, threw a mug of paraffin over the door and set it alight. Then he broke a window and pushed a paraffin-soaked, lighted shirt through it. He had also draped a Union flag over the church railings, and a passing milkman, who saw this, commented, 'That's a bad business.' The defendant replied, 'It will give them something to talk about.'

Other forms of communal antagonism flourished: homes, churches and halls were daubed with slogans; soccer fans clashed; Orange and nationalist bands provoked conflict, either by infringing on disputed territory or by evoking abuse from passers-by. Belfast Corporation had to discontinue band concerts in Falls Park in west Belfast because musicians were being abused for playing 'God Save the Queen'. However, many people disapproved of such behaviour: on two occasions local Falls residents, armed with hurley sticks, chased the hooligans away, just as a number of Protestants helped to clean up the statue of Saint Gabriel at the Holy Cross Catholic Church, Ardoyne, which had been daubed with red-white-and-blue paint and obscene slogans.

Another recurrent feature of the period was the communal tension which usually accompanied elections in Northern Ireland. In October 1964 the Nationalists demanded in Stormont that those responsible for 'rowdyism' at election meetings in Enniskillen, Dungannon, Coalisland and other places be prosecuted. Sam

Napier of the NILP compared the election campaign in west Belfast with Smethwick.[13] He claimed that a leaflet had been distributed which asked people if they wanted a Catholic for a neighbour. An NILP candidate complained that he and the republican candidate had been prevented from speaking by Unionist supporters after the announcement of the result in one Belfast constituency, and that his car had been attacked as he left the count.

During the Westminster general election of 1964 the Ulster Liberal Party contested Fermanagh and South Tyrone. Its candidate was harassed by Unionist supporters, but harassment was even more intense the following year when Albert McElroy, the Liberal president, contested Enniskillen during the Stormont general election. At a meeting in Derrygonnelly in November 1965, a crowd of fifty Unionist supporters surrounded the Liberals, preventing them from speaking. Stones, eggs and snowballs were thrown and the candidate and his election agent were assaulted. A few days later a similar incident occurred in Enniskillen; this time the RUC held back the crowd but the wires to the loudspeaker were cut and McElroy had to abandon the meeting. (These incidents showed the determination of Unionist supporters to prevent any challenge to their party from another Protestant; they reacted more strongly to McElroy, a Protestant clergyman, than to the Liberal candidate the previous year. By Fermanagh standards, that candidate had been alien and exotic. He was a Dublin-born Catholic called Giles Eden Fitzherbert, educated at Ampleforth College, Christ Church, Oxford, and the Harvard Business School. His wife was a daughter of the novelist Evelyn Waugh.) A crowd of youths sang the Irish national anthem and a republican song, 'Kevin Barry', outside the courthouse in Derry during an election count in 1965 and had to be restrained from attacking a Unionist procession. In 1967, Gerry Fitt was surrounded by Paisley supporters when he lodged his nomination papers for a municipal election. A Union flag was draped over his shoulders and on leaving, he was again surrounded and hit over the head. In 1968 the Independent and Liberal candidates were heckled after the count at a by-election in Lisnaskea, County Fermanagh.

One of the principal causes of communal conflict was the provocative use of flags and emblems. Sometimes this resulted in violence, sometimes not, but in all cases what was involved was a very symbolic assault on the other community, such as when an Orange arch over the Coleraine–Dungiven road was burned in July 1962. At the same time three Royal Air Force men were beaten up for interfering with an Orange arch at Lisnarick, County Tyrone. As these cases show, such provocations were by no means confined to the Protestant community. In July two Catholic girls were arrested for singing a republican song during the Twelfth celebrations and a Union flag which had flown near the entrance to Moira Demesne in County Down disappeared. This followed a dispute caused by a request from the management of a local poultry-processing factory for the removal of a Union flag from the roof of the plant, where it had been placed by a section of the workers. In June 1964 a trainee nurse was bound over in Belfast for producing an Irish tricolour pennant during an Orange demonstration. In November a County Donegal motor mechanic was also bound over after having 'forgotten' to remove a tricolour from his car before crossing the border. The same month a tree in Bessbrook, County Armagh, from which a tricolour had been flying, was felled by an explosion, and there was a debate in Stormont about the fact that a Union flag had been flown over a school which was being used as a polling station. In March 1965 a youth was jailed for failing to pay a fine imposed after he had set fire to a Union flag at a demonstration in Clonard in Belfast. In June another youth was fined for having set fire to some red-white-and-blue bunting in Portadown, County Armagh. In July forty-seven employees of a religiously-mixed Belfast linen mill walked out after the management removed flags and bunting put up to mark the Twelfth. In March 1966 two youths were fined after a gang had gone into a Protestant area waving Irish tricolours and singing republican songs. In October a forty-six-year-old man was jailed for nine years; he had threatened a Catholic householder with a revolver and warned him not to interfere with Twelfth street decorations that had been fixed to his house. In Stormont, Austin Ardill, Unionist MP for Carrick, felt it necessary to scotch a newspaper report which claimed that Girl Guides were prohibited from carrying the Union flag in Keady, a mainly Catholic town in County Armagh.

These factors of elections, and flags and emblems as causes of sectarian conflict came together in 1964 when Ian Paisley achieved considerable prominence by appearing to force action by the authorities against the republican election headquarters in Divis Street in the Falls Road area of Belfast. An Irish tricolour had been placed in the headquarters window and Paisley announced that if the police did not remove it, he would lead a demonstration into the area and do it himself, an action which would, inevitably, have led to serious rioting. The rioting happened anyway. On the orders of Minister of Home Affairs Brian McConnell the RUC broke into the premises, in front of a large crowd, and removed the offending emblem. Nationalists, republicans and Protestant liberals were angered; they claimed that the flag could have provoked no one since it was displayed in a solidly Catholic area. Paisley, it was argued, had gone out of his way to draw attention to this particular flag in order to provoke just the kind of conflict which had occurred.

The police had, in fact, taken a similar action a year earlier, when a parade down the Falls Road, to commemorate the two-hundredth anniversary of the birth of Wolfe Tone, was prevented from carrying the Irish tricolour. The legal position was that, under the Flags and Emblems (Display) Act of 1954, the display of the Union flag was protected in all circumstances and other flags and emblems could be banned if in the opinion of the police they were likely to provoke a breach of the peace. This gave the RUC a wide area of discretion, which they seem to have utilised with remarkable inconsistency. Similar action was taken against tricolours displayed at election meetings in Enniskillen and Coleraine, but on the Sunday following the rioting they took no action against a republican march down the Falls Road, carrying the tricolour. Republicans in Newry and Armagh were prosecuted in 1964 for organising Easter Rising commemorations at which the tricolour was carried, while in October 1964 the RUC in Newry refused to take action against a tricolour displayed in the window of the local republican headquarters, despite the fact that the republicans had tried very hard to provoke them. The flag had been put there in place of a smaller one, against which the police had said they would take no action since it was made of paper and did not count as a flag. In 1965 the Easter Rising commemoration in Belfast again carried a tricolour and no action was taken. But in Waterfoot, County

Antrim, a ban was imposed and the police allowed themselves to be cast in a sectarian light. The *News Letter* of 19 April 1965 reported:

> In reply to a remark by Mr Caughey [the organiser of the march] that the police allowed Orange processions to pass through Nationalist areas in Dungiven, Carnlough and Annalong, County Inspector S. S. Hopkins . . . said that they would never try to interfere with people who were carrying 'the flag of this country'.

The Divis Street riots, with their petrol bombs, water cannon and armoured vehicles deployed against crowds of protesters, were a dress rehearsal for what was to come later. At the time, however, most anti-Unionists saw the events as the result of a manoeuvre by the Unionist Party to ensure the election of its candidate, James Kilfedder. The violence was seen as an episodic phenomenon and not as an indication of a deeply rooted problem for Northern Ireland society.

In 1966 communalist incidents took on a more serious character than usual. There was a clustering of cases of arson, desecration, violence and intimidation. This, of course, was the year of republican fiftieth-anniversary commemorations of the Easter Rising of 1916 and of the controversy over the naming of the new bridge over the River Lagan in Belfast, when the governor, Lord Erskine, provoked Paisley's wrath by blocking a plan to call it Carson Bridge. It was also the year of the Cromac Square riot, of the blowing up of the Nelson Pillar in Dublin, and of the emergence of the UVF. In September, Lord Chief Justice Lord MacDermott told the grand jury at the opening of Belfast City Commission that 'it has been a period of some tumult, some rioting and violence . . . You may well reach the conclusion that the gunman has come amongst us again.' During the following months there was serious vandalism, directed against churches, schools, clubs, halls and so on. January saw an outbreak of teenage gang warfare in Belfast city centre; in February petrol bombs were thrown at an RUC landrover in west Belfast, at Unionist Party headquarters in Glengall Street, Belfast, and at a Catholic school on the Falls Road; in April the Catholic Holy Cross Girls' Primary School in Ardoyne was petrol-bombed, a hoax bomb was left on the steps of Bangor Town Hall in County Down and a telephone kiosk in Smithfield, Belfast, was blown up; in May the opening of a new school in Armagh was disrupted by a bomb scare.

There was an outbreak of intimidation and sectarian attacks. In June, Unionist MP Nat Minford claimed that he had received threats to his life by telephone and telegram after he had denounced Paisleyism. In July, on the eve of the Twelfth, a Catholic man who lived in a Protestant street was seriously injured by a gang of some thirty to forty youths. Threats were made to burn him out and the windows and window frames of his house were smashed. In September a nun, returning to Belfast after thirty-five years abroad, was attacked twice during two months' holiday and two Catholic families were intimidated out of their homes off the Donegall Road, Belfast. In October two more Catholic families were intimidated out of Percy Street off the Shankill Road. In July the tenants' association in Turf Lodge, west Belfast, denied reports that Protestant families in the district were being intimidated.

The most horrifying aspect of the violence of 1966 was the responsibility of the UVF. A Protestant widow died in a blaze caused by a misdirected petrol bomb, an innocent Catholic was shot dead as he drunkenly sang republican songs and three Catholic barmen were shot, one of them fatally. The killings were shocking not only because they were brutal and unjustified but also because they were so arbitrary. This arbitrariness was a result of the UVF's incompetence; Paisley's newspaper, the *Protestant Telegraph*, was justified in pointing out the background of these incidents in 'the hell-soaked liquor traffic'. In 1969 loyalist extremists helped to precipitate Terence O'Neill's resignation by bombing installations at the Silent Valley reservoir in the Mourne Mountains. They were able to take advantage of a political crisis which should be understood in the light of the events of 1966; but such political significance should not be read back into the actions of the UVF in that year.[14]

Paisleyism, however, was of crucial political importance. In the early to mid-1960s it was justifiable to portray Paisley as little more than a spoiler, on the fringes of Northern Ireland society. But the emergence of the civil rights movement enabled him to move to centre stage; he articulated the fears aroused in the minds of very many Protestants by the civil rights movement. Sarah Nelson has summed up their response with admirable clarity:

When the civil rights movement emerged a few Protestants were prepared to make a leap of trust and accept that Protestants must change both their attitudes and their policies. A larger group felt Catholics could never be trusted, that their demands must be fought to the end. The rest were to varying degrees unwilling to accept that Protestants had any major responsibility for Catholic inequality, for past bitterness or future reconciliation. Civil rights offered them no proofs of Catholic loyalty, and challenged their definitions at every point by putting the blame squarely on the majority. The movement also said: 'You are not the sort of people you claim to be, fair and freedom loving: you are frauds or hypocrites.' People's definitions of themselves were fundamentally challenged.[15]

Also, more basically, the very fact of Catholic mobilisation after 5 October 1968 was profoundly alienating for many Protestants. An example of this was the former Liberal supporter who wrote to Albert McElroy on 23 October 1968 asking to be removed from the Liberal mailing list

> because you *must* know that after Derry the position here is crystallised between orange and green and any compromisers have *no* chance . . . in this hour when every thinking person should come down off the fence. I take my stand alongside Rev. Ian Paisley mainly because I haven't caught him out in any lies yet and because he is obviously the only spokesman the true Ulsterman has.
>
> I am a bus conductor and I wish you could see the brats from St Patrick's School, Banbridge, singing 'What will we do with Ian Paisley – Burn Burn Burn the bastard', and now of course their latest hymn of defiance, 'We shall not be moved'. Well today I moved a few of them all right – OFF. I suggest you get out and have a look at Ballymurphy or Turf Lodge estates. Oh yes a few dreamers need to work amongst the minority for a few weeks.[16]

Paisleyism had two effects; it limited the room for manoeuvre of O'Neill and his supporters in the Unionist government and party, but it also undermined trust in O'Neill among civil rights supporters. Just as the right wing of unionism saw the Irish Republican Army (IRA) looming behind the civil rights movement, the left wing of the civil rights movement saw Paisley behind O'Neill's shoulder and interpreted the prime minister's hesitations and evasions as concessions to extreme loyalism. This made any reasonable settlement of their grievances impossible. There simply was not enough faith or mutual trust to consider what kind of concessions they might accept, or which the Government could concede. This lack of trust, however, should not be too narrowly attributed to the effects of Paisleyism. By 1968, O'Neill had, quite independently of Paisley's actions, succeeded in alienating most Catholics. Paisleyism was important in providing the nationalist community with an explanation for what it saw as unacceptable in O'Neillism – it was believed that Paisley's pressure, together with that of the 'backwoodsmen' in the Unionist Party, had frustrated the prime minister's weak liberal instincts. This reinforced the communalist divide within Northern Ireland and it was an important part of the process whereby Catholic and Liberal Protestant opposition to the Government took to the streets – no other effective means of pressurising the Unionist administration had been found and O'Neill had done nothing effective to deal with the mounting frustration.

O'Neill's policies of economic development and political and cultural integration with Britain failed because of three fundamental weaknesses:

1 His economic strategy, as set out in the Matthew and Wilson Plans,[17] involved concentration of investment in 'growth centres' which would provide the initial impetus to stimulate the economy on a wider geographical basis. What this boiled down to was a grandiose scheme for the 'new town' of Craigavon, planted right in the middle of the Protestant heartland and named after a Unionist hero. Catholics, and especially those living west of the River Bann, saw this as a deliberate denial of investment to their areas, especially since the actual growth which was achieved failed even to turn Craigavon into a viable entity.

2 O'Neill tells us in his autobiography that he waited twenty-one months until he felt secure enough to invite Lemass to Belfast and of the secrecy he thought necessary in carrying out the operation. He is less candid about his often-repeated opposition, during the months beforehand, to negotiating with Dublin until the southern government recognised the constitutional status of the north. The meeting was not simply a surprise sprung upon his colleagues but a sudden reversal of a tenet of unionism that he had always seemed to endorse. It is hardly surprising that

34

although he caught the imagination of large sections of the public, he provoked suspicion and opposition within his own party.

3 The logic of extending the Unionist Party into the middle ground would have been to win over the many middle-class Catholics who wanted no part of the Nationalist Party and its fixation with the border. But the traditions of the Unionist Party were strongly anti-Catholic and there was no real evidence that it was changing or that the Orange Order had ceased to play an important role within it. O'Neill made no significant attempts to confront this aspect of his party until 1969, when it was already too late. In January 1966 the *Irish News* noted the fact that when the president of the Antrim Unionist Association said that it was 'impossible' for Catholics to join the Unionist Party, O'Neill, who spoke after him, made no reference to the remark. There were other apparent cracks in his liberal façade.

Despite the 'modernism' which he counterposed to traditional unionism, many of his speeches about economic regeneration appealed to those same traditions. In his 'Pottinger' speech of November 1962, in which as finance minister he set out the main lines of his economic policy, he summoned up the ghosts of the signatories of the Covenant of 1912 and commended the spirit which motivated them as one which must now drive 'Ulstermen' on to new initiatives and development. His speeches are full of references to the hard-working, enterprising, straightforward people of Northern Ireland; the new Ulster would, it seemed, be built on the solid foundations of the Protestant work ethic and it would still, he assured his listeners, be the 'Ulster of Carson and Craig'. He often reiterated his determination to uphold the Union and his opposition to Irish unity. But he went further: in a speech to the Scots-Irish Association of Philadelphia in September 1963 he stressed the separate identity of the northern Protestants. The Scots-Irish of the north, he claimed, were as different from the rest of the Irish people as 'chalk from cheese'.

There were other significant actions. O'Neill's speech of May 1969, in which he said that if Catholics were given good jobs and houses they would behave like Protestants, was a serious blunder which has often been quoted. But two years earlier, in May 1967, he had to apologise to Stormont for having read to the House a forged letter purporting to come from a 'loyal Falls Road Catholic', which claimed that Catholics were instructed from the pulpit not to employ Protestants and to boycott Protestant shops. In 1964 he joined the Ahoghill Royal Black Preceptory number 173 and became entitled to wear the black collarette as well as those of the Orange Order and the Apprentice Boys of Derry. That year he was also prominent in the celebrations of the fiftieth anniversary of the Larne gun-running.[18] All of this meant that Catholics were not just being asked to embrace modernisation and reconciliation. Quite apart from the problem of whether or not the Unionist Party would open its doors to them, they were being asked to swallow part of a tradition that was alien to them. It was hardly surprising that the Nationalists returned to hostility to the Government in 1966 after a flirtation following the Lemass visit. In October, D. MacDonnell, writing a political commentary in the *Irish Weekly* in October 1966, discussed the disputes within the ruling party:

> The only divergence of opinion amongst these groups is the means to their common end . . . the perpetuation of the intolerant ascendancy of the Unionist Party and its masters in the Orange Order.
>
> Mr O'Neill's method has been to camouflage his Government's policy of discrimination from the outside world by expressions and gestures of friendship across the Border, coupled with hopes of better relations in some undetermined future era. One would look in vain for a single positive step by his Government towards ending discrimination.

Later that month James O'Reilly, Nationalist MP for Mourne, said that O'Neill was 'a man of fair words and few actions' who had 'done nothing to set the machinery of reform in motion', and Austin Currie, the young Nationalist MP for East Tyrone, said that O'Neill realised what was necessary and had spoken of building bridges and partnership, 'but unfortunately he has given no indication that he is tackling the problem or is going to do so'. A month later Harry Diamond, RLP MP for Falls, accused O'Neill of evasion. His attitude had 'brought a halt to any prospect of reform'. Diamond's colleague Gerry Fitt was more generous, saying that he thought that the Government wished to introduce some 'simple reforms' but were being held back by the backwoodsmen of its own party. He reminded O'Neill, however, that 'people who were suffering injustice were not prepared to wait forever'. In February 1967 Patrick Gormley, Nationalist MP for Mid-Londonderry, echoed the idea that O'Neill was being held back by his party and called on him to 'honestly admit the bigotry within it'. In April, Eddie McAteer, Nationalist MP for Foyle and leader of the Nationalist Party, was angered by a television interview in which, he claimed, O'Neill had taken the credit for the Nationalists becoming the official opposition. He threatened that they would withdraw and said: 'The harsh fact remains that Captain O'Neill is simply a reincarnated Lord Brookeborough with a rather more plausible face.'

Disillusion in O'Neill had a number of causes. Exaggerated hopes about change were shown to be false by the communal conflicts of 1964 and 1966. The 1965 Stormont general election showed that the Unionist Party was more firmly in control than it had been since 1949. And a return to political mudslinging could only be expected after the rather artificial good will that followed the Lemass visit in January 1965. But in 1962 there had appeared to be a real break with the past. The IRA cease-fire removed one source of communal bitterness and there was widespread dissatisfaction with the old politics. The middle ground became more substantial and was occupied not just by the NILP but by the Liberals and groups within the Nationalist and Unionist camps. The growth of a left wing – admittedly small – showed that some, mainly university-educated, young people were responding to political ideas quite outside the traditional frame of reference. This helped to create a new opposition which, frustrated by the lack of real change, sought for new ways to bring it about.

The new opposition politics was created by dissatisfaction at the failure of the Unionists to solve the economic problems of Northern Ireland and by the irrelevance of Nationalist politics to such issues. But it was an episodic phenomenon which did not touch the roots of communalism in Northern Ireland society. The continuation of grass-roots sectarian conflict showed that the potential for another bout of communal polarisation still existed.

THE NEW OPPOSITION

There's many a victory decisive and complete
Has meant a sight less fighting than a hardly fought defeat;
And if people do their duty, every man in his degree,
Why defeat may be more glorious than a victory needs to be.

quoted in the *Belfast Labour Chronicle*, February 1905

In 1945 Nationalist politicians in Northern Ireland assumed that the changed political situation put a united Ireland within their grasp. As they perceived it, the Unionists were Tories, therefore the new Labour government at Westminster was bound to oppose them. With a minimum of persuasion the Government could be brought to see that this meant supporting Irish unity. The new importance of the United States as ally and benefactor of Britain would make this more likely by giving the Irish-American lobby strong influence. It was such thinking that lay behind the creation in 1945 of the Anti-Partition League (APL),[1] which was set up to co-ordinate the Nationalist MPs at Stormont and to build a grass-roots political movement that would unite the entire Catholic community behind them.

The APL was launched by Nationalist MPs and senators in a series of public rallies throughout the nationalist areas of Northern Ireland, beginning in January 1946. At these, the triumphs of the past and heroes long dead were summoned up to support the claim that Ireland was about to break the last fetter that tied it to the British Empire. Despite the rhetoric, the activity of the APL was fairly prosaic. Led mainly by Catholic professional men and organised by small businessmen, with the support of the clergy, the APL concentrated on electoral activity, which meant registering Catholics to vote, scrutinising the registrations from the 'other side', and putting together an election machine. The APL sought support from the rest of the Irish nation and was partly responsible for the anti-partition campaign of the late 1940s and early 1950s.

The high point of this campaign came after the declaration of a republic by the Dublin government in 1948. The withdrawal of the south from the British Commonwealth provoked Westminster's Ireland Act of 1949, which for the first time guaranteed the position of Northern Ireland within the United Kingdom. The anti-partition movement in the south mounted a massive campaign involving all the main political parties and culminating in the Mansion House Conference of 1949, which set up a fund to help finance anti-partition candidates in the north.

In response the Unionists called a general election and made the 'threat' of southern 'interference' the main issue. They were returned to power with an increased majority, having wiped out the NILP's parliamentary representation. In this polarised situation the Nationalists retired to abstentionism and ineffectuality. Although the APL standing committee was retained as a form of liaison between Nationalist MPs, senators and notables of the Catholic community, there was a return to the tradition of independent politicians operating from purely local power bases without any form of permanent party organisation. The attempt to create a movement to unite and mobilise the Catholic community was abandoned.

The situation in Belfast was different, but not qualitatively so. The APL made no attempt to challenge the existing representatives of the minority in the city, who sailed under a variety of flags, all claiming some association with Labour politics. There were defectors from the NILP who set up branches of the southern Irish Labour Party, and there were Independent Labour, Socialist Republican and Republican Labour candidates at different times. This nomenclature had three purposes: it facilitated a certain amount of voting across sectarian lines in mixed constituencies; it accommodated individual Protestants who had been won over to a left–nationalist standpoint; and it was indicative of the fact that the Catholic traditionalist stance of the APL on social welfare issues did not appeal to urban Catholic workers. Effectively, however, these were usually local machines supporting individual politicians, similar to the organisation of rural Nationalist politics. Two of these politicians, Harry Diamond, Stormont MP for Falls, Belfast, and Jack Beattie, Westminster MP for West Belfast, were useful to the APL in helping to forge links with a group of Labour backbenchers at Westminster who called themselves the Friends of Ireland.[2] Not all of these MPs were Irish nationalists and the basis of their collaboration was not against partition but against what they saw as the oppressive and discriminatory aspects of Unionist rule in Northern Ireland. Another theme, pursued especially strongly by their main spokesman, Geoffrey Bing, in his best-selling *Tribune* pamphlet of 1950, *John Bull's Other Ireland*, was the responsibility of Westminster, under the Government of Ireland Act 1920, for the operation of devolved government in Northern Ireland. This, they argued, made it incumbent on Westminster to intervene to check on the discrimination practised by Unionists and to impose reforms.

Although some of the APL's most important allies were implicitly at odds with the view that the only problem in Ireland was partition and the only remedy reunification, there was plenty of scope for uniting to harry the Unionists at Westminster and to agitate about discrimination. But there seems never to have been any discussion about the long-term incompatibility of their aims and the alliance broke up in the wake of the Ireland Act of 1949. For the next decade Nationalist opposition in Northern Ireland concentrated on maximalist and fruitless agitation for Irish unity. The episode is instructive; the Nationalists were happy to adopt a tactical line of agitating about discrimination but their commitment to this line proved to be very fragile. They seemed to think of discrimination not as an issue demanding reforms within Northern Ireland but as a means of exposing unionism and of justifying their denial of the legitimacy of the Northern Ireland government. At the first setback they reverted to their fundamental commitment to Irish unity. It is a characteristic which, on the one hand, gives a measure of the extent to which the civil rights movement differed from the nationalist tradition, and on the other helps explain why sections of that movement reverted to anti-partitionism during the crises of 1969–1972.

The early 1950s saw Irish nationalism still riding the tide of emotionalism created by the Ireland Act. The Dublin government tried to make partition an international issue and failed. The Irish-American lobby failed to shift Washington from its non-interventionist policy. The anti-partitionists in Britain failed to punish Labour by mobilising the Irish vote against it. Nationalist politics in the north lapsed into another bout of abstentionism and extra-parliamentary action, which merged into the IRA campaign of 1956–62.

The founding leaders of the APL, people like James McSparran MP, Thomas Campbell KC, MP, Cahir Healy MP, and Senator James G. Lennon, were staid, not to say ponderous: they were socially and politically conservative men who were very traditional Catholics and nationalists. In contrast the new leader of nationalist Derry, Eddie McAteer, who was in his early twenties when first elected to Stormont in 1945, had a vivid rhetorical style and a degree of political imagination which was not common within the ranks of the APL. In his pamphlet of 1948, *Irish Action*, he proposed a campaign of civil disobedience which was to have included traditional Irish sanctions like the boycott, but also more light-hearted tactics like gumming up the operations of officialdom by 'acting stupid'. 'Chuckle your way to freedom,' he advised. 'It is still a little risky to twist the British Lion's tail. Just tickle it.' Despite this advice there was nothing light-hearted about politics in Northern Ireland in the 1950s. The instinct of nationalists embarking on extra-parliamentary action was not to adopt McAteer's proposals for civil disobedience but to indulge in communalist pageantry. McAteer himself was involved in a number of clashes with the RUC over the carrying of the Irish tricolour. Communal hostilities were further exacerbated by a series of incidents in which Orangemen insisted on attempting to march through nationalist streets. The commemoration of the 150th anniversary of the 1798 Rising of the United Irishmen in 1948 and the coronation of Queen Elizabeth II in 1953 were further occasions for displays of conspicuous disunity.

The creation of the APL had not changed the practice whereby the selection of Nationalist candidates in rural areas was in the hands of local conventions. As long as the Nationalist leadership was unchallenged, this worked in its favour, but it created an opportunity for Sinn Féin, who nominated candidates for all twelve Westminster constituencies and then challenged the conventions to select a Nationalist and split the Catholic vote. This effectively blackmailed the Nationalists into conceding the right to contest Westminster seats to the republicans. Since Northern Ireland legislation prevented Sinn Féin from contesting Stormont seats as abstentionists, there was a tacit division of labour whereby the Nationalists held their seats in the Northern Ireland parliament, while after 1955 the minority community had no representatives at Westminster.

However, after 1959, Catholic opinion had turned against an increasingly futile IRA campaign which had become little more than a series of isolated attacks on individual policemen. Militant republican tactics had failed but the frustrations within the Catholic community remained and were shared by increasing numbers of Protestant opponents of the Unionist Party. This meant that the 1960s saw another period of experimentation but this time with a broader, more fragmented and more heterogeneous opposition movement. The IRA cease-fire in 1962 cannot be credited with the responsibility for creating the conditions for the emergence of this new opposition, but it did mark a major watershed in Northern Ireland politics.

Immediately after the IRA cease-fire there was a split in Sinn Féin; a number of older leaders left and there were reports that they intended to start a new republican party. But instead they retired to the sidelines and the new leadership devoted fresh energy to public political activity. The new leaders of the movement were Tomás Mac Giolla, acting president of Sinn Féin, Cathal Goulding, chief of staff of the IRA, Tom Mitchell, the disqualified MP for Mid-Ulster, who became director of elections, and Seán Ó Brádaigh, secretary of Sinn Féin. After the 1970 split, Mac Giolla, Goulding and Mitchell went with the Official Republicans and Ó Brádaigh with the Provisionals, but at this time there was a general consensus among republicans about the new direction. Seán Mac Stíofáin, later chief of staff of the Provisional IRA, has recorded in his autobiography the pleasure with which he greeted Goulding's appointment and his support for the turn to politics. It was not until 1964 that he began to be concerned about Marxist influences within the leadership.

On the surface, however, it appeared that little had changed within the republican movement. In 1962 the Easter Rising commemorations in Belfast and Newry attracted large crowds, although in Newry it was noted that most of the hundreds who turned out preferred to line the route rather than march. In Milltown cemetery in Belfast, Sean Keenan gave the oration: 'One day the appeal of those crying from the grave [will] be heard not only by the faithful few, but by all Ireland. Then Ireland, like a giant waking from its slumber, [will] throw off the yoke of tyranny and wonder why it [has] borne it so long.'[3] In Newry, Christopher Loy voiced the same unchanging message. The country, he said, had been divided against the wishes of the overwhelming majority and allegiance was due to neither of the usurping governments. One American writer evoked the atmosphere of decay and isolation that surrounded the republicans in the early 1960s: Sinn Féin was a

demoralised party – defensive, self-pitying and self-righteous . . . [It] has been reduced to the stage of being led by a waxen-faced, middle-aged Government clerk named Tomás Mac Giolla. His party's headquarters, in a run-down building in a lower-class section of Dublin, are airless, unpainted and dusty; and they reek of disinfectant. Scattered throughout the two small offices are old pieces of furniture, ancient maps of Ireland, ragged banners and stacks of yellowing literature.[4]

The main focus for the republicans in 1962 was the campaign to obtain the release of IRA prisoners still held in Belfast and in British jails. Political prisoners release committees were set up all over the north, uniting various strands of nationalist opinion. Among those lobbying on behalf of the prisoners were the Ulster council of the Gaelic Athletic Association (GAA), the AOH in County Tyrone, the Old Fianna Veterans' Association, Dublin Corporation, one hundred members of Dáil Éireann, twelve Stormont and twenty-five Westminster MPs, as well as three trade-union national secretaries. Among the Stormont MPs who were most prominent in the campaign were: Joseph Stewart, MP for East Tyrone and leader of the Nationalist Party in Stormont; Harry Diamond, the Socialist Republican MP for Falls; and Gerry Fitt, the recently elected Independent Irish Labour MP for Dock.

Through their skill at pageantry and their front organisation, the National Graves Association, the republicans established a monopoly on the commemoration of such symbolic anniversaries as the birth of Wolfe Tone and the Easter Rising. This enabled them to parade, at least twice a year, as the leaders not of a faction but of a nation, and helped to create the ambiguous situation in which, while Catholics would not vote for them in any significant numbers, they retained a secure niche within the nationalist community of Northern Ireland. The importance of such pageantry for the IRA in the early 1960s was underlined in a talk given in 1972 by Billy McMillen, commanding officer of the Official IRA in Belfast following the split with the Provisionals in 1970. He claimed that in 1961 the total membership of the IRA in the city was twenty-four and they were equipped only with two short arms. They did, however, have flags, and they were asked by the organisers of the Wolfe Tone bicentenary commemoration in 1963 to supply a colour party for the Belfast parade. The Government imposed a ban on the carrying of the Irish tricolour, and in the face of a large force of RUC the then commanding officer, Billy McKee, accepted the decision of the parade organisers and withdrew the flag:

> The parade . . . marched up the Falls Road headed by an IRA colour party minus the tricolour to the hoots and jeers of a couple of hundred onlookers. The humiliation and embarrassment of the Volunteers was acute and McKee's refusal to sanction the carrying of the tricolour created bitter resentment . . . The tricolour was to play a central part in the future developments in Belfast, especially in re-awakening the dormant nationalism that slumbered in the hearts of the people.[5]

The following Easter there was no interference with the tricolour, but in October 1964 it was the focus of the Divis Street riots and in 1966, on the fiftieth anniversary of the Easter Rising, 'the Belfast staff saw . . . a golden opportunity to drive a coach and four through the notorious Flags and Emblems Act'. 'Thousands' of tricolours and 'miles' of green-white-and-gold bunting festooned nationalist Belfast, large crowds marched and watched and 'although no great material benefit accrued to the IRA . . . there was general satisfaction that progress had been made in dispelling the deadening apathy that had immobilised the people for so many years'. McMillen was careful to present this activity as defiance of the Flags and Emblems Act and an assertion of the civil right to carry the tricolour. He also stressed the IRA's success in overcoming apathy and mobilising Belfast Catholics, but there must be a large suspicion that much of what happened was the result of fairly apolitical communal polarisation, focused on the emotive issue of nationalist symbols.

In other ways, too, republicans were reluctant to break from their traditions. Despite the cease-fire, a number of incidents showed that military activity had not been totally eliminated. In March 1963 a young man was killed and another injured in an attempt to blow up an old IRA memorial in County Cork. The IRA denied that this was one of its operations but the dead man was buried with full republican military honours and the Irish Republican Publicity Bureau admitted that they were IRA volunteers who had been trying to forestall an unveiling by President Eamon de Valera. In July 1963 a republican meeting in Waterford town protested at the arrest of 'young freedom fighters' who had been training in the hills outside Dungarvan. These were a Belfast man and two others who were arrested in possession of uniforms, arms and ammunition. During the trial the Belfast defendant interrupted to say that the arms were for use 'against British forces in the six occupied counties'. In October six young men were held after RUC raids in the Falls Road area of Belfast. In January 1965 explosions cut off the electricity supply at Abbeyleix, County Laois, during a visit by Princess Margaret and Lord Snowdon. In the summer of 1965 the IRA fired on a visiting Royal Navy torpedo boat in Waterford harbour. In January 1966 a young Dungannon man was charged with collecting information on the use of explosives, anti-personnel mines and rocket launchers. Four other teenagers were arrested with him and charged with possession of two bayonets and a copy of the *United Irishman*, the republican movement's newspaper. In March 1966 there was an attempt to set fire to the home of the British military attaché in Dublin. A few days later the Nelson Pillar in O'Connell Street, Dublin, was toppled by an explosion.

Other incidents in 1966 included a campaign of sabotage in south Kilkenny for which the well-known republican, Richard Behal, admitted responsibility. There were scuffles in O'Connell Street during the Easter Rising commemoration in Dublin, as gardaí tried to seize a banner bearing the legend 'Óglaigh na hÉireann' (Irish Volunteers, the Irish title of the IRA). In September shots were fired over the grave of Patrick McManus of Kinawley, County Fermanagh; he was described as commanding officer of the IRA's south Fermanagh unit. In late 1966 an IRA unit broke up a British Army recruiting lecture in a Catholic boys' school on the Crumlin Road in Belfast; its members smashed a film projector and injured British officers who were present. In February 1967 a man was found tarred and feathered and tied to a lamppost in Leeson Street in the Lower Falls; a statement from the Belfast IRA claimed that he had been giving information to the RUC. In October the RUC alleged that during a raid on the Sean McCaughey Club in Oldpark, Belfast, they found a number of young women drawn up in military formation and responding to commands. Prominent members of the republican women's organisation, Cumann na mBan, were recognised. In September 1968 the RUC alleged that the IRA had been responsible for raiding a house in Sultan Street in the Lower Falls and demanding the householder's legally held firearms.

Not all of these incidents were particularly serious. The five Dungannon teenagers seem to have been simply young romantics. Gerry Fitt and Harry Diamond claimed in Stormont that the alleged Cumann na mBan parade was actually an Irish language class. Richard Behal was disowned by the IRA leadership as were those responsible for blowing up the Cork monument and the Nelson Pillar. Allegations by the authorities, north and south, that a resumption of the IRA military campaign was imminent were strenuously denied by the Irish Republican Publicity Bureau. J. Bowyer Bell helps to clarify the reasons for this ambiguity about militarism:

> Without the IRA the Movement would be a fraternal society, a clan of the alienated, not a force for change. Without the IRA the Movement would wither and die. Thus the IRA was maintained; organisers travelled the hinterland, training camps were held, equipment was polished – and there was no action, the IRA was building with sand. Recruits drifted through a revolving door of idealism, boredom and departure. Units dissolved or squabbled. Pressed for money, for time, for men, Dublin GHQ had to move ever faster on the treadmill even to shore up the Army much less to enlarge it.[6]

In a *Belfast Telegraph* interview of 10 February 1967, Cathal Goulding, IRA chief of staff, admitted that there had been unauthorised activity by splinter groups. This was because of the maintenance of the cease-fire: 'Men who had been engaged in military training wanted to put it to use. If you train a horse you have to race him. We weren't able to race these people so they raced themselves.' The new leadership had adopted a strategy aimed at involving the republican movement in agitation on social and economic issues, with a final goal of a united socialist republic. Militarism was not to be abandoned but it was to be used in a different way. As one commentator put it, the new strategy 'involved abandoning the strict theoretical divison between "military" and "political" action and their combination in a much more subtle blend in which they would fully complement each other'.[7] Sean Garland, one of the key members of the new leadership, put it this way: 'There are no longer two different types of Republicans; physical force men and politicians. We in the Republican Movement must be prepared to take the appropriate educational, economic, political and finally military action.'[8] In practice the strategy could not be implemented as the theory predicted. The old distinction between physical force and political action reflected the simple fact that the first was illegal and the second was not. Involvement in both became difficult because open political action exposed the small numbers of volunteers to police attention, threatening the security of the movement's covert activities. And since all this was being carried out by a secret organisation that did not even make all of its own members privy to the thinking of its inner councils, what appeared on the surface was highly ambiguous. This ambiguity could be interpreted either as evidence that the IRA was being kept in readiness for a renewed military campaign, or as a tactic to keep the organisation together while its direction was fundamentally changed. The security forces and governments on both sides of the border held the first view, but sections of the republican movement favoured the second. Seán Mac Stíofáin has recorded his disillusion with Goulding's leadership and in retrospect he saw developments during the 1960s as a justification for the Provisionals' split in 1970. But even at the time, elements in the IRA warned about reformism and an abandonment of militarism.

A group of left-wing oppositionists in Cork published a duplicated magazine, *An Phoblacht*,[9] which in March 1966 berated the leadership:

> Republican leaders will talk their heads off on the subject of the IRA fighting for Irish freedom when they appear at some commemoration or other. But they make no preparations for such a struggle; and in private conversations with them, it became very apparent that they haven't a clue how such a war is to be waged and they have no desire to find out.

In October 1967 they excoriated the 'present trend towards a total reliance on non-violent methods'. The involvement of the republican movement in the civil rights movement will be examined later and it will be made clear that the evidence does not point to any intention of exploiting the latter movement for subversive purposes. The publishers of *An Phoblacht* seem to have been right: behind the façade of a continued verbal commitment to militarism and the occasional 'racing' of volunteers, the leadership had turned away from any perspective of a renewed military campaign.

After the May 1962 Stormont general election an *Irish Weekly* editorial commented: 'It is clear that . . . the policy of more vigorous tactics, employed by the [Nationalist] Party at Stormont in the last Parliament, has won recognition and would seem to indicate that Nationalists want political opposition at Stormont rather than any policy of abstentionism.' Despite this, as with the republicans, the surface appearance was very little different. Eddie McAteer told a victory rally in Derry that the election results represented a 'new rising tide of strong nationalism in the north', and Irish tricolours were carried in the victory parade and flew from many houses, including McAteer's. Shortly after the election, Cahir Healy, the eighty-five-year-old MP for South Fermanagh, addressing a Gaelic League *feis* in Newcastle, County Down, said that 'the Irish language was the badge of their nationality and where it was being neglected or put aside the spirit of nationality receded'. This kind of statement showed how much the Nationalists were caught up in a very traditional Catholic–Gaelic interpretation of nationalism and were suspicious of influences from outside. In June 1964, James O'Reilly MP, speaking at a *feis* in County Down, said that while youth was 'kicking over the traces in other countries – seeking thrills in outlandish fashions and habits – we can be thankful that the *feiseanna* show an Irish way of life that is satisfying and sound'.

The differences between the Nationalist Party and the republicans were not so much about policy or ideology as temperament. Constitutional nationalism in the south was the adaptation of republicanism to the empirical realities of running a small, poor, independent state. Constitutional nationalism in the north could appear like republicanism without the maximalism and idealism that made people willing to kill and die for the unity of Ireland. As Ian McAllister points out, the Nationalist Party had

> a half-hearted commitment to constitutional politics. They failed to organise and restricted their activities to enclaves where they possessed a numerical majority. Moreover they frequently abstained from parliament and continued to emphasise partition to the exclusion of other social issues affecting the welfare of their supporters. In many ways this solution . . . was the worst they could have adopted, for it left them open to attack from all sides. Unionists accused them of being quasi-revolutionaries, moderate Catholics of not adequately seeking to redress their grievances, and militant Republicans vilified them for not having the courage of their convictions to oppose partition by force.[10]

There was a fatalism about the Nationalists that prevented them from making any real effort to break out of this vicious circle. Eddie McAteer, leader of the party from 1964, saw things in terms of a broad historical perspective:

> You have this cyclical appearance of the Irish struggle for freedom. At times there's a constitutional movement; then they weary of it because you cannot accomplish very much by talking peacefully. When they weary of constitutionalism, then there is an outbreak of violence. At times we wander about in such matters as civil rights, civil liberties, and so on, and at an earlier period in our history in the great agrarian conflict over the ownership of the land . . . But all these, I insist, are side issues, really. You have the old racial-colonial struggle going on, and this is the key to the whole problem.[11]

The Nationalists maintained two contradictory principles: on the one hand they rejected the legitimacy of the Northern Ireland constitution; on the other they acquiesced in and worked within it. But the two principles were not held together in the kind of intellectual tension which can produce creative politics, but by the absence of a critical faculty. They usually simply did not notice that what they were doing was contradictory. In so far as they did notice, they attempted to resolve the contradiction through futile gestures – like blanking out the word 'leader' on the door to the office of the leader of the opposition at Stormont, and refusing to take the salary.[12]

The Nationalists still looked on the other political forces in

Northern Ireland with suspicion. In April 1962, Joseph Stewart, refuting suggestions that there had been a pre-election pact with the NILP, said that Labour's policy on the fundamental issue of national unity was 'no different from that of the Ascendancy Party'. In June, when forcing a division on the nomination of Sir Norman Stronge as Speaker at Stormont, Eddie McAteer said that he was 'not an expert on Orange mysticism, but he thought that the Black Preceptory of which Sir Norman was the head contained a darker distillate of Orangeism and was even more anti-Catholic than the parent Orange Order'. In June 1964 the Nationalists put down an amendment to a Stormont bill to disqualify Orangemen from participation in local government. Even when they made what were meant to be conciliatory gestures to the Protestant majority, they insisted on their own terms. Joseph Connellan MP, speaking at a Nationalist meeting in south Down in February 1965, said that

> so many changes were taking place in the outlook of intelligent people everywhere that it would be a glorious gesture if the Protestant people of the North decided to return to the fold of nationalism . . . Protestants would be no strangers in the field of nationalism. Their Northern ancestors, pioneers of democratic thinking, were the founders of Irish nationalism . . . Several thousand of the more educated Protestant people had . . . quietly voted for Nationalist candidates . . . It is deplorable that they have not so far publicly identified themselves with our work.

To be fair to the Nationalists, their crusted antiquity and suspicion of the modern world was shared to a large extent by their Unionist opponents. A little vignette conveys this: McAteer asked a question about the computer which had recently been acquired by Stormont and requested that members should be 'allowed to peer into the belly of the monster'. Replying, the finance minister, Herbert V. Kirk, said that members would have the machine explained to them and that it was 'close to a thing of black magic'. There were some signs that the Nationalists were aware of the changing world in which they lived. At an AOH demonstration in March, Joseph Stewart said that young people realised that this was 1962 and not 1690 but he interpreted that change as making the downfall of unionism imminent: 'The sooner our Unionist friends realise that the writing is on the wall and [do] not favour the action of Unionists in Government and local government levels, the better.' At the same rally P. S. Donegan TD (Teachta Dála, member of the Dáil) warned the Unionists to be prepared for the ending of the border in the European Economic Community (EEC) and Senator P. J. O'Hare forecast that the 'props that support partition would soon be swept away'.

When Eddie McAteer succeeded to the leadership of the Nationalist Party in June 1964, he was fifty years of age and was described by the *Irish News* as 'young'. Within the party's frame of reference this was accurate, but from the perspective of the new layer of university-educated young Catholics there was little to choose between McAteer and Cahir Healy, who was now approaching the end of his forty-year stint as Stormont MP for South Fermanagh. Shortly before McAteer's election, the twenty-seven-year-old John Hume had written a series of articles in the *Irish Times* which lambasted the Nationalist Party for its 'irresponsible' leadership:

> There has been no attempt to be positive, to encourage the Catholic community to develop the resources which they have in plenty, to make a positive contribution in terms of community service . . . Unemployment and emigration, chiefly of Catholics, remain heavy, much of it no doubt due to the skilful placing of industry by the Northern Government. But the only constructive suggestion from the nationalist side would appear to be that a removal of discrimination will be the panacea for all our ills. It is this lack of positive contribution and the apparent lack of interest in the general welfare of Northern Ireland that has led many Protestants to believe that the Northern Catholic is politically irresponsible and therefore unfit to rule.[13]

In the autumn of 1964, Cahir Healy defended the party from criticisms that it was out of touch with the younger generation. He claimed that it was 'difficult to find places for all the clever, aspiring young men who are hammering at our door'. But only one clever, aspiring young man – Austin Currie – appeared. He held the Stormont seat of East Tyrone for the Nationalists at a by-election in July 1964, increasing the majority from 815 to 1,296. Aged twenty-four, Currie had been born near Coalisland in County Tyrone, the eldest of a family of eleven and the son of a lorry driver. He had won a scholarship to St Patrick's Academy, Dungannon, and went on to graduate in politics and history at QUB. He first made his mark as president of the New Ireland Society – an important arena for innovative nationalist thinking. Although many of his contemporaries went on to be active in the civil rights movement and later still joined Currie in the Social Democratic and Labour Party (SDLP), he was alone in beginning his political career in the Nationalist Party. To do so he had to submit himself to an archaic procedure – the Nationalist nominating convention. It is worth quoting from a contemporary description of the convention that picked Currie to give a flavour of Nationalist politics at the grass roots in this period:

> Who are they, these delegates shouldered with the responsibility of selecting a candidate to hold the Nationalist fort in East Tyrone? There are over seventy of them, comprising the public representatives of the area – County Councillors and Rural District Councillors (there are no urban areas in the constituency), the registration agents, the men who mind the machine by keeping the register and attending the revision sessions, and finally two delegates from each church area. These have been selected earlier in the day at a meeting held after Mass and most come pledged to support a particular candidate as long as he is in the fight.

The meeting was presided over by Senator Lennon and agreed on its own rules of procedure and the conditions to be imposed on aspiring candidates. Nominations were taken from the floor and the prospective candidates had five minutes each to address the convention.

Voting was by secret ballot and by an exhaustive procedure in which those with the lowest number of votes were eliminated until one candidate had an absolute majority. Outside, 'men loiter around the street in small groups. The Sunday suits, the Pioneer pins, the *fáinnes*, the parked Volkswagens, the sporadic guffaws'. Someone 'looks up at the tall chimney of the hall and comments that the "white smoke will be coming soon"'. A delegate comes out to give the result of the first ballot:

> Those outside speculate on how the transferred votes will go, and defend their own predictions while those inside decide the issue. This sequence is repeated from time to time as another man goes out on each count. At the third vote one of the throng outside produces a notebook and starts offering odds on the remaining

52

candidates. He is soon holding a fistful of notes. At last the hall doors open and this time it is not a solitary delegate slipping out, but a surge of humanity. 'Currie has it.'[14]

In his convention speech Currie had stressed his 'acceptability to the conservative and radical elements in the constituency'. In an early speech in Stormont, in November 1964, Currie bowed to traditionalism by saying that the Union flag was 'not the flag of this country'. However, a year after being elected he made a speech at a *feis* in Newcastle, County Down, in which he pointed out the changes taking place in the 'political, cultural and social life of Ireland'. They must 'welcome useful and progressive change, while maintaining the customs, traditions, attitudes and way of life which distinguish us from the rest of the world'. Two months later he announced plans to create a 'more intensive and democratic movement' in the constituency. He was dissatisfied with the lack of a democratic grass roots and he hoped to involve many of the younger generation. But not all of his colleagues agreed that new initiatives were necessary. Joseph Connellan, speaking in Newry, denied that nationalism was declining or that it was sectarian. They must be radicals like the United Irishmen – 'They had no academic degrees and did not pose as intellectuals.'

However, the tide of events was running Currie's way. There was increasing pressure north and south of the border for Nationalists to adopt a more positive and active role in Northern Ireland political life. Conor Cruise O'Brien records a discouraging trip that he made on behalf of Frank Aiken, foreign affairs minister in the Lemass government:

> The object was to convey to various nationalist/anti-Unionist/ Catholic leaders and publicists the wish of Mr Aiken and the Dublin Government that they should take a more active part in public life, cease to boycott local official ceremonies, and associate with Protestants to a greater extent. Most of them heard me with resignation, but without manifest assent. A typical comment was that, although Frank Aiken had been born in Armagh, he had been away from it a long time.[15]

During 1963 the influential Dublin Catholic political review *Hibernia* carried out a campaign in its columns for a new nationalist attitude towards the realities of Northern Ireland. In the February issue Henry Heany, assistant librarian at QUB and a former president of the QUB Catholic Students' Association, called on the Nationalist Party to recognise the legitimacy of the Northern Ireland state and government. He demolished most of the historical myths erected during the anti-partition campaign and argued that recognition would be beneficial to the nationalist cause because it would be more in tune with reality. An editorial in the same issue argued that 'recognition' simply meant recognising the actual existence of the northern government, not necessarily approving of its actions, and pointed out that 'the Holy See recognises Gibraltar, though obviously not conceding the abstract right of British occupation'. In the June issue there was an article by the director of the Abbey Theatre, Ernest Blythe, born in Magheragall, near Lisburn in County Antrim, and the only northern Protestant to have been a member of a Dublin cabinet. He called for the appointment of a consul general to be based in Belfast, 'whose presence would put beyond doubt Southern recognition of the powers and rights of the Northern Government'. Another benefit would be that his attendance at official functions would teach northern nationalists 'by example how in the national interest they ought to meet the minor ceremonial difficulties inherent in the situation'. In the December issue of *Hibernia*, William Patrick, in his column on northern affairs, referred approvingly to a speech made in October 1963 by Gerard Newe, secretary of the Northern Ireland Council of Social Service and a leading Catholic of conservative views. He had reminded northern Catholics of their church's doctrine that 'civil authority called for respect because of its Divine origin, even when those elected . . . to exercise that authority might come from a political party or group to whose views as individuals they did not subscribe'.

Within Northern Ireland the Nationalist Party was being pressed by a new organisation, based mainly in Belfast – National Unity. It should be noted that the Nationalist Party did respond positively to one of the aims of National Unity – the creation of a democratically structured, grass-roots party, with individual membership and local branches. In November 1964 plans were announced for the Nationalist Party to 'step into the twentieth century', with individual membership and an annual conference. The party would also examine the 'sacred cow' of refusing to become the official opposition at Stormont. Following the meeting between Terence O'Neill and Sean Lemass in January 1965, the Nationalists did, in fact, become the official opposition. In May 1966 the first party conference was held. It passed resolutions calling for: electoral reform to bring Northern Ireland into line with Britain; the abolition of discrimination and the introduction of competitive examinations for all government and local authority appointments; substantial increases in grants to voluntary schools; legislation to bring about equal opportunities for all citizens and an extension of the north–south talks. However, by this time conciliation was already turning sour and McAteer hinted that the party might have to review its position as the official opposition because of government reluctance to 'accept ideas not arising from the narrow limits of their own front bench'. Party organisation was sketchy and it never matured into a genuine, widely organised party based on grass-roots democracy.

The Nationalists responded to events in the early 1960s in much the same way as they had in 1945. Any alteration in the status quo was seen as threatening the existence of the 'artificial' state and the rule of the 'undemocratic' Unionist Party. Their endless variations on the same theme indicated that their political tradition did not contain the resources that would enable them to come to terms with the solidity of Northern Ireland and the resistance of the majority to Irish unity.

Alongside the Nationalist Party there was the smaller nationalist group, National Unity, founded in 1959, which was confined to Belfast and most strongly represented among the QUB-educated Catholic middle class. Ian McAllister, in his study of its successor, the National Democratic Party (NDP), defined the two prongs of the organisation's policy:

> National Unity based its appeal firstly, on the need to make reunification conditional on consent and, secondly, the need for a united opposition. The notion of the consent of majority was a recognition that not only Protestants but a substantial number of Catholics were apathetic to the ideal of Irish unity. Any 'new nationalism' in the Province would therefore have to spring from the integration of the two politico-religious traditions, 'and not from the domination of one by the other'. The aim of creating a united opposition from the existing fragmented nationalist groups made

55

the Unity movement a focal point for the co-ordination of these groups and aroused hopes that a united opposition was an attainable goal.[16]

The thinking behind National Unity's approach was outlined in 1964 by its chairman, John Duffy. He pointed to three main factors: first, the realisation that resort to arms by a minority group was 'neither . . . legitimate nor successful'; second, that the people of the Irish Republic had 'lost much of their enthusiasm for reunification . . . There is now in the South a fully developed political system which conducts its controversy almost entirely in terms of domestic issues' – this meant that the drive for Irish unity now had to come mainly from the north; and, third, Nationalists in Northern Ireland had played into the hands of unionism by

> relying too much on Catholic support and by allowing nationalism to become identified with gaelic games, the language revival and the affairs of the Catholic Church. The habit of having 'after Mass' meetings to select delegates for Nationalist conventions is an abuse which is damaging both to the church and the nationalist cause . . . Again Unionists are well pleased with the Nationalists' refusal to become the vehicle of effective opposition on the almost unbelievable grounds that this would amount to 'co-operation', involving 'recognition of the present constitutional position'.

Duffy saw glimmerings of hope in the emergence of a new generation of educated younger nationalists who rejected the negative attitudes of the Nationalist Party. What was needed was an overhaul of nationalist organisation and a re-examination of its political philosophy. He outlined a structure for a democratically organised nationalist party which would enable new ideas and new people to come forward:

> The open policy debate which would then ensue both at local association level and at annual conference would radically reshape nationalist thinking . . . One almost certain development would be the discarding of present preoccupation with the rights and wrongs of drinking toasts to the Queen . . . A more concrete development might be the acceptance of the Nationalist role as official opposition at Stormont.[17]

An example of such new thinking was Duffy's proposal, in 1963, that the Stormont parliament should be given greater powers. He pointed to the difficulties that Stormont's circumscribed economic powers created for matching economic policy to Northern Ireland's special difficulties and the poor quality of political life which resulted from the parliament's lack of prestige.[18]

National Unity's aspirations, therefore, were for a reorganisation of nationalism, a restructuring of its political philosophy and a new and more attractive offer to Unionists of a united Ireland in which they could share. What this programme boiled down to, in practice, was an immediate aim of reorganising nationalism. In April 1964, National Unity invited all elected Nationalist representatives to a conference in Maghery, County Armagh, to discuss the creation of a united party with democratic structures. However, the elected representatives were only encouraged to attend by a threat that if they did not, the assembly itself would create such an organisation. The meeting agreed on the creation of a National Political Front to co-ordinate elected representatives and grass-roots activists and to prepare the ground for unity. But the new body was soon racked by disagreements over whether or not to contest the Westminster seat of Fermanagh and South Tyrone at the next general election.

Two years earlier National Unity had declared its intention of contesting the Westminster constituencies rather than permit republican domination to continue. But the Nationalists were reluctant, and when the National Political Front backed an Independent Nationalist candidate in Fermanagh and South Tyrone, this ensured a Unionist victory and also the destruction of the front. However, these events stimulated a challenge to the mainstream Nationalist Party from Patrick Gormley, MP for Mid-Londonderry, and his brother, Thomas Gormley, MP for Mid-Tyrone. The former had stood against McAteer for the leadership of the Nationalist Party but was soundly beaten. The brothers shared many of National Unity's ideas; they believed that Nationalist thought

> had been too rooted in the past and must adapt itself to current changes and needs. They argue that a more rational approach to politics should replace their old emotional approach. Therefore . . . the party should change its emphasis from arguing the . . . merits of partition to arguing the more relevant economic shortcomings of the six counties. The Gormleys, for instance, do not like to see their

party forced into an anti-Protestant position every time their old policies are subject to scrutiny; nor do they like the trend of abdicating the nationalist position in Westminster elections to the 'renegade' Sinn Féin Party.[19]

In October 1965, Patrick Gormley said that Northern Ireland needed 'more socialist measures', and in November he helped to organise a democratic party organisation in his constituency. Addressing this body, he called for the creation of an organised political party to 'put forward a realistic programme of political action for the social development of all the people of Northern Ireland'. In 1967, Thomas Gormley became the first Nationalist MP to attend a royal garden party at Hillsborough, the governor's residence in County Down, held in honour of Princess Margaret and Lord Snowdon; in 1972 he joined the Alliance Party.

With the break-up of the National Political Front, National Unity adopted a policy of going it alone and it set up a properly organised party. It concentrated initially on the Belfast area, where it would be treading most lightly on the Nationalist Party's toes; branches were set up in north, west and east Belfast, and in south Antrim. The organisation was at first called the 'National Party' but in June 1965 it adopted the title National Democratic Party. From the start, however, the organisation bent over backwards to avoid disputes with the Nationalist Party; the first announcement by the new party said that it intended to 'link up with and eventually merge with the Nationalist Party'. In November 1965 it decided not to contest any of the seats held by Nationalists. Throughout its existence the party hankered after the nationalist unity that had eluded it in 1964. In September 1966 the Nationalists set up a committee to consider how to achieve unity and this was welcomed by the NDP. Nationalist observers attended the NDP conference and a joint action committee of the NDP and the Nationalist Party was set up. In February 1967 they issued a joint statement declaring that neither party would organise in a constituency already organised by the other and that each would call on their supporters to work for the other party.

A year later Ben Carraher, assistant secretary of the NDP, speaking at QUB, said that it was 'ludicrous' to have three nationalist parties. He called for a 'mass party [with a] radical social policy [to] present their case to all creeds'. He pointed out that as the population of Northern Ireland was redistributed, they were in danger of losing votes to other anti-Unionist parties if they did not broaden their appeal. However, by June 1968 the agreement of February 1967 was in tatters. The Nationalists had maintained that where an MP represented a constituency, this meant that it was 'organised' by them, even if no democratic, grass-roots organisation existed. The NDP repudiated the agreement because it effectively confined the party to Unionist areas. By this time the NDP had one Stormont MP and twenty-eight representatives in ten local councils. It controlled local government in Strabane, County Tyrone, and Downpatrick, County Down, but it was manifestly a small party facing major obstacles. One indication of this was its failure to attract the Gormley brothers and John Hume. As Barry White says, 'it should have been a natural home' for the latter, but the self-denying ordinance that kept the NDP out of Nationalist-held constituencies meant that he could not join. In 1966 the NDP asked Hume to stand as its candidate in the Westminster general election, but he 'was going for an important role in a mass movement and the NDP, overloaded as it was by teachers and intellectuals, did not have the makings of a winning combination'.[20]

The NDP's difficulties were not only with the Nationalists; in its stronghold of Belfast it was challenged by Gerry Fitt's RLP. The political differences between the two groups were narrower than those between the NDP and the Nationalists. The RLP had a left-of-centre policy on social and economic issues and it had a grass-roots organisation. However, according to Ciaran McKeown, 'the NDP saw Gerry Fitt as merely a more able version of the one man bands whom minority politics tended to throw up . . . Far from trying to recruit him, the National Democrats saw his brilliant lonerism as a block to the development of organised Catholic minority politics'.[21] For his part, Fitt ridiculed the NDP for its intellectualism and lack of the common touch. He 'pictured them sitting round a table saying to each other, "Think of a big word to impress the people in the Pound Loney – no that's not big enough, give us a longer one."'[22]

In December 1965 the NDP announced its intention of contesting the West Belfast Westminster constituency at the forthcoming general election. Its candidate was the first to be nominated and it began canvassing ahead of any other party. However, the RLP nominated Fitt for the constituency shortly afterwards, and in March he publicly attacked the NDP for putting up 'a young schoolteacher with absolutely no experience of politics' and for its attitude that 'they were the only spokesmen for the nationally minded electorate. In effect they are one more splinter party.' By the middle of March the pressure on the NDP had been successful. Its own canvassing returns had shown that Fitt had a better chance of winning, and after a meeting in which Eddie McAteer pleaded with the party to stand down, it withdrew its candidate. The party came under similar pressure during the run-up to the Belfast City Council elections the following year. It was obvious that both groups would suffer if they ran against each other and a meeting was organised to work out a division. However, the pact broke down; Fitt accused John Brennan, the NDP's only MP, of putting up candidates in Falls. In the event the Unionists benefited from a split vote but the RLP increased its representation at city hall, while the NDP failed to make gains which it had expected.

The two aims of the NDP were to unite and to renew nationalism. It failed to achieve either because these aims were incompatible. Nationalist MPs did not need a democratic party or sophisticated policies because personal election machines and anti-partitionist rhetoric were enough to get them elected. Gerry Fitt needed socialist rhetoric and an organised group of supporters, but he did not need the NDP, whose complex ideas and high principles simply got in the way of his instinctive political cunning. And because the NDP put such a high value on unity, it was always at the mercy of less scrupulous politicians. In any case, nationalist politics could not be renewed through unity with the Nationalist Party, but only by replacing it. That task took a combination of the civil rights upheaval and the emergence of a skilful and determined politician in John Hume. Members of the NDP then supplied the organisational muscle to build the new nationalist party – the SDLP – which they were incapable of creating.

In May 1962, Gerry Fitt, who had been a member of Belfast City Council since 1958, won the religiously-mixed Stormont seat of Dock in Belfast. He stood as an Independent Irish Labour candidate and his campaign emphasised bread-and-butter issues. He accused his Unionist opponent of trying to turn the election into a 'sectarian political wrangle' and challenged him to debate the economic situation in Northern Ireland instead. Fitt had been associated with the Irish Labour Party when it was organised in Northern Ireland during the 1950s. In 1962 he joined with another former member of that party, Harry Diamond, leader of a splinter group called the Republican Socialists. Their new organisation was called the Republican Labour Party.

Fitt claimed to be a Connolly socialist; speaking on 'Socialism and Republicanism' in University College Dublin in February 1967, he said that the Irish socialism that James Connolly had envisaged had not evolved because of partition, which 'isolated the industrial North from the agricultural South'. The only solution was to integrate the Labour movements on both sides of the border. In August he spoke at a commemoration for Sir Roger Casement. He said that

[the] best way to honour Casement and Irish patriots was to make certain that conditions in Ireland were brought into line with what they fought for. Casement had fought injustice in the Congo and had supported James Connolly on the streets of Dublin in 1913. I believe that the uniting of the progressive forces in Ireland would bring about a standard of living comparable with any other country in Europe.[23]

None of this was particularly original; Connolly was a favourite icon of the Irish left in the 1960s and was often used to provide a nationalist slant for socialist social and economic policies. Much of the same kind of rhetoric could be heard from left-wingers in the Irish Labour Party, the NILP and the republican movement. However, Fitt used it with great skill to present just the right degree of non-sectarian imagery to wrong-foot his opponents and rivals, while not straying too far from what was acceptable to his core support among Catholic Belfast voters.

In other ways he was quite a conventional nationalist politician. In September 1962 he expressed concern at the showing of a 'vice' film in Belfast. In November 1963 he attacked the appointment to the National Assistance Board of a deputy Grand Master of the Orange Order who had 'stirred up opposition to St Malachy's College using its sports ground on Sundays'. In October 1965 he protested at the decision of Belfast City Council's General Purposes

Committee to allow the Grand Orange Lodge of Ireland to incorporate the city's arms in a special badge. In September 1966 he attended a concert given in Belfast by the popular Glaswegian Irish singer Glen Daly, where he was presented with a pennant by members of the Andersonstown Glasgow Celtic Football Club Supporters' Club. He promised to take Saturday off to 'see his favourite team – Celtic – play'.

The NDP and the NILP tended to assume that the RLP was simply a personal vehicle for Fitt, similar to the organisations maintained by rural Nationalist MPs. In fact the RLP proved to be independent enough to expel Fitt and his colleague Paddy Wilson when they helped to set up the SDLP in 1970. However, it did not survive long afterwards and it is evident that it was not a fully developed political party. But what it lacked in democratic structures and internal intellectual life, it made up for in sheer political shrewdness. Ciaran McKeown, when he was a member of the NDP, was given a glimpse of the RLP in action during the 1967 Belfast City Council elections:

> Gerry's machine was actually more of a 'party' . . . than the NDP Executive . . . It was fascinating to hear the realpolitik amongst these genuine ward politicians, who were prepared to sacrifice a great deal of time, money and effort to get their men in . . . They were also a little dubious lest Gerry's ring craft be compromised by too close an association with 'a bunch of green teachers', as they characterised the NDP. Moreover, these men had no pretensions about appealing to 'moderate Protestant opinion' – but they were genuinely concerned about the ordinary Catholic and Protestant working-class people, and felt that Gerry as a 'socialist' would do more for the Protestants than their own Unionist representatives.[24]

Fitt's greatest triumph was his victory in the West Belfast constituency in the Westminster general election of March 1966. He had shrewdly calculated that his Labour rhetoric would catch the mood of popular support for Harold Wilson's seventeen-month-old government. The 1964 contest had shown that the Unionists could be beaten; James Kilfedder won the seat with 41.2 per cent of the vote, while Harry Diamond for the RLP had won 28.3 per cent, William Boyd of the NILP, 24.3 per cent and Billy McMillen, the republican candidate, 6.2 per cent. The republicans and the NILP were persuaded to stand down and the NDP, after much heart-searching, also withdrew. This left a straight contest between Kilfedder and Fitt. The poll was 74.8 per cent, practically the same as 1964. Fitt won 52 per cent and Kilfedder 48 per cent; Fitt's majority of 2,011 was in line with his own predictions. The difference between Fitt's 1966 result and the total RLP and republican percentage in 1964 was 6.8 per cent. Most of this must have come from former NILP voters, who were largely Protestants. This underlines the success of his campaign in depicting him as 'the standard-bearer of Labour', although an incident, reported in the *Belfast Telegraph* on the afternoon of election day, ensured a maximum Catholic turnout. Two nuns were photographed being jeered by Protestants outside a polling station: 'The psychological impact of this on Catholic voters may have contributed powerfully to the peculiar blend of religious and political loyalties which carried Gerard Fitt to Westminster.'

Fitt's election had a greater impact than the sum of his, or his party's, contributions. It was not just that he had broken a more than ten-year-old Unionist monopoly on Northern Ireland representation at Westminster, but he was the first representative of the Catholic minority to go to Westminster with a firm intention of using the place as a sounding board for its grievances and determined to press the government and parliament of the United Kingdom to take their responsibilities towards Northern Ireland seriously. On flying out to take his seat in April 1966, he announced that he would be trying to get the British Representation of the People Act extended to Northern Ireland. Speaking at QUB seven months later, he 'reminded the Government that the Northern Ireland Constitution arose from a British Act of Parliament, which could be changed by the British Parliament'. Speaking at a Connolly Association conference in London the following spring, he pledged that if after four years he had not achieved anything, he would seriously consider whether or not to return to Westminster. He went on:

'What I ask for is that British standards should be made applicable to Northern Ireland. I cannot conceive any MP denying me those rights. Some day the crunch has got to come in Northern Ireland affairs and this is the overall responsibility of the British

Government.' When it did come it should come within the lifetime of the present Parliament and Socialist administration. The British Government had taken a stand against the Smith regime in Rhodesia. 'How much more necessary that it should take a stand against the Stormont Government.'[25]

Fitt's victory gave added emphasis to the idea that the way to achieve redress of its grievances was for the minority in Northern Ireland to act positively and to seek to communicate with potential allies outside, not to engage in a fruitless, symbolic rejection of the state. The emergence of a more positive and constructive nationalist opposition opened up another possibility – that a grand coalition of opposition parties might actually get a majority at Stormont and oust the Unionists from power. On the face of it, the Unionist vote might have proved vulnerable to a united opposition, in a situation of widespread discontent with the Unionists and demoralisation in their ranks. In 1953, 1958 and 1962 they received less than 50 per cent of the total votes cast at 47.5 per cent, 43.6 per cent and 48.6 per cent respectively;[26] these figures, however, should be treated cautiously. There were unofficial Unionist candidates who polled between 5 per cent and 13 per cent in all the elections except in 1962 and 1965. In addition these figures only offer a comparison for those constituencies in which there actually was an election. In 1958 the Unionists had twenty-five MPs elected unopposed, in 1962 there were twenty, and fourteen in 1965. The figures for 1965 show that if these vast reservoirs of Unionist support had been contested in 1958 and 1962, the overall opposition percentage would have been reduced. In 1962 the total Unionist vote was 143,740, but in 1965 it went up to 191,896, an increase of 48,156. The total opposition vote in 1962 was 152,134, reducing to 132,693 in 1965, a reduction of 19,441.[27] The margin of 18,715 between the Unionist increase and the opposition decrease can best be explained by the contests in these six seats. Nevertheless, until 1965 the opposition was making real progress and had a reasonable hope that the Unionists could be successfully challenged by parliamentary means. But the advent of O'Neill, combined with a favourable turn in the economy, averted this possibility. He successfully stopped the leakage of Unionist votes to the NILP and focused attention on pressure for specific reforms rather than an alternative government. But the period between

1962 and 1965 illustrates the crucial role which might have been played by the two non-nationalist opposition parties, the NILP and the Ulster Liberal Party.

The Stormont general election of May 1962 produced an apparent stalemate. Only two seats changed hands – Gerry Fitt won Dock and Mid-Tyrone returned to the Nationalists. The Unionists had thirty-four seats and the NILP and the Liberals retained four seats and one seat respectively. But, as the *Round Table* of September reported, 'in an unguarded moment', Lord Brookeborough called the result 'a draw'. The NILP had made major gains: its total vote had gone up from 37,000 in 1958 to 77,000 and its total majority in its seats had risen from less than 6,000 to over 8,000. The four Labour seats were in Belfast, where the situation was even more striking. While the Unionists held seven seats, their total vote was 67,450 compared to Labour's 60,170. As Charles Brett pointed out, there were some 5,049 business votes in these eleven seats, 'not many of them, I am pretty sure, vote for Labour'.[28] The *Round Table* reckoned that Labour 'must be an even more formidable contender for the control of Belfast in five years' time'. Labour was helped by a number of factors. The election, for once, was relatively free from sectarian flag-waving and the Government chose to fight on Labour's strongest ground – the economy. But for the trend towards Labour to continue, these three factors – a low level of sectarianism, a concentration on economic issues and continued failure by the Government to tackle them satisfactorily – would have to proceed uninterrupted. This was an unlikely scenario: in the event, sectarianism did raise its head again and the Government succeeded in winning back some of the ground it had lost on economic issues. But Labour had another major problem. If it was to progress much further, it would have to resolve some of the contradictions implicit in its position. Since its adoption of a pro-partition policy in 1949 and the split of its nationalist wing, it had become the party of a section of the Belfast Protestant working class. For it to proceed much further it would have to clarify whether it was a Protestant and Unionist party, or a secular party seeking to transcend the divisions between Orange and Green.

The task was not quite as formidable as it might appear. There have always been significant class-based tensions within the

Unionist bloc, and from time to time there have been large-scale rebellions of Protestant workers against the leadership of the Unionist Party. A considerable degree of class consciousness has, in fact, coexisted with sectarianism. As Sarah Nelson puts it:

> There was a general knowledge, especially in Belfast, of the political arguments used by democratic socialists, and sporadic but repeated willingness to break with Unionism by actually voting for a party which asserted that social and economic struggles were more important than sectarian ones. Each generation also stored up its memories of strikes and industrial agitation, which again at least made them familiar with the methods and arguments of militant protest, and fuelled their suppressed resentments against the view traditional leaders took of their deprivation.[29]

In 1962 the liberal Unionist Robin Bailie claimed that in many Belfast Orange lodges a majority of members were socialists rather than Unionists, and the official history of the order in Belfast noted that 'the Belfast County Grand Lodge is much less conservative in politics than other County Lodges and its large industrial worker membership dictates that it speaks concernedly on matters that affect to help, or hurt, people whose living is in the factory rather than the farm'.[30] Orangeism was not incompatible with Labour voting – it was not even incompatible with promoting the social and economic interests of Catholics as well as Protestants – but it was fickle support which the NILP could never consolidate. The degree to which Labour could benefit from it depended on the general level of sectarian tensions, on discontent over social and economic issues, principally over unemployment, and on the extent to which Labour was perceived as rock solid on the constitutional status of Northern Ireland. It was not impossible for Labour to consolidate its support among Orange workers, but it was very difficult to do so while at the same time opening up the party to members and voters who supported it on a non- or anti-sectarian basis. So many conflicting factors had to be juggled that it was impossible for the party to map out a strategy that would ensure success.

The 1962 election had demonstrated increasing support for the NILP from voters who supported it as a party that opposed the sectarian character of Northern Ireland politics. This was expressed most coherently by its adherents in Northern Ireland's small cultural and artistic world, such as the shipyard playwright

Sam Thompson. His play *Over the Bridge* had created controversy in 1960 when the board of the Group Theatre had demanded substantial changes in the script, forcing the resignation of the artistic director, James Ellis. The board had been fearful of the effects of Thompson's frank portrayal of sectarianism in the shipyard, but the play was switched to another venue and played to large audiences and general acclaim. Speaking in 1962, Thompson gave a direct political point to the critique of Northern Ireland society presented in his play:

> We are in danger of ending up as a tribal community of processions and primitive ceremonies – international freaks with half the community starving and the other half emigrating . . . It was typical of the Unionists that they were always marching somewhere – not forwards, of course, but always backwards into history.

In June 1963 his play *The Evangelist* opened in the Grand Opera House. It was an attack on bible-thumping intolerance and fairly openly directed against Ian Paisley. The *News Letter*'s drama critic summarised Thompson's philosophy as 'ordinary decency and love and understanding against false and commercialised religion'.

This 'ordinary decency' has to be borne in mind when assessing the NILP's response to what were to become the civil rights demands. Frank Wright points out that the NILP's manifesto for the 1962 general election contained provisions for the revision of electoral law to bring it into line with that in the rest of the United Kingdom, the creation of an impartial boundary commission and the abolition of the ratepayer franchise in local government elections. During the Cromac by-election in Belfast in December 1962 there was evidence that the NILP was conscious of the need to reach out across the sectarian divide in a more positive way. Cromac was a heterogeneous constituency. Although dominated by middle-class Unionist voters, it also contained large numbers of mostly Catholic, working-class voters and the liberal-minded university area. In this constituency the only effective challenge to the Unionists would come from a party which succeeded in pulling together dissatisfied and mainly liberal Protestants with a major chunk of the Catholic vote.

A speech made by the NILP candidate, Cecil Allen, showed that the party was sensitive to the issues about which Catholics might be expected to be concerned. He made the usual references to the Unionists and their flute bands, sectarian slogans and old hatreds and prejudices, then condemned the governing party's 'absolute barrier to Catholic membership and shabby treatment of the Mater Hospital'.[31] He stressed that the NILP's primary concern was with the economic situation; 'However, the problems of discrimination, no matter from what quarter, and of religious tension are just as great.' Allen was a prominent trade-unionist of Protestant stock and represented the secular, democratic socialist wing of the NILP, which was close to the traditions of British Labour. This grouping was strengthened by the adherence of a small number of educated, professional people, many of them from a middle- and upper-middle-class background. The contribution made by some of these people outside the political sphere in later years is testimony to their intellectual quality: Charles Brett was to become chairman of the Northern Ireland Housing Executive, and has made major contributions to architectural history; Brian Garrett became a prominent solicitor and broadcaster; Vincent Hanna became a well-known television journalist; and Turlough O'Donnell became a judge.

Charles Brett has eloquently explained the reasons why he joined the NILP:

It was clear that my sympathies were overwhelmingly on the side of those less privileged than I had been. In general I strongly approved of the policies of the post-war Labour government . . . I felt that the working people of Ulster would benefit from fuller parity with the welfare state as understood in Labour Britain: so that the traditions of Irish nationalism and republicanism did not attract me. On the contrary I felt myself to be very much a European and an Internationalist. I was therefore left with a straightforward choice . . . I could join the deeply entrenched Unionist Party and endeavour to lever it leftward from inside; or I could join the tiny and feeble Northern Ireland Labour Party . . . The latter alternative was almost quixotic in practical terms, certainly in the short run, but it was honourable, straightforward and challenging. Moreover the smugness and self-satisfaction of Unionists at all levels, and the overbearing way in which they ran their one-party state, would seem today almost unbelievable; so that it appeared a positive public duty to stand outside and bung bricks at them.[32]

Brett was chairman of the NILP's policy committee, which also included party secretary Sam Napier and parliamentary leader Tom Boyd. They worked out a series of fairly sophisticated policy documents, which although inspired by the ideas of British Labour, were an independent application of Labourist ideas to Northern Ireland conditions. Brett attributed much of the party's success in the 1962 election to its programme, *Ulster Labour and the Sixties*. He believed that many electors were attracted by its approach not only to questions of economic policy and unemployment but also on hire-purchase law, consumer protection, ground rents and housing.

The 1964 programme, *Signposts to the New Ulster*, retained this emphasis on economic policy and better administration. However, it also elaborated policies on two areas of civil liberties: it attacked the Government's delay in introducing a legal aid scheme comparable to the system in Britain; and it also called for a review of the death penalty and advocated not merely a restriction on its use, as in Britain, but its total abolition. Throughout the 1960s, while concentrating on economic matters, the NILP plugged away at many of the issues that were taken up by the civil rights movement. Its 1963 conference called on the Government to extend the local government franchise to everyone over the age of twenty-one. In 1965 David Bleakley MP attacked the Government for not locating Northern Ireland's second university in Derry. In 1965 the party conference opposed the Special Powers Act. In 1966 Tom Boyd made a plea in Stormont for financial aid for the Mater Hospital and later that year Vivian Simpson MP sought suspension of the writ for a by-election in the QUB seat, pending abolition of the university seats. In 1967 the NILP conference called for an inquiry into religious discrimination and electoral gerrymandering. In March 1968, Sam Napier called on the O'Neill government to substitute deeds for words on such issues as housing allocation, discrimination in employment and restrictions on the franchise.

An NILP statement of 1967, published in the newsletter of the London-based Campaign for Democracy in Ulster (CDU) summarised the party's record:

> The NILP has always been opposed to discrimination on religious or political grounds and, particularly since 1959, has included statements against such discrimination in all its policy proposals.

Resolutions opposing discrimination have been adopted by successive annual Party conferences and Northern Ireland Labour
Members of Parliament have both sponsored and supported anti-
discrimination legislation in the Northern Ireland Parliament. In
1965 the NILP issued a statement on electoral reform calling for a
revision of Parliamentary boundaries . . . and for elections to be
based on the principle of one man one vote. In December 1966 the
NILP, jointly with the Northern Ireland Committee of the Irish
Congress of Trade Unions, made representations to the Northern
Ireland Government in the form of a joint memorandum calling for
electoral reform and a deputation sought to press the principles of
the document on the Northern Ireland Government.[33]

Nevertheless, the NILP saw the emergence of the CDU and the
increased interest shown by Westminster Labour MPs as a very
mixed blessing. Jack Hassard, a Dungannon NILP councillor who
had a good local record on civil rights issues, complained about the
visit of three British CDU-supporting MPs who toured Northern
Ireland in April 1967. They had, he said, only talked to 'Green
Tories'. The fact that Gerry Fitt had masterminded the tour was
another source of irritation.

Paddy Byrne, secretary of the CDU, visited Northern Ireland in
August 1967 and had a meeting with members of the executive
committee of the NILP. He was greeted warmly, not least because of
his long-standing friendship with Tom Boyd, which dated back to
their mutual involvement in work for the republican side in the
Spanish Civil War. But he was left in no doubt about the NILP's
deep reservations about the CDU's activities. Indeed its members
gave him the impression that they considered the CDU to be a 'damn
nuisance'. They made four points:

1 Outside attacks . . . were generally looked on by the majority of
people in Ulster as 'interference' and had the effect of uniting people
behind the government and away from Labour.

2 We should be more pro-Ulster in our approach and not always be
indulging in carping criticism. We should be seen as the true friends
of Ulster, that is our reforms would benefit all the people and we
should press for fair shares for Ulster in the allocation of factories,
etc . . .

3 We must not appear to be attacking the constitutional position.

4 We should work more closely with the NILP. The visit of the three MPs . . . and what they considered open siding with the Nationalists was bitterly criticised.[34]

Such criticisms were not unanimous, and when Byrne asked for their views on the progress of O'Neill's reforms, other differences emerged. A majority criticised O'Neill for moving too slowly on reform but also for not contemplating reform in local government, where grievances were most acute. A minority rejected the notion that O'Neill was doing more than stalling for time and believed that his reformism was no more than a hollow pretence. The meeting resulted in agreement on a number of points to bring about a closer liaison between the NILP and the CDU, but in a letter to Paul Rose MP, written on 21 August 1967, Byrne reported that he had found the NILP's attitude 'baffling'. The guarded nature of the agreement between the two groups was brought out in a letter to Byrne from Sam Napier, dated 14 August, which reported a positive response by the party's executive committee to the meeting, and said that they would submit a statement for inclusion in the CDU newsletter, but went on to say that they 'would like an assurance that the text of this would either be printed in full or only amended with their consent'.[35]

As a political party operating in a complex situation, the NILP could not see things in the same way as the CDU, which was a single-issue campaign based outside Northern Ireland. Indeed it says much for the openness and flexibility of both sides that relations were developed at all. However, by 1968 the NILP was committed to a series of wide-ranging reforms of electoral law, of electoral boundaries, of housing allocation, and to dealing with discrimination. The *Joint Memorandum on Citizens' Rights in Northern Ireland* of 1967 was as full a programme of reform as any brought out by an explicitly civil rights group. And the Northern Ireland Society of Labour Lawyers' pamphlet, *Discrimination – Pride for Prejudice* of 1969 was as sweeping an indictment of the Unionists and as passionate an appeal for civil rights as any of the publications of that time. Why, then, did the NILP not take the leadership of what was to become the civil rights movement? Very largely because, as a party which was oriented to parliamentary methods, it was not a suitable instrument for creating a mass extra-parliamentary movement; indeed most of its leaders were incapable of imagining such a course of action. The party, however, might have become an *alternative* to the civil rights movement by achieving its aims through parliament. A government led by, if not entirely composed of, the NILP did seem a possibility in the aftermath of the 1962 election. However, by 1966 it was abundantly clear that the party was incapable of ousting the Unionists.

The NILP was severely damaged by the 'Sunday swings' scandal of November 1964, when three of its six councillors voted in Belfast City Council to keep children's playgrounds closed on Sundays. This was in direct contradiction to the party's manifesto commitment during the council elections earlier in the year. The incident provoked bitter disagreement within the party, including the parliamentary party. One of its four MPs, William Boyd, was also one of the rebellious councillors and another, David Bleakley, supported him and blocked his expulsion from the parliamentary party. A compromise was reached and a split averted but this simply underlined the party's divisions. Charles Brett commented at the time that 'due to outside pressures the Executive Committee was afraid to . . . give a ruling on the interpretation of an entirely unambiguous sentence in the party's policy statement'. Frank Wright explains the significance of the dispute:

> What was so devastating about 'Sunday Swings' was not only that Catholics were troubled . . . but that it forced a public split between those Protestants who considered sabbatarianism to be a religious question . . . and those who considered that adherence to sabbatarianism was symptomatic of Protestant bigotry. It was on implicit agreement to differ about questions of this kind that the unity between the different groups in the NILP had been based . . . It is difficult to see how the issue could have left the NILP altogether unscathed.[36]

The party's 'equivocal solution of expelling and then readmitting the . . . councillors both shook the "Unionist" credentials of the NILP and "liberal" middle-class support simultaneously'.[37]

The NILP suffered a setback in the 1965 Stormont general election, but this should not be attributed too narrowly to the Sunday swings dispute. The sectarian polarisation created by the Divis Street riots was still operating and a fall in the unemployment rate deprived the NILP of its major issue. It should also be noted that in Terence O'Neill the NILP had a more formidable opponent than Lord Brookeborough. The new prime minister had a record of achievement on economic issues and his reforming image made him a much more credible repository for the votes of those Protestants who hoped to overcome sectarianism but were not committed socialists. Bew, Gibbon and Patterson, in *The State in Northern Ireland 1921–72*, have argued that O'Neill's strategy was designed principally to reunite the Unionist bloc by winning back from the NILP Protestant workers who were disaffected over unemployment. There is certainly evidence that in the 1965 election O'Neill made special efforts to challenge the NILP. Charles Brett testifies that the prime minister 'personally campaigned against the Labour candidates with more energy than he devoted to most other causes'.[38] After the election O'Neill expressed satisfaction that 'the rising tide of Labour had been well and truly turned'. In later years Sam Napier waxed bitter about O'Neill's campaign. He claimed that the premier had toured the Labour-held Belfast wards of Woodvale and Victoria in his official car: 'By convention no leader of a party would stoop to such tactics.' Napier also claimed that O'Neill smeared the NILP as anti-partitionist: 'He told people who lived in kitchen houses – imagine a Prime Minister – that Harold Wilson controlled the Northern Ireland Labour Party's policies and that Wilson was also anti-partitionist.'[39]

The NILP was partly a victim of circumstances, partly a victim of its own blunders and partly the victim of a deliberate attempt by O'Neill to stop its progress. In whatever way responsibility is measured, one salient fact emerges: by 1966 Labour had failed and its failure was one more factor in the inexorable process that was forcing opposition onto the streets.

The NILP was not the only party offering a radical, non-sectarian alternative; during the early 1960s the Ulster Liberal Party experienced a modest revival. Organised Liberalism in Ulster had broken up during the Home Rule crisis and by the time the Northern Ireland parliament was established it had ceased to be an electoral force. In 1958, however, a small group formed the Ulster Liberal Association – later the Ulster Liberal Party. It elected as chairman a clergyman from Newtownards, County Down, the Reverend Albert McElroy. For more than a decade he personified Liberalism in Northern Ireland. McElroy was born in Glasgow in 1915 and moved to Toomebridge, County Antrim, with his parents in 1930. He began his political involvement in the Fabian Society at Trinity College Dublin in the mid-1930s. He was active in the NILP and supported Harry Midgley's breakaway, pro-Union Common-wealth Labour Party in 1943. When Midgley went over to the Unionist Party in 1947, the Commonwealth Labour Party disinte-grated and McElroy returned to the NILP. But by then he was moving towards Liberalism. His election address as Labour candi-date in North Down, during the Westminster general election of 1950, made the point that 'the tragedy of Irish politics is the virtual absence of any Liberal tradition. Labour, whose appeal transcends sectarian bitterness, must champion liberalism in thought and practice'.[40] After a period in Glasgow and after studying theology in Oxford, he returned to Northern Ireland as Minister of New-townards Non-Subscribing Presbyterian Church. With a private income and a respectable position, he was well placed to lead the tiny Liberal forces. His attractive personality, humour, and talent as a communicator soon made him a well-known public figure.

The most important breakthrough for the Liberals came when Sheelagh Murnaghan, a Catholic barrister, won a seat in the Stormont parliament at a by-election in 1961 for one of the QUB seats. McElroy had stood for the QUB constituency in 1958; this was a favourable seat for the Liberals because of its educated electorate and the fact that in university elections the single transferable vote system of proportional representation was used. He won 13 per cent of first preferences but failed to get enough transfers to beat the Unionists to the third seat. The 1961 by-election was a straight fight with the Unionist candidate, and Sheelagh Murnaghan received 52.5 per cent of the vote. She went on to hold the seat at the general election of 1962; afterwards the secretary of the Ulster Unionist Council commented that 'the Liberal got in as a result of a large poll [of QUB graduates] from across the water where there has been an upsurge in favour of the Liberals'. This was not the whole explanation since Murnaghan's surplus was sufficient to elect an independent, Charles Stewart QC, and the party's domestic support was demonstrated in September 1962 when they won a borough council by-election in Bangor, County Down. However, when McElroy contested another by-election for QUB, in the more polarised atmosphere of November

1966, he was defeated by 749 votes, winning 44.4 per cent of the vote.

Although its revival was a result of contemporary factors, the Ulster Liberal Party still embodied the traditions of the party's past. In December 1962, McElroy claimed that it represented the

> heritage of Ulster Radicalism, of the brave men and women of '98, of the Rev J. B. Armour of Ballymoney . . . With them the driving force was passionate belief in the fatherhood of God and the universal brotherhood of man. They were no timid Whigs but full-blooded Radicals who got fighting mad at injustice, religious bigotry, smugness and cruelty. Our community needs to be shaken out of its dull conformity, out of its parochial indifference to the forces that are struggling all over the world for a world civilisation based on democracy, justice and peace.[41]

McElroy had moved significantly from the pro-Union views of his Commonwealth Labour Party days, and now, like a true Ulster radical, he wanted to see a united Ireland. He saw this coming about through the EEC, in which 'the border would disappear and there would be a levelling of social services'. Despite his chiliastic enthusiasm for a 'world civilisation', McElroy was anxious to present the Liberals as a 'broadly based, classless, non-sectarian party' which had won votes in the Cromac by-election 'from [Catholic working-class] Markets to [mixed, middle-class] Malone'.

Throughout the 1960s, the Ulster Liberal Party, like the NILP, was moving towards a more and more explicit endorsement of what were to become the civil rights demands. But in the case of the Liberals the shift in perceptions can be traced more easily. In 1964 McElroy wrote a broad attack on Ulster unionism. It made no reference to specific reforms but did focus on the undemocratic character of Northern Ireland:

> This community, of course, is not a normal democratic society. The permanent Tory majority at Stormont helps to underline its abnormality. For political democracy to work implies the existence of an opposition that does become the Government from time to time, with the existing Governments recognising this probability . . . Political monopolies, like any other kind of monopoly of long standing, are bad for the community, and even for the monopolists themselves.[42]

At this point McElroy, like the NILP, was emphasising the need for an alternative government to the Unionists rather than demanding a series of reforms from the Government.

As we have seen, after the 1962 general election it did seem possible that a coalition of oppositional forces might have ousted the Unionists; had this come about the Liberals would have been an important connecting link between the NILP and nationalists, helping to smooth over their mutual suspicions. McElroy was well placed to play the part of honest broker: his correspondence shows the trust he inspired among nationalist politicians such as James Connellan MP, and Ernest Blythe in the Irish Republic. During his 1966 election campaign Father Denis Faul and Austin Currie were active in canvassing on his behalf and Gerry Fitt donated £10 to his campaign. Michael McKeown of the NDP persuaded his party to give him a clear run.

Following McElroy's defeat, there was an increased emphasis by the Liberals on civil rights. It was now fairly evident that the Unionists were not going to be dislodged, but at the same time there was a swelling of grass-roots protest, largely initiated by, or focusing on, the republicans. McElroy held no brief for republicanism; in March 1966 he described Paisleyism and republicanism as 'twin brothers [whose] appeal is to blind unreason'. However, he strongly defended the right of republicans to hold commemorations of the 1916 Easter Rising and condemned as 'extremists' those who suggested that 'orderly and friendly processions in sympathetic areas will provoke anyone'. He spoke out against the ban on the Republican Clubs in March 1967 and against the prohibition of the commemorations of the 1867 Fenian Rising and the Easter commemoration in Armagh, appearing on the platforms of protest meetings along with republicans and nationalists. In September 1966 he challenged the attorney general, E. W. Jones, on the issue of discrimination in jobs and housing against Catholics in Enniskillen, Dungannon, Omagh and Derry. His election address for the QUB by-election in November 1966 denounced 'unjustifiable' discrimination in jobs and housing and said that 'machinery for investigation of complaints [was] essential'. He called for the abolition of the university seats to be accompanied by universal franchise and proportional representation.[43] In his presidential address to the

October 1967 conference of the Ulster Liberal Association he called on O'Neill to

Make a generous grant to the Mater Hospital without strings.

Meet 100% of the costs of voluntary schools without conditions.

Introduce a Government-sponsored Human Rights Bill . . .

Introduce legislation obliging local authorities to remove obscene and offensive slogans.

Introduce real electoral reform – one man one vote plus proportional representation in local government and Stormont elections . . .

Pursue a dynamic policy of economic co-operation with the rest of Ireland.

Repeal the Special Powers Act.

Expand the Privy Council to be representative of all shades of opinion.

Throw the sectarian bigots out of the Parliamentary Party.

Resign, himself, from the Orange Order and its ancillary organisations to show that he is Prime Minister of all the people.[44]

The Ulster Liberals, like the NILP, had links with their counterparts in Westminster. But whereas agitation on discrimination in Northern Ireland was mainly confined to the back benches of the British Labour Party, the front bench of the Liberals spoke out on the issue. Commenting on the visit of the Nationalist deputation to Westminster in July 1962, Eric Lubbock MP said that when they had seen Jo Grimond they had 'made out a *prima facie* case for the existence of discrimination'. Interviewed on Ulster Television in August 1962, Grimond himself said, 'Yes, I think there is discrimination.' Speaking in Belfast in 1967, Jeremy Thorpe MP said that there was 'growing impatience and intolerance at Westminster over the slow pace of reform in Northern Ireland'.

In December 1965, Sheelagh Murnaghan presented a bill at Stormont which would have made it a criminal offence to discriminate on grounds of race, creed, colour or belief, and would have set up a human rights commission to investigate allegations of discrimination. It was supported by NILP, Nationalist, NDP and RLP MPs and by her fellow QUB member, the Independent Charles Stewart. However, in February 1966 it was rejected by Stormont. She made three further attempts to bring forward such a bill; the third bill dropped criminal sanctions against discrimination and would have made the human rights commission more of a conciliatory and negotiating body, but it too was rejected. Her final attempt came in January 1968, but in February, Stormont refused a second reading by twenty-two votes to eight.

The Liberals had made valiant efforts to advance the cause of reform and reconciliation in Northern Ireland. They had tried to play their part in constructing a wide-ranging parliamentary alternative to the Unionists, but they had failed to achieve this, or even to make any significant electoral breakthrough. They had, from 1965 onwards, pressed determinedly for acceptance of reforms by the Government and had played an important part in drawing attention to the grievances of the minority community. They had successfully used their links with the British Liberals to give legitimacy to the complaints. All had been to no avail.

The launching of street marches by the Northern Ireland Civil Rights Association (NICRA) in 1968 could be seen as a logical consequence of the closure of every other channel for bringing about reform, but it divided the Liberals. A biography of McElroy comments:

> Many Liberals joined the movement and participated in the protest marches in the belief that this was the best way to force the Stormont government to introduce reforms. Albert McElroy was not one of them. McElroy remembered all too clearly the results of mass marches held by the Fascists, Nazis and other extremists in the 1920s and '30s. He knew that it was easier to get people onto the streets than to get them off again and dreaded the descent into bloodlust that the protests might bring.[45]

McElroy's Liberal colleague, Claude Wilton, took a leading part in the Derry Citizens' Action Committee (DCAC), but this was a consequence of his personal prestige as a champion of the rights of Derry Catholics. The Ulster Liberal Party, like the NILP, was committed to parliamentary action and it was not, and could not have become, a vehicle for mass protest.

The unemployment problem led to increasing involvement in politics by a trade-union movement that had always been cautious about any initiatives which might divide its rank and file. In February 1962 the Northern Ireland Committee of the ICTU called a one-day strike against the Government's 'pay pause'. The shipyard, and engineering and aircraft factories were closed as twenty-five thousand workers marched to a rally in the Ulster Hall, Belfast. In August the committee gathered some one hundred thousand signatures on a petition for the recall of Stormont to discuss unemployment and it proposed to send a batch of these petitions to arrive on Brookeborough's desk each morning, together with a copy of the Unionist manifesto which had promised action to increase employment.

The improved environment for trade-union political activity was shown by a march organised by Newry trades council in October 1962, in which Belfast contingents outnumbered the local participants. In this mainly Catholic town, two of the speakers were the Nationalists Eddie Richardson and James Connellan. They were given a good reception by the staunchly Protestant workers of Shorts aircraft factory and the Queen's Island shipyard. The disenchantment with the Government felt by many of these traditionally Unionist workers had been shown in Belfast City Hall some weeks earlier. A contingent of 150 aircraft shop stewards created pandemonium when the Unionist majority on the city council amended an NILP resolution about the plight of industry so that it praised, rather than condemned, the Government's efforts over unemployment. At the end of October a demonstration of three thousand to four thousand trade-unionists marched to Stormont on the day the Hall Report was debated. It was a smaller march than had been expected but it left the shipyard and the aircraft factory deserted and involved trade-unionists from Newry, Larne, Bangor, Newtownards and other towns. They called on the Stormont parties to 'lay aside party political bickering and sectional interests' and assured them that the unions would 'co-operate in all measures that are aimed at achieving . . . full employment and prosperity'.

The trade-union movement had some success in mobilising its members on narrowly social and economic issues but it trod carefully since it was all too well aware of the divisions within its membership. As the 1960s progressed, the unemployment situation improved as sectarianism revived, and the trade-union movement retreated once more from any public political role.

The Belfast and District Trades Union Council was less restrained. It spoke out on issues that were relatively safe, such as council rents, and joined in the condemnation of the Unionist Party's 'sectarian tactics' and record on unemployment. But in December 1962 it approved a document from the London-based National Council for Civil Liberties (NCCL), which condemned the Government's continued refusal to abolish the Civil Authorities (Special Powers) Act and called for an investigation into alleged discrimination against Catholics. In 1966 it wrote to Minister of Home Affairs William Craig, calling for legislation against discrimination and incitement, electoral reform, control over arms held by members of the Ulster Special Constabulary (B Specials), and economic development. The trades council was in a better position than the Northern Ireland Committee of the ICTU to take such initiatives because trade-union branches which disapproved of its policies simply refrained from affiliating, or disaffiliated; like the east Belfast branch of the Electrical Trade Union, which withdrew from the council in 1966 because of its support for an Easter Rising commemoration. Betty Sinclair, the trades council secretary, explained that they had taken part to honour a former member of its executive – James Connolly; this was unlikely to persuade trade-unionists who supported the Unionist Party to become involved in the council.

Betty Sinclair was a veteran Communist who later became chairman of NICRA. The NCCL document originated with a resolution to its annual conference from the Connolly Association, an organisation for Irish workers in Britain that has always had close links with the Communist Party of Great Britain. Communism in Northern Ireland was upheld by the Communist Party of Northern Ireland (CPNI); the party was created by a split in the former Communist Party of Ireland over support for the Allied war effort following Hitler's invasion of the USSR in June 1941. The CPNI felt sufficiently encouraged by political developments in 1962 to launch a membership drive. Its main emphasis was on opposition to entry into the EEC and it organised a meeting in Belfast with speakers from its fraternal parties in Britain and the Irish Republic to oppose British and Irish membership. It proposed to flood the factories with leaflets inviting all who opposed the EEC to join the ranks of the party.

University-based protest was fairly weak in Belfast; there was a small branch of the Campaign for Nuclear Disarmament, but even during the trauma of the Cuba missiles crisis in October 1962, it mustered only fifty people on a picket of the United States consulate, and there was a small group of Trotskyists within the NILP's youth group, the Young Socialists. But the general picture is clear – left-wing movements were tiny, weak and isolated. They had a structure of priorities and a view of the world which had little purchase on the consciousness of other Northern Ireland citizens.

The years between 1962 and 1968 saw a more determined, broader and more sophisticated assault on Unionist domination than had occurred at any time since the creation of Northern Ireland. The opposition forces were divided and could only with great difficulty have come together to offer an alternative to the ruling party, but it was a real possibility. However, such a course of events was cut across and diffused by O'Neill's premiership. This was partly through a deliberate strategy, partly because his more conciliatory image was sufficient for most of the dissident middle-class voters who had dallied with the NILP and the Liberals, and partly because his economic policies and increased sectarian polarisation staunched the haemorrhage of working-class Unionist voters. In any event, O'Neill's success in the 1965 Stormont general election was an important turning point. He had blocked the emergence of any alternative to the Unionist Party but his moderate image gave hope that he might sponsor the necessary reforms. Albert McElroy believed in this possibility; in his 1967 presidential address to the Ulster Liberal Party he said:

> Everything depends on the calibre of O'Neill's character. There are those who argue that he is a weakling and/or a prisoner of his own tradition. My personal view is that he means well, that he has the latent strength of character and that up to the present he has been largely a prisoner of the tatty Ulster Tory tradition.[46]

Events would show that McElroy's hopes were not to be fulfilled. O'Neill did not promote sufficiently far-reaching reforms sufficiently early to avert a turn to street politics.

THE CAMPAIGN FOR SOCIAL JUSTICE
AND THE CAMPAIGN FOR DEMOCRACY IN ULSTER

> The British Labour Members,
> this Miller, Orme and Rose,
> have come across to Ulster
> to pick and rake and nose.
> For Gerry Fitt has told them
> in this they must not fail,
> but we will tell them Derry's walls
> are not put up for sale.
> They talk of segregation, discrimination too,
> but face the facts, dear Gerry,
> for we have news for you.
>
> We're proud of our wee Ulster,
> we always take a stand,
> for Protestants the Union Jack
> will fly across this land.
>
> *from* 'Gerry's Walls' by James Young

The Campaign for Social Justice (CSJ) was to be instrumental in founding NICRA some years later and it helped to prepare the ground for the emergence of a mass civil rights movement. The CSJ's origins are important, however, not only in this context but also because they illustrate the way in which an issue – housing – was crucial in the mid-1960s as a catalyst for the political developments which created the movement. The CSJ was important also for its orientation to British politics through its relationship with the CDU.

The CSJ grew out of the Homeless Citizens' League (HCL) founded in Dungannon in May 1963. The HCL was created and led by Conn and Patricia McCluskey, who were also to be the founders of the CSJ, and arose out of a challenge to the housing policy of Dungannon Urban District Council by a group of young Catholic housewives. In May 1963 forty of these young women submitted a petition to the council; they told a reporter on the *Dungannon Observer* that they were living in cramped and insanitary houses, or with relatives, because of their inability to get other accommodation. They complained that Protestants were getting houses almost as soon as they applied and council houses were being given to Protestants who came from other areas, while the petitioners had, in some cases, made seven or eight applications without success. A few days later sixty-seven women picketed a council meeting, provoking what the *Dungannon Observer* called a 'stormy session'. On 24 May the HCL was formed at a meeting chaired by Patricia McCluskey.

The grievances that led to the formation of the HCL were localised. The overall record on housing in Northern Ireland was creditable. A great effort had been needed to replace housing that had been destroyed during World War II. As Hugh Shearman pointed out in his government-published handbook, *Northern Ireland*, the amount of housing stock lost during World War II – fifty thousand units – was almost the same as the number of houses built between 1919 and 1939, so that Northern Ireland was in much the same position in 1945 as it had been at the end of World War I. The Government responded by revising housing legislation in order to facilitate house-building by local authorities, by providing subsidies to public- and private-sector house-building, and by setting up the Northern Ireland Housing Trust (NIHT) to supplement the efforts of local councils. Between June 1944 and December 1964, 45,920 council houses were built and the NIHT erected 28,513, while 3,102 were built by other public bodies. The total of new permanent dwellings, including those in the private sector, was 124,878.[1] This was a good record when compared with the 100,000 new dwellings which the 1943 Northern Ireland Housing Survey showed were needed.

This overall expansion of housing did not mean that there was no scope for grievances. In fact it heightened them by making it possible for those who were not benefiting to compare themselves with those who were, and by creating new expectations which some councils did not satisfy for some sections of their populations. Needless to say, these dissatisfied groups were mainly Catholics in the lower income brackets. In the first place the housing programme was closely linked to industrial expansion, which meant that it tended to be focused on those areas and among those sections of the population which were key factors to economic growth. As long as the new factories, and therefore a large proportion of the new houses, were concentrated east of the River Bann, and Protestants continued to be employed in proportionately larger numbers than Catholics, there was continuing scope for feelings of grievance among the minority community.

Feelings of grievance about housing allocation, therefore, were not just created by discrimination against Catholics. The sectarian dimension was influenced by geographical location and income levels. For example, the best of the new housing was provided by the NIHT and it was allocated fairly when Protestants and Catholics in similar circumstances were being considered, but there was a definite bias against the lower income groups. One study found that when the average income levels of NIHT tenants were compared with the average for the community as a whole, it was apparent that the NIHT catered mainly for 'the middle paid workers'.[2] This excluded more Catholics than Protestants, since a higher percentage of low-income families were Catholic. However, the overall figures for housing allocation did not show discrimination against Catholics. Richard Rose found that when the housing of Protestants and Catholics in the same income groups was compared, there was a slight bias of 4 per cent in favour of Catholics. When family size was considered, there was a bias of 12 per cent against Catholics. Nevertheless, 'Catholics still constitute 78 per cent of all large families in public housing'.[3] This finding was used by Unionists and their supporters in later years to dispute the claims of the civil rights movement. However, both John Whyte and Charles Brett, in their respective studies, pointed out that Rose had not excluded the possibility of individual cases of discrimination by local councils. These, while not proving generalised discrimination, were acute irritants creating discontent far beyond the boundaries of the authorities concerned.[4] Whyte found that allegations of discrimination in housing were made, almost exclusively, about local authorities west of the Bann, where Unionist–Nationalist rivalries were most intense. There are records of numerous disputes from this area during the early 1960s.

In December 1963, Councillor J. J. Donnelly of Enniskillen

Borough Council alleged that out of 179 houses built by the council, 178 were tenanted by Protestants. Nearly a year later the Senate was told that out of 231 houses built in Enniskillen, only 20 had gone to Catholics. In early 1965, Austin Currie complained that 17 out of 19 houses allocated in Cookstown had gone to 'Government supporters', and Senator P. J. O'Hare called on the Government to 'sack' Lisnaskea Rural District Council for having given a three-bedroomed house to an unmarried man, while rejecting the application of a widow and her sons who were living in a condemned hovel. The successful applicant, he said, was a Unionist who had been put on the list the day before the decision was made. The custom of many councils of allocating houses by vote in council meetings led to a number of clashes. Councillor John Curran walked out of a meeting of Lisnaskea council in November 1963 after a house was allocated to a man who was 'in a fairly good house', while a more needy Catholic applicant was rejected: 'Would they not take the man off the bog bank,' he asked, 'and do what he was asking for once?'[5] In March 1965, Lisnaskea Rural District Council ignored a plea from the Fermanagh Welfare Committee to let a house to a father of four who was about to be evicted from his existing accommodation. The council members were asked to 'examine their consciences' by a Nationalist councillor, but voted to let the house to another applicant. In May that year another Nationalist commented: 'It's the old, old story of no Catholic need apply' when Lisnaskea council voted to give a house to a Protestant who had been waiting for two years, over the head of a Catholic who had been waiting for ten years. The same month Enniskillen Rural District Council voted to let six new houses to Protestants, ignoring a plea on behalf of a Catholic family 'living in terrible circumstances'.

The Government could, on occasion, appear to be embarrassed at the actions of some of these Unionist councils. In 1963 the Minister of Health and Local Government, William J. Morgan, 'deplored' a remark made by the housing committee chairman at Enniskillen Borough Council that houses should only be let to the 'right' people. However, a month later he refused a demand that local authorities should be asked to submit their housing allocation policies for approval. When Cahir Healy asked in February 1963 that councils be issued with simple instructions on housing allocation because 'some people get houses in a month and some are kept waiting for ten years, depending on the influence they can bring to bear on local councillors', the minister replied that the only standard laid down in the act was one of need, but took no action on Healy's request. In 1965, when Senator P. J. O'Hare called for curbs on those councils that discriminated in housing allocation, J. L. O. Andrews, for the Government, replied that the only answer was to build more houses, more quickly. So while the Government did not stand over the actions of some councils, it was clear to anti-Unionists that it was not going to intervene.

In these west of the Bann local authorities, housing allocation became an intensely politicised issue, which militated against any resolution of particular disputes. Nationalists saw each one as another turn of the screw against the Catholic community, while Unionists were all too ready to dismiss them as no more than partisan propaganda. Such disputes would be particularly intense where there was a real prospect of shifting the local balance of power: in other words, where the two sides were evenly balanced numerically, or where a Unionist minority held power because of the electoral system. It is not surprising, therefore, to find Dungannon as the focus of a major battle over housing.

Dungannon was evenly balanced between Protestants and Catholics. (The CSJ claimed a slight Catholic majority, with 50.3 per cent.) But control of the council was firmly in Unionist hands. There were three wards, each of which returned seven councillors: the bulk of the Protestant population was in the East ward and the bulk of the Catholics in the West ward; the Central ward had only about half the population of each of the other two, but returned the same number of councillors and had a Protestant majority. The result was that fourteen Unionists were elected from the East and Central wards, while the West ward returned seven anti-Unionists. Any major expansion of housing could bring about a shift in the political balance of the council and Catholics were keenly aware of this. They tended to assume that any dragging of council heels in housing provision was linked to Unionist determination that its electoral position should not be eroded. As Mike Tomlinson has put it:

The practice of discriminatory housing allocation had a direct political vitality: to Catholics it appeared as the crucial practice by which Unionist councillors guaranteed votes and automatic re-election, and it seemed to explain why they themselves were so badly housed.[6]

In other words it did not lead to demands for a general increase of housing provision but to a struggle over allocation of the existing housing stock. The HCL did not, however, express the grievances of Dungannon Catholics as a whole, but of a particular section – young married couples, and families living with relatives or in inadequate accommodation. Much of the council's housing effort was devoted to slum clearance and Catholics benefited dispropor-tionately from this, since they were disproportionately affected by slum conditions. But there were many Catholics who were not eligible for rehousing under slum clearance; some had been made homeless by rehousing of relatives with whom they had been living and were prevented from moving with their relatives to new council homes by the housing regulations. They saw the council's allocation policies as unjust and unacceptable.

A HCL delegation to Stormont in 1963 outlined what it saw as the discriminatory housing policy of Dungannon council:

> Since the war 194 houses have been built for normal letting [as distinct from slum clearance]. All were let to Protestants, none to Catholics. (In the same period 128 houses have been let in rehousing families under slum-clearance schemes: 26 to Protestants, 102 to Catholics.) Between the end of the war and May 1950 there were 275 Catholic families on the Council's waiting list for houses. At the present time there are 400 names on the waiting list. Not one has got a house from the Urban District Council.
>
> When the houses built since the war (194) were let, 112 Protes-tants were taken from outside the urban boundaries and given houses. Virtually all members of the Homeless Citizens' League have been born and reared within the urban boundary, except for a couple of cases where a Dungannon person has married a newcomer to the town.
>
> The Council owns a grand total of 411 houses. Of these 200 are let to Protestants and 131 to Catholics.[7]

The council housing committee defended its record by pointing to the overall housing record in Dungannon and suggesting that it corresponded, in terms of allocation, to the proportions of Protes-tants and Catholics in the town. However, it did not distinguish between NIHT provision and that of the council, or between slum clearance and other lets. It pointed out that the allocation of houses had been left to officials and attacked Nationalist councillors for absenting themselves from the council for nearly seven months in protest over a GAA pitch, which meant that they were not present when crucial decisions on housing were taken. One Unionist councillor put the figures at 229 council houses to Protestants and 138 to Catholics, with 180 NIHT dwellings to Protestants and 212 to Catholics, but he did not distinguish between slum clearance and new lets.

What was new about the HCL, however, was not the complaints which it voiced but the fact that it took direct action. A local estate of some fifty prefabricated houses was due to be cleared and demolished as part of the housing programme and its residents were being rehoused at the time of the HCL's agitation. Appeals were made for the vacated prefabs to be given to homeless families but the council replied that plans were already under way to demolish them to make room for further development. However, the HCL made enquiries and discovered that the Ministry of Health and Local Government had received no proposals for redevelopment and that a public inquiry would be necessary before it could take place. This meant that there would be a considerable period of time before demolition of the prefabs was necessary. The HCL moved thirty-seven families into the prefabs as they were vacated – some former tenants co-operated by handing over their keys. The council decided to take legal action to evict them and threatened that the squatting tenants would be taken off the housing list altogether, and a number of the prefabs had their electricity cut off.

However, the new occupants were delighted with their homes and messages of support flooded in from all over Northern Ireland. The squatters got widespread publicity, and a degree of sympathy, in the Northern Ireland press. A *Belfast Telegraph* editorial commented on 4 September 1963:

> For all its financial assistance and encouragement, the feeling persists that Stormont should adopt a tougher line with those local authorities whose building programmes fall short of requirements. When persuasion does not produce results stronger means are justified. The Dungannon Council's post-war housing record is not one of signal achievement. In these circumstances it is negative to

assert that the squatters 'will not be considered' when houses become available. The objective is to provide houses for all those in need. Meanwhile the efforts to overcome the immediate difficulties should be tempered by humanity.

The *Belfast Telegraph* saw the problem as one of the total amount of housing being provided rather than in terms of allocation policies, but it left no doubt that the HCL had succeeded in wrong-footing the Dungannon Unionists.

In September the HCL sent a delegation to meet the Minister of Health and Local Government; it was led by Conn McCluskey and accompanied by Joseph Stewart MP. Subsequently the minister wrote to the delegation informing its members that he had held a meeting with the council chairman, William Stewart, the housing committee chairman, J. Purdy, two other councillors and the town clerk. The minister's parliamentary secretary and some ministry officials had also taken part and there was reference to a meeting with prime minister Terence O'Neill, so obviously the affair was being taken seriously. A three-point agreement had been reached; this involved an extension to the Ballygawley Road housing scheme, to be completed as soon as possible, and in the meantime, although the squatters would be obliged to vacate the prefabs and would not be considered for rehousing until they did so, no steps would be taken to evict them and squatters who co-operated with the council would be fully eligible for rehousing at Ballygawley Road. This was perceived by the HCL as a victory but it should be noted that neither the squatting nor the compromise threatened the political balance in Dungannon. The prefabs were in the West ward and the squatters were to be given houses in the predominantly Catholic Ballygawley estate, also in the West ward. The council's response to the squatting had been bureaucratic and insensitive but it was not prompted by fears of its electoral position being eroded. Indeed on 18 September the *News Letter* was able to find evidence of the positive features of Unionist rule in the affair:

Here is an instance where, by reason of the compact nature of the territory [of Northern Ireland], there can be greater interest and sympathy at the top for a purely local difficulty than one could imagine might be given by a more distant executive control . . . There is something indeed healthy about an administration in which such care can be taken to find an acceptable sympathetic solution to a human problem.

The HCL and its campaign were significant for the development of the civil rights movement in a number of ways. Up until that time complaints by Catholics about discrimination tended to be contained within their own areas. Nationalist councillors would make ritual denunciations for the record and for a few lines in the local press and in the *Irish News*. The ill feeling and polarisation produced by such incidents helped to keep the Catholic vote mobilised but it could never actually change anything. The HCL forced the council to back down and got a number of families into new homes. Part of the reason for its success was that it went over the head of Dungannon Urban District Council and took a coherent, well-presented case to the Stormont authorities. The HCL also cut across the leadership of local Catholics and highlighted some of its inadequacies. Shortly before the creation of the HCL, a newly elected West ward councillor, William Doherty, was reported as being undecided about whether or not to take his seat. His sponsors, Councillors Peter Donnelly and Jack McRea, had been boycotting meetings for six months in protest at the council's decision not to provide facilities for Gaelic games. Another West ward councillor, Brian Morrison, had decided to return to the council to join the opposition which was being provided by an Independent, Jim Corrigan, and an NILP councillor, John Murphy. He said that the four abstentionist councillors had made a laughing stock of the ward and had not succeeded in embarrassing the Unionists. The picket of the council by the housewives helped Doherty to make up his mind and he attended the council meeting, pledging his support to their campaign. But the Unionists were able to point to the boycott and Nationalist non-participation in housing decisions to deflect criticisms of their own policies.

Two of the HCL's main demands were for a points system for housing allocation and an end to residential segregation in council housing, so it was embarrassing when it emerged that there had been a 'gentleman's agreement' between Unionist and Nationalist councillors on the allocation of houses. The Independent councillor, Jim Corrigan, revealed at an HCL meeting that the prefabs had been allocated on a fifty–fifty basis and that when a tenant left the prefabs the vacated house was allocated to a new tenant of the same denomination. This enabled a Unionist councillor to claim that since twelve Protestant families were leaving the prefabs, twelve extra Catholic families could be accommodated who would not have been housed under the gentleman's agreement, so the Catholics should feel grateful instead of complaining about discrimination. He did not explain how the council's policy of demolishing the prefabs fitted in with this claim.

At the HCL's first public meeting Councillor James Donnelly claimed that he and the other Nationalist councillors had been fighting on the housing issue for eight years and that their boycott had been about housing as well as about the council's refusal to allocate a Gaelic pitch on the new playing fields. However, Malachy Sweeney took up the record of the Nationalists and criticised the custom whereby Catholics were chosen as tenants for 'Catholic' houses and Protestants for 'Protestant' houses: 'This gentleman's agreement,' he said, 'should be done away with. I would like to see the councillors fighting every house on its merits. Doesn't matter where it is . . . people had a right to live in their own town and I say that they should break the agreement.'[8] His statement was met by cheers and applause from the audience. Such a response was an indication of the way in which outside events were changing perceptions in Northern Ireland, so that practices that had been accepted for decades were now coming under attack. A letter in the *Dungannon Observer* of 21 September 1963 reflected these new attitudes:

Surely the Nationalist Councillors of Dungannon could not, even for some possible immediate gain, acquiese in something which is so blatantly against the spirit of the times? What's not acceptable in South Africa or Birmingham, Alabama, is surely not going to be acceptable as applicable on a religious basis in Dungannon, Co. Tyrone?

The HCL arose at a time when the Black civil rights movement in the United States was headline news around the world. The way in which it had captured the popular imagination was reflected in a photograph in the *Dungannon Observer* of 21 September 1963 showing a fancy-dress parade in Dungannon. Two little boys, one with his face blacked, held up a placard that read:

We are pals from Alabama,
Where they say we can't agree.
Is there really that much difference,
When you look at him and me?

Members and supporters of the HCL made a direct parallel with their own situations. One woman who was interviewed on the first picket of the council said:

> They talk about Alabama. Why don't they talk about Dungannon? Why don't they open their eyes and see what's going on here? Take the Killyman Road Estate for example . . . dozens of houses and not a Catholic to be found amongst them. It's a cut and dried case of religious discrimination.[9]

Placards displayed on the picket included slogans like 'Racial discrimination in Alabama hits Dungannon' and 'If our religion is against us, ship us to Little Rock'. 'P. F.' suggested, to the *Dungannon Observer* in a letter, that Freddie Gilroy, the Belfast-born boxing champion, should follow the example of Floyd Patterson, who had gone to Birmingham, Alabama, to throw his weight behind the campaign against discrimination and prejudice.

Councillor Corrigan referred to the surprise which he had encountered among liberal Protestants at some of the events in Dungannon. He compared this with Senator Bobby Kennedy's reaction in the United States when a delegation of Black civil rights leaders had outlined the reality of discrimination in the United States:

> No one should be under any illusions. There are class barriers, race barriers and religious barriers in most countries. No one should condone them. Meek acceptance is not enough. The internal divisions in the North of Ireland have done more harm to the whole of Ireland than has partition, which was partly a result of those internal divisions in the first place.[10]

Two months later Corrigan commented on the massive civil rights march which had taken place in Washington DC on 28 August 1963: 'But perhaps the issue which has been so powerfully underlined in Washington this week . . . can be better appreciated in the North of Ireland than in Britain. There has been a continual struggle in the six counties for the rights of the minority.'[11] A letter in the *Dungannon Observer* of 7 September concluded that the minority in Northern Ireland were 'white negroes', who were in the same position as Blacks in the Southern United States. Another letter in the same issue drew a direct lesson from events across the Atlantic and called for 'a march on the town in which all victims of discrimination and all sympathisers will take part'.

It was to be five years before such a march actually took place and during the intervening period agitation on the civil rights issue was to be dominated by the CSJ which, although it grew directly out of the HCL, did not initiate direct action nor even try to mobilise a popular campaign. Its activities were confined to publicity and to lobbying politicians at Westminster. The founders and leaders of the CSJ, Conn and Patricia McCluskey, were initially motivated by what they saw as the ineffectuality of Nationalist opposition in putting the case of the Catholic minority. Patricia McCluskey was to recall: 'I saw a television show . . . between a Nationalist MP and Mr Faulkner and the Nationalist, who had the best case, made such a poor showing. He asserted all the wrongs but had no statistics to back them up . . . Mr Faulkner just walked rings round him and made a fool of him.[12]

The success of the HCL further highlighted the weakness of Nationalist opposition. The McCluskeys told Vincent Feeney how

as news of what had been achieved in Dungannon spread through Ulster, [they] were deluged with letters. The messages were all the same: how had they won this concession from Stormont? This reaction surprised the McCluskeys, and they quickly realised that there was a tremendous yearning among the Catholic people for organisation and leadership. There and then they decided to establish a group of educated people who would articulate the frustrations of the minority.[13]

The membership of CSJ was restricted to a group of thirteen professional people and although it was avowedly non-sectarian, membership was entirely Catholic. The name 'Campaign for Social Justice' is significant: although, as we have seen, the Black civil rights movement in the United States was making a tremendous impact when the CSJ was founded, the term adopted was not 'civil rights' but 'social justice', a term which was given a wide currency by Pope Pius XI in his encyclical, *Quadragesimo Anno*, of 1921. The adoption of this name said something about the background of the

93

members of the CSJ, drawn as they were from the educated Catholic middle class, trained in Catholic schools and colleges. Patricia McCluskey said: 'The people who were into Social Justice at the beginning were all second generation, if you like, educated . . . People like my husband and myself would have been the first generation at boarding school, secondary school, university.'[14] One CSJ member, Brian Gregory, remembered that when Bernadette Devlin, at a civil rights meeting, had attacked 'middle-class, middle-of-the-road, do-gooders' he had turned to his friend Conor Gilligan and said, 'That's us!'[15] The membership included two consultant surgeons, two general practitioners, an architect and a science professor. There were two councillors, one from Armagh, the other from Enniskillen, and two others were involved in political organisations: one was on the committee of National Unity, the small nationalist ginger group, the other was secretary of the RLP. Two were prominent in the Freedom from Hunger Campaign. One was an English-born woman who had lived in Northern Ireland for twelve years.

The CSJ was officially launched at a press conference held in the Wellington Park Hotel, Belfast, on 17 January 1964. A statement issued at the time said:

> The Government of Northern Ireland's policies of apartheid and discrimination have continued to be implemented at all levels with such zeal that we . . . have banded ourselves together to oppose them.
>
> Our first objective will be to collect comprehensive and accurate data on all injustices done against all creeds and political opinions including details of discrimination in jobs and houses and to bring them to the attention of as many socially minded people as possible. A booklet will be published for the widest circulation in which we will feel no need to select or slant our facts for the best effect, our case being so strong that the presentation of the unvarnished truth will be sufficient . . . Our aim is, we think, both basic and Christian but, nevertheless, has not been realised here for hundreds of years, namely equality for all.[16]

Conn McCluskey, challenged on the basis that all the members were Catholics, replied that five or six Protestants who had been approached had approved of their idea but had been unwilling to join. He felt that they had been intimidated. Brian Gregory added that a great many right-thinking Protestants did not know the facts.

The CSJ announced that it intended to make 'as full use as funds allow' of newspaper, poster and leaflet publicity outside Ireland, availing of the services of an advertising consultant. 'In this way we will force all the disturbing details of life over here to the attention of the British and American people so that it can never again be said that they were unaware of what was happening in Northern Ireland.' No approach was intended to the Northern Ireland government, but the CSJ members hoped that publication of the 'facts' would lead 'decent Ulster people [to] say it was time for the community to live in a proper manner'. Patricia McCluskey said that 'it was housing which brought us into this, but then the jobs situation came with housing and the whole picture is really frightening'.

The CSJ differed from previous organisations which sought to highlight the grievances of the Catholic minority in the extent to which it directed its efforts at influencing political opinion in Britain. 'My heroes,' said Conn McCluskey, 'are all the people belonging to the British National Council for Civil Liberties who are democrats and liberals and have something we Irish haven't, a bit of objectivity.'[17] Brian Gregory has said how, at the inaugural meeting of the CSJ, someone had suggested that they try to capture the Nationalist Party; Conn McCluskey said that he was not interested in the Nationalist Party, that it was powerless.[18] At the first press conference Conn McCluskey dissociated the CSJ from approaches being made by the Nationalist Party to the British government and to politicians at Westminster on the discrimination issue. Conor Gilligan recalled that the CSJ did not want to be 'contaminated' by any Northern Ireland politicians, except Gerry Fitt. The tradition of Nationalist politics was to link the grievances of the Catholic minority to Irish unity, but the CSJ members were not concerned with ending partition. 'Somebody else can solve the border question,' said Brian Gregory. 'We were concerned with the rights of people living here.' He did admit, however, that most of the CSJ people would have had aspirations for eventual Irish unity.

In the view of the CSJ the 'kernel of the Ulster problem' was that:

1 The Northern Ireland Parliament which is subject to the authority of Westminster, has refused since it was set up by Britain to give justice to the minority, and steadfastly ignored the appeals of the Parliamentary representatives of the minority.

2 The Government of Ireland Act which set up the Northern Ireland Administration had a Section 5 which was designed to give protection to the minority. It has failed to do so.

3 Every attempt to have the grievances of the minority discussed at Westminster was defeated by the existence of a 'convention' which prevented discussion of matters which were within the competence of the Parliament of Northern Ireland.

Successive British Governments, both Tory and Labour, have failed to protect the minority in Northern Ireland.

To us the solution seems for the Westminster Parliament to make long overdue amends to the Government of Ireland Act, 1920, in order to afford protection to the religious minority, as was originally intended.[19]

Just as the HCL had gone over the head of Dungannon Urban District Council and had taken its case direct to Stormont, the CSJ intended to go over the head of the Unionist government and to appeal directly to Westminster and to political opinion in Britain. And just as the HCL had been able to present a well-researched and well-presented case, which the Dungannon Unionists had been unable to refute completely, the CSJ intended to concentrate on presenting what it saw as the facts about discrimination in Northern Ireland, believing that a simple presentation of its evidence would be sufficient to discredit the Stormont authorities and to bring about reform.

The CSJ published five pamphlets: *Why Justice Cannot Be Done; Londonderry. One Man, No Vote; What the Papers Say; Legal Aid to Oppose Discrimination – Not Likely!; Northern Ireland. The Plain Truth;* and a second edition of *The Plain Truth.* It also published a regular *Campaign Newsletter*, which consisted mainly of extracts from newspapers, which enabled it to pass on items published in Irish newspapers which would not have been covered in the British press. The first pamphlet – *Why Justice Cannot Be Done* – arose out of the efforts of the CSJ to use the courts to challenge what it saw as religious discrimination. It had received legal advice to the effect that no legislation of the Unionist government contravened the

Government of Ireland Act 1920 and that the act did not offer a means of obtaining redress for complaints of discrimination. This opinion was contradicted by Prime Minister Sir Alec Douglas-Home when he visited Northern Ireland in the spring of 1964. At a press conference he suggested that anyone with such complaints could take action in the courts under Section 5 of the act, which prohibited the Stormont authorities from discriminating on grounds of religion. The CSJ wrote to Sir Alec asking how the act could be used to obtain redress. The pamphlet reproduced the correspondence and showed that the prime minister was unable to give any concrete advice to back up his claim. The Home Office was unable to help either. A letter to the CSJ, dated 30 June 1964, stated:

> The matters in this letter appear to the Secretary of State to be within the field of responsibility which the 1920 Act has entrusted to Stormont and it would not be proper for him to comment upon them. Her Majesty's Government has no legislation in view to amend the above Act.[20]

Londonderry. One Man, No Vote reiterated the Nationalist case against the local government electoral system in Northern Ireland's second-largest urban centre. What was new, however, was the use of the name 'Londonderry' – an indication of the CSJ's determination not to be drawn into secondary issues, such as the dispute over the name of the city and county. The pamphlet outlined the well-known gerrymandering of the city, whereby a one-third Unionist minority of the population elected two-thirds of the councillors. It went on to describe the way in which the city had been allowed to decline while investment in new industry was concentrated east of the Bann. It explained how Londonderry Corporation was unwilling to upset the political balance by extending the city boundary in order to build new houses, despite the fact that all the available land in the Catholic-dominated South ward had already been built on. It summarised the allocation of houses in the city, providing comparative lists of Catholic tenancies and those of 'others'. These indicated a large disparity: the total of Catholic tenancies was 924, while 'others' was 2,212. A similar comparison was made for corporation employment, with contrasts being drawn not just between the overall numbers of Catholics and

Protestants, but between the total value of salaries earned by Catholic and Protestant employees – £20,400 and £94,004 respectively. It went on to show how the electoral boundaries for the Northern Ireland parliament had been arranged so that Foyle returned a Nationalist who was, however, 'neutralised' by the creation of a City of Londonderry constituency which stretched far out into the Unionist-dominated countryside.

What the Papers Say sketched in the background to the formation of the CSJ and went on to elaborate on why it wished to involve British public opinion:

> If through publicity we could procure what must surely be the very reasonable achievement of universal adult suffrage in local or regional government[21] then our position would be immeasurably strengthened. Our people could then begin to have allocated to them their fair share of housing built with public funds. As the law now stands deprivation of housing offends not alone against basic human rights but also limits the voting and therefore the political power of our people in their own community . . .
>
> Pressure of British opinion, properly directed, could force the Government here to ensure that the minority get public employment at least in fair proportion; and could ensure the removal of any bias against Nationalists and Catholics because of their political or religious convictions.

It went on to provide quotations from *Le Monde*, the Manchester *Guardian*, the *New Statesman and Nation*, the *Belfast Telegraph*, *Tribune*, the *People*, and the *Sunday Express*, illustrating the CSJ's claims about discrimination in Northern Ireland.

Legal Aid to Oppose Discrimination – Not Likely! recounted the efforts of the CSJ to use the courts to obtain redress for discriminatory actions by local authorities. It recalled the episode with Sir Alec Douglas-Home. Two members of the QUB Faculty of Law, J. McCartney LLB and H. G. Calvert LLM, had put forward the same idea in 1965, and in October 1966 it was advanced by the Northern Ireland attorney general, E. W. Jones QC. McCartney outlined some relevant sections of the Government of Ireland Act and Calvert pointed to the legal aid scheme, which had been introduced in November 1965, and had suggested that it provided a way in which working-class Catholics could seek legal redress. The CSJ decided to fight a test case, and in November 1965 instructed a solicitor to commence proceedings against Dungannon Urban District Council on behalf of John Patrick McHugh, a Catholic textile worker who alleged discrimination against him in housing allocation. This had obliged him to take unsatisfactory accommodation outside the two boundaries. When a legal aid application form was lodged with the Law Society of Northern Ireland, its secretary wrote back asking under which heading the action was being taken. Consequently,

> Rather than prejudice the application by submitting it in the wrong way, [the CSJ's] solicitor advised [it] it would be safer to consult Senior Counsel about the method to be used . . . Senior Counsel advised [it] that technicalities in the law might make it impossible for Mr McHugh to take direct action against Dungannon Urban District Council, and that it would be better if the action were brought by a ratepayer in the Council area. Mr Anthony Sheridan, a working man and a ratepayer, aggrieved at the misuse of Council powers in the allocation of houses, offered to be the plaintiff and Legal Aid was applied for on his behalf.

However, the application was refused on the grounds that 'the proceedings to which the application is related are not proceedings for which Legal Aid may be given'. No further information about the reasons for the rejection was given.[22] The case was eventually appealed to the legal aid committee of the Law Society of Northern Ireland, but the refusal was upheld because the applicant had 'not shown reasonable grounds for taking or being party to proceedings'. Legal advice given to the CSJ indicated that litigation taken as far as the House of Lords, 'where their opponents would undoubtedly force it', could cost up to £20,000: 'Therefore, denial of Legal Aid amounts to denial of access to the courts. This effectively prevents most Northern Ireland citizens from taking Sir Alec's advice.' As Kevin Boyle and Tom Hadden put it, they had 'reverted to the view that, after effort[s] with local lawyers, none of whom appeared to have any fire in their bellies, there was no future in legal redress'.[23] The CSJ was forced back to its contention that discrimination could only be dealt with through action by Westminster under the Government of Ireland Act 1920. It pointed out that the British government had recently applied the Prices and Incomes Act of 1966 to Northern Ireland, despite the fact that it dealt with matters devolved to Stormont. The pamphlet urged the Westminster government to take up the request of the CDU for a royal commission on Northern Ireland affairs.

The Plain Truth was a broad exposé of Unionist rule. It explained the meaning of gerrymandering and the other devices whereby 'one Conservative or Unionist vote is often equivalent to two opposition votes' and went on to detail discrimination in Derry, Enniskillen, Lurgan and Dungannon, providing statistics on housing, voting and employment. The second edition of *The Plain Truth* was an expanded and updated version, which added maps and charts and a broader historical and political analysis. It was published in 1969 and also gave information on the setting up of NICRA and detailed the events in Derry on 5 October 1968. It also reproduced extracts from two letters written to Patricia McCluskey by British Labour leader, Harold Wilson, in July and September 1964, deploring religious discrimination and supporting the idea of new and impartial procedures for the allocation of council houses and public appointments. The CSJ regarded these as a major coup. Patricia McCluskey said: 'He wrote just before the election saying that if he were returned he would settle things out for us. We more or less used that letter and published it as often as we could on Harold all over England.'[24]

In assessing the most important aspects of the CSJ – its publications – it is important to note both their similarities to and differences from an earlier wave of literature about the disabilities of Catholics in Northern Ireland, that of the anti-partition movement of the late 1940s and early 1950s. *The Plain Truth* and *Londonderry. One Man, No Vote* are in many ways reminiscent of the 1945 pamphlet by Cahir Healy MP, *The Mutilation of a Nation: The Story of the Partition of Ireland*. Healy also provided a comparative chart of salaries paid to Protestants and Catholics in public appointments and details of gerrymandering in counties Fermanagh, Armagh, Tyrone and Derry. His use of snippets of news reports and quotations from politicians is very similar to the style adopted by the CSJ. A more systematic treatment of the issues of gerrymandering and discrimination was provided in the 1957 book by Frank Gallagher, *The Indivisible Island: The History of the Partition of Ireland*, which summarised much of the postwar anti-partition propaganda. Again, in content and style, the CSJ's literature was strongly reminiscent of Gallagher's book. Such material would be part of the cultural background of the members of the CSJ, and it often formed the basis for articles in the *Irish News* and *Irish Weekly* and for speeches and pamphlets by Nationalist politicians. So pervasive was the style of presentation that members of the CSJ may well not have been conscious of it as a particular source for its ideas on discrimination; it would appear to be simply common sense as well as common knowledge.

There was one striking difference between Healy's pamphlet and the CSJ's most directly comparable publication, *The Plain Truth*, and this was in the amount of attention paid to the law-and-order aspects of discrimination. *The Mutilation of a Nation* gave equal prominence to the Special Powers Act and to the RUC and B Specials as it did to gerrymandering and discrimination in public appointments (housing was not yet a grievance). The first edition of *The Plain Truth* devoted only one paragraph to the issue of law and order, and while the second edition gave it more attention, prompted by the incidents in Derry and at Burntollet, it added little in the way of substance. The CSJ seems to have been relatively unconcerned about disabilities that were geared specifically to republicans as distinct from other opponents of unionism. The section of the second edition of the pamphlet dealing with law and order did, however, begin by referring to the disparity between the numbers of Protestants and Catholics in the RUC.

The CSJ's propaganda made more sophisticated use of tables and diagrams, including such statistical devices as histograms, than the anti-partitionist propaganda and tended to rely heavily on comparative tables of Catholic and Protestant numbers in public housing and appointments, but it seems never to have considered the possibility that factors other than deliberate discrimination could account for the disparity. The facts and figures on the RUC ignored the way in which tradition and communal pressures have kept Catholic applications for membership of the force extremely low. On education it accepted the right of Catholics to have their own separate system: while it highlighted the greater costs imposed on the Catholic community, it did not examine the question of whether or not it might be better to accept an integrated state system. On public appointments it was able to show that highly questionable recruitment procedures were operated by some local authorities but it did not consider the full range of factors which might explain disparities in civil service recruiting – for example, the practice of many Catholic schools in preparing their pupils for the examinations of the imperial and Irish Republic civil services while not encouraging applications to the Northern Ireland civil service. It criticised local authorities and the NIHT for their segregated housing estates, but ignored the extent to which residential segregation arose from a deliberate choice by tenants.

These aspects of the CSJ's arguments should not, however, be allowed to detract from its undoubted successes. Unionists never answered satisfactorily the CSJ's points about Catholics being housed mainly through slum clearance by Dungannon Council and the restraints on house-building programmes by Londonderry Corporation and others in situations where there was a potential for new housing to alter the balance of political power. In later years this seriously undermined the credibility of Unionists at a time when they were unable to maintain political stability. In the mid-1960s, however, it made little difference. They held political power and could afford to allow the CSJ to have a few propaganda coups. Catholics were a minority of the electorate, gerrymandering denied them the power which ought to have been given them in a small number of local government areas, but it did not affect their position at Stormont. By 1964 it was clear that the NILP was losing ground again to the Unionists, so the prospect of a grand coalition of opposition parties which could oust the Unionists was not on the cards.

The political system in Northern Ireland, based as it was on the Westminster model of parliamentary democracy, gave complete power to a governing party elected by an electoral majority. But unlike Britain, the majority and the minority were set in the concrete of religious and communal identity. Those who held power and those who were denied it could never change places. Had the courts operated on the American model, they might have offered a counterbalancing force, as they did for the Black minority in the Southern states. As Richard Rose puts it: 'In a representative assembly the majority wins, the minority must always lose. In the courts, by contrast, judges are not meant to count heads but to weigh arguments.'[25] The demonstration by the CSJ that the courts did not offer a means of obtaining redress was significant. It eliminated the last prospect of advance by constitutional means within Northern Ireland. But there was still another forum that could be appealed to – the Westminster parliament. This made the links established by the CSJ with a section of the British Labour Party of key importance.

It was fortunate for the CSJ that simultaneously with its own launch a group of activists in the British Labour Party was making the first moves in the creation of the CDU. The success of the CDU in winning the support of over one hundred members of both houses of parliament, mostly from the Labour Party but with the backing of some Liberals, gave the CSJ an audience within British politics that would have been very difficult for it to achieve on its own.

Prospects did not appear bright in 1964. C. Desmond Greaves, leader of the Connolly Association, which was to be an important ally of the CDU and the CSJ, wrote in 1963:

> Despite signs of a revival of interest, Ireland remains very much a *terra incognita* to the British working-class movement. Can it be, one imagines the trade unionist saying in his capacity as tourist, that this place that looks so similar and whose people palpably speak English can really be politically so different? His first reaction may be to attempt to wreath the Irish picture into the British framework. This does not work. He may now conclude that Ireland is incomprehensible. He will be assisted in that view by all the organs of propaganda available to reaction in Britain.[26]

Kevin McNamara, MP for Kingston-upon-Hull North (later Hull Central), recalled that in the early years of the Labour government, 'if a Minister of State went over there, such as Alice Bacon, one was taken over by the Government, set up in Stormont Castle or in Holywood House. It was all laid on.'[27] National executive committee reports to the Labour Party conference in these years reflect the way in which the party in parliament took up the issues of deprivation and unemployment in Northern Ireland. There was concern about the refusal of the Stormont government to recognise the ICTU and the harm this was doing to the achievement of planning agreements, but no awareness was shown of Catholic complaints of discrimination.

One factor which began to change this situation was, ironically, the success of the Unionists in the 1964 Westminster general election. They swept the board, sending a solid phalanx of twelve MPs to the House of Commons, where they took the Conservative whip. Since Labour was returned with a majority of only four, this threw a spotlight onto the links between the Unionists and the Conservative opposition. Harold Wilson was to comment acidly on this a couple of years later: 'There have been cases, when majorities were smaller than at present [after the 1966 general election], when a government could have fallen with a Northern Ireland vote on Rachmanism in London, although nothing could be said about housing conditions in Belfast.'[28] Wilson endorsed anti-Unionist sentiment within his party when he wrote to Patricia McCluskey in July 1964:

> We work closely with our colleagues of the Northern Ireland Labour Party. Like them we deplore religious and other kinds of discrimination, and we agree with them that this should be tackled by introducing new and impartial procedures for the allocation of houses, by setting up joint tribunals to which particular cases of alleged discrimination in public appointments can be referred, and indeed, by any other effective means that can be agreed.[29]

On closer reading, this was not a programme for action by Westminster, nor a promise to override the prerogative of the Stormont parliament and government. This is confirmed by a second letter that Wilson wrote in September 1964 in which he expressed agreement with the CSJ on the importance of the issues it was raising and assured Patricia McCluskey that

> a Labour Government would do everything in its power to see that the infringements of justice to which you are so rightly drawing attention are effectively dealt with. We recognise however that this is no easy task.
>
> We believe that before steady progress can be made in the effective solution of these problems there must be changes in the Parliamentary representation of Northern Ireland, both at Westminster and Stormont. Our colleagues in the Northern Ireland Labour Party are, as you no doubt already know, strongly opposed to any kind of discrimination. They are fighting the forthcoming General Election on a completely non-sectarian policy which strives for the betterment of our people without distinction. Because of this we are convinced that the most immediately helpful way of fur-thering the cause for which you are campaigning is to give active support to the Northern Ireland Labour Party candidates in their fight.[30]

Making the will-o'-the-wisp of an NILP electoral breakthrough a precondition for action by the Labour government was a safe way of putting off any action whatsoever. But by endorsing the CSJ's complaints, Wilson was helping to stimulate the greater interest in Northern Ireland which was developing among his own backbenchers and increasing their determination to put pressure on his government. Other factors were referred to by Kevin McNamara:

The resurgence of nationalism after 1966 led by a new generation of nationalist leaders. Austin Currie would be one, Fitt's Republican Labour Party . . . Eddie McAteer for example came over here and sought to embarrass Heath and Wilson and had all sorts of undertakings made to him. Mary Holland writing articles in the *Observer* excited the minds of people.[31]

The beginnings of a new coalition in Britain of groups interested in Northern Ireland can be traced back to 1962. In August of that year, Fenner Brockway, the leading figure in the Movement for Colonial Freedom, spoke in Dublin to the Nigerian Union of Britain and Ireland. He was an old-fashioned Independent Labour Party supporter of a united Ireland, who had been imprisoned with Eamon de Valera during World War I, but his speech showed how the 'wind of change' in the old British Empire had created political categories within which Ireland could take on a new significance for the British left. He called for a 'self-reliant, independent and united Ireland'; it was time for the people of both parts of Ireland to cease 'begging from Westminster'. They ought to adopt the alternative of the 'united economy and dynamism which the newly independent countries were feeling.'[32]

The main Irish nationalist organisation in Britain, the Anti-Partition of Ireland League (GB), was also taking note of a changing world. At its annual general meeting in November 1962 the league decided to change its name to the 'United Ireland Association' and switched its emphasis from partition to fostering changes that were already taking place:

If both Ireland and Britain join the Common Market the divisions between the 26 Counties and Six Counties will be weakened. Membership . . . will give the people of both parts of Ireland a more outward looking attitude and a change of heart which must in time lead to a realisation of the ridiculousness of the artificial barriers now dividing our people. Our work in the future should be directed to bring about better relations between Irish people on both sides of the border.[33]

In December 1962, Martin Ennals, general secretary of the NCCL, visited Northern Ireland to investigate the situation. In 1936 the NCCL had sponsored an independent commission of inquiry into the Special Powers Act, which condemned its use against political opponents of the Unionist government. In London, in 1948, the NCCL organised a conference on human rights. A report to the conference included a section on Northern Ireland which described the situation there as 'very grave'. It pointed not only to the continuation of abuses under the Special Powers Act but also to the recent alterations in the local government franchise which deprived large numbers of people of their previous voting rights and introduced plural voting for others, and said that 'jerrymandering [sic] of electoral boundaries both for local councils and for the Northern Ireland Parliament is grossly unfair'.[34] The report recommended an NCCL investigation into conditions in Northern Ireland but this appears not to have been acted upon, so that Ennals's visit was an indication of renewed interest. In June 1962 the NCCL's annual general meeting had adopted a resolution, moved by the Connolly Association, calling on the council to set up an impartial inquiry into civil liberties in Northern Ireland and for pressure to be put on the Government for a public inquiry into the operation of the Government of Ireland Act. As a result of the Ennals visit, the NCCL called for a reform of the electoral system in Northern Ireland, a new boundary commission for Stormont constituencies and local government wards, abrogation of the Special Powers Act, and a royal commission on Stormont, including its relationship to Westminster as it had evolved since the Government of Ireland Act.

The organisation which had prompted this new interest in Northern Ireland by the NCCL, the Connolly Association, is a group which is generally thought to have close links with the Communist Party of Great Britain; its title commemorates Ireland's best-known Marxist socialist and 1916 martyr, James Connolly. Although a small organisation, it was able to exert significant influence in the early 1960s due to its having a regular monthly newspaper, the *Irish Democrat*, which sold widely among Irish immigrants, and its considerable political experience dating back to the 1930s. The association is a strongly anti-partitionist body. A pamphlet published in about 1962 presented the partition of Ireland as a device by 'British Imperialism' to weaken Ireland politically and to exploit the island economically. In considering ways in which partition could be fought, the association urged unity between Irish anti-partitionists and the British Labour movement and discussed immediate steps which could be taken:

> It must be obvious that the greatest obstacle to turning out the Brookeborough Government is the way it has barricaded itself in Stormont behind a mountain of anti-democratic legislation.
>
> Consider the gerrymandering, the restriction of the franchise, the special powers act, the religious and political discrimination, the control of education . . . Then there is the refusal to recognise the Northern Ireland Committee [of the ICTU] . . . These restrictions of the freedom to speak, work and organise against the Unionists must be swept away. If they were swept away, the confidence engendered among the nationally minded population would become boundless, and the effort to attain unity would be enormously strengthened.
>
> The Westminster Parliament has the power to compel Lord Brookeborough to restore Democracy. So let us demand that it does so.[35]

The Connolly Association, like the CSJ, had recognised in Section 75 of the Government of Ireland Act 1920 a possible weapon against the Unionists. C. Desmond Greaves later recalled discovering Section 75 and consulting the left-wing QC, D. N. Pritt, about it. It was Pritt who highlighted the fact that power over Northern Ireland was reserved to the Westminster parliament, not the Government. The association then decided to press for an inquiry into the working of the act.

The CDU had its origins in a not dissimilar group of Irish exiles. An impression has gained ground in the intervening years that the CDU was founded in, and was restricted to, parliament. The list of over one hundred MPs and peers who sponsored the CDU was one measure of its success, but it was not in itself the CDU. The CDU was created and kept alive by a group of rank-and-file members of the British Labour Party who were mainly, though not exclusively, of Irish origin. They provided an activist base which was essential for the more public campaigning of the MPs.

The CDU was launched at a meeting in a Streatham public house in London in early 1965. The meeting was sponsored by the Streatham Labour Party, whose secretary, Bill O'Shaughnessy, became the founding secretary of the CDU. Its founding vice-president, Paddy Byrne, recalled that the name was chosen because the initials were 'crisp and neat and had the appeal of initials like CND which was then riding high'.[36] Although there were objections to the use of the word 'Ulster', it was adopted because it was 'well known and understood in Britain'. In a brief history of the CDU, written in 1970, Byrne stressed:

> CDU is a British organisation, based largely in the Labour Movement. When we wish to extend our organisation, or arrange meetings, we contact the local Labour Party and not Irish organisations . . . We have always claimed that we are concerned only with obtaining full British democratic standards for the people of Northern Ireland, to which they are entitled as British subjects. We hold that the 'Border' is irrelevant to the issue . . . As far as CDU is concerned, the Tory-Unionists who rule Northern Ireland can build a wall around the six-counties if they wish, but we do insist that all citizens on the British side of the wall enjoy full British standards.[37]

The original aims adopted by the CDU were:

> To secure by the establishment of a Royal Commission a full and impartial inquiry into the administration of Government in Northern Ireland, with particular reference to allegations of discrimination on religious or political grounds in the fields of housing and employment and into the continued existence of the Special Powers Act.

> To bring electoral law in Northern Ireland at all levels into line with the rest of the UK, and to examine electoral boundaries with a view to providing fair representation for all sections of the community.

> To amend the Race Relations Act to include discrimination on religious grounds and to press for its operation throughout the whole of the UK, including Northern Ireland.[38]

About the time of the formation of the CDU, Paul Rose, MP for Blackley in Manchester, made a speech in the House of Commons about discrimination in Northern Ireland. His interest in the subject had been stirred when he addressed an Irish group in Manchester in 1962. He had gone to speak on civil liberties but 'what I learned there made me resolve to visit the province and when I was asked about Northern Ireland at the 1964 General Election I gave a solemn promise to do so'.[39] Paddy Byrne approached Rose and he agreed to become president of the CDU. Through his efforts the list of parliamentary sponsors was built up and a separate CDU group, with its own structure and meetings, was set up in parliament.

Rose's non-Irish background made him an excellent front man for the CDU. Byrne, who was the real driving force of the CDU, could not have claimed such disinterested credentials. A Dubliner, he had a long record of left-wing and republican activism in Ireland. He had been a member of the Republican Congress, the most important left-wing nationalist movement in 1930s Ireland, and he was active during the Spanish Civil War in promoting support in Ireland for the Spanish republic. At the time of the launching of the CDU he had been living in Croydon in London for about twelve years and was a leading member of the local Labour party; later he became a councillor. He began as vice-president of the CDU but in 1967, when Bill O'Shaughnessy moved to Manchester, they swapped jobs and Byrne became secretary. His motives for involvement were firmly socialist; in the draft of an unfinished pamphlet he expressed the hope that Belfast workers, 'freed from the fear of what would befall them if Ulster were not kept "Protestant", would vote according to their class interest and return not one but perhaps five socialists to Westminster'.[40] Other important CDU members included Ken Graham, Oliver Donoghue and Mick Melly. Graham was a Londoner, editor of the left-wing newspaper *London Voice*, and a member of the Streatham Labour Party. For a time he was the organiser of the CDU. Donoghue had emigrated to London in the 1950s from Portlaoise in the Irish Republic, where his father had been a prominent republican. He was a member of the Streatham, and later the Hammersmith, Labour parties. Melly was a Sligoman who also emigrated in the 1950s; he came from a prominent trade-union family and was a member of the Maidstone and then of the Putney Labour parties, and of the Clerical and Administrative Workers' Union.

The public launch of the CDU took place in the House of Commons on 3 June 1965. The meeting was chaired by Lord Brockway and attended by twenty of the sixty MPs who were sponsors. A message was read from Sam Napier, secretary of the NILP, and the meeting was addressed by Paul Rose, Patricia McCluskey and Bill O'Shaughnessy. Rose highlighted the anomaly of Labour MPs being accused of interference when they raised issues of discrimination in Northern Ireland, while no limit was put on the rights of Unionist MPs to speak and vote on British matters. Patricia McCluskey described discrimination in housing and the plight of Belfast's Mater Hospital. Bill O'Shaughnessy stressed the importance of winning support from the British Labour movement, although the CDU would welcome support from other quarters if it were offered.

Three years later a memorandum to the central committee of the CDU, dated June 1968, showed that the success of the campaign in attracting parliamentary sponsorship had not been matched by success in building up the mass support outside parliament which was one of its original objectives. A Manchester branch had been started and it had a couple of successful meetings before 'the tide receded, largely because of internal problems'.[41] Contacts were made with Birmingham, Liverpool, Nottingham, Oxford and other places, but none of these resulted in the setting up of a CDU branch. Apart from another brief period of life for the Manchester branch in 1969, the CDU's organisation and activities were confined to London. This did not, however, define the limits of its contacts and influences. Paddy Byrne's correspondence between June 1967 (when he took over as secretary) and October 1968 (when events in Derry transformed the situation) shows a wide range of organisations and individuals who were in touch with the CDU. There were letters from and to a large number of constituency Labour parties and branches of the Young Socialists, correspondence with the Movement for Colonial Freedom, the Connolly Association, the Haldane Society (of Socialist Lawyers), the Electoral Reform Society, Liberal branches in Hampstead and in the University of Edinburgh, with societies of emigrants from counties Sligo, Donegal, Cavan and Galway, with groups in the United States and New Zealand, and in Ireland with the NILP, the NDP and the Council of Labour in Ireland. There was a regular and friendly correspondence with Conn McCluskey and the CSJ. It can also be said that the CDU MPs had some success and had shown not a little ingenuity in exploiting loopholes in the House of Commons procedures in order to ventilate the grievances of anti-Unionists in Northern Ireland.

Three events kept up the momentum of the CDU during these years. The first was the election of Gerry Fitt to Westminster. He worked closely with the CDU within and outside parliament, and as a socialist he was a more natural ally than a Nationalist would have been. The second was a visit to Northern Ireland in April 1967, suggested and organised by Gerry Fitt, by three CDU MPs – Paul Rose, Maurice Miller (Glasgow, Kelvingrove) and Stan Orme (Salford West). They intended not only to investigate conditions in Northern Ireland but also to 'inform a wide spectrum of citizens of Northern Ireland of the activities at Westminster of Labour Members interested in Northern Ireland'.[42] The tour included Belfast, Coalisland, Dungannon, Strabane and Derry. They met the executive of the NILP, shop stewards from Harland and Wolff, the officers of Belfast trades council, the CSJ, and representatives of the Ulster Liberal Party, the Derry branch of the NILP, the RLP, and the NDP. Paul Rose recalled that 'in some areas we were met by bands and led to the rostrum set up in the middle of the town like conquering heroes. Even the pubs closed. In Strabane virtually the whole town turned out at eleven at night, and television cameras were thrust upon us at one in the morning'.[43] They reported that

> there was a ready response at all the meetings to the simple statement of principle that the Members of Parliament demanded the same rights and privileges for Northern Ireland as in their own constituencies as an integral part of the United Kingdom. A policy which respects the right of Irishmen ultimately to decide their constitutional status for themselves, but recognises Westminster's overriding obligation to ensure democratic government in the province, is one which would commend itself to large sections of the people, both Protestant and Catholic, in Northern Ireland.
>
> It is therefore considered that the Government should set up a Royal Commission to investigate the operation of the Government of Ireland and the Ireland Acts.[44]

The third event that sustained the momentum of the CDU was a conference held in the Irish Club, Eaton Square, London, on 28 January 1968. Seven resolutions were passed, all unanimously, and these provide a good indication of the strategy of the CDU and its allies at this time. Manchester CDU proposed that the conference call on the British government to use its powers under the 1920 act to 'ensure that all citizens of Northern Ireland shall enjoy the equality of rights and privileges enjoyed by all the people of the remainder of the UK'. The NILP moved a resolution on the economy, proposing a programme of government action to deal with unemployment. The Electoral Reform Society moved that the conference demand a return to the original voting system in Northern Ireland, using the single transferable vote in multi-member constituencies, as a necessary addition to the granting of one man, one vote and equal electoral areas. The central committee of the CDU proposed the launching of a national fund to aid the civil rights movement in Northern Ireland. The Connolly Association proposed a Bill of Rights to take the form of amendments to the Government of Ireland Act. The London area committee of the CDU called on the British government, in view of the increasing civil strife in Northern Ireland, to suspend Stormont and impose direct rule through the governor. Finally, Gerry Fitt moved that 'this conference calls on the Members of Parliament at Westminster, who are supporters of the CDU, to use whatever measures are available to question the legality of the convention whereby they are unable to discuss matters relating to Northern Ireland'.[45] This resolution pinpointed what was the most important battle and the most significant failure of the CDU and its allies in the period between 1965 and the events in Derry on 5 October 1968.

The section of the Government of Ireland Act on which the CDU, the CSJ and the Connolly Association pinned their hopes was brief but appeared to be comprehensive:

> Notwithstanding the establishment of the Parliament of Southern and Northern Ireland, or anything contained in this Act, the supreme authority of the Parliament of the United Kingdom shall remain unaffected and undiminished over all persons, matters and things in Ireland and every part thereof.[46]

The Ireland Act of 1949 having recognised the existence of an independent republic in the twenty-six counties of southern Ireland, the effect of Section 75 was now restricted to the six counties of Northern Ireland. What Section 75 meant to the CSJ and the others was summed up by Patricia McCluskey: 'We got out the 1920 Act and we read it, and the 1920 Act said clearly that

Westminster had the last word, and we said this is where the seat of power lies and they must be made aware of their responsibilities.'[47]

However, there were complex questions of constitutional law and practice about how Section 75 could be given practical effect. Martin Wallace, in a lecture to the Faculty of Law at QUB in 1966, discussed these:

> There is of course power under Section 75 of the 1920 Act for the British Parliament to pass whatever legislation it likes, applicable to Northern Ireland. In practice the original division of responsibilities has changed in response to changing situations. The Imperial Parliament has on a number of occasions included a clause indicating that an Act applies to Northern Ireland. The convention has always been, however, that the latter step is taken only with the agreement of the Northern Ireland Government where it seems to impinge on transferred services. In August 1966 Miss Alice Bacon, Minister of State at the Home Office, indicated that there was no present intention of breaching that convention. She pointed out that Section 75 preserved supreme authority to the United Kingdom Parliament, but that it did not give the Government of the United Kingdom authority over transferred matters. She said she thought it would do harm to the relations between the two Governments to pass legislation on transferred matters against the wishes of the Northern Ireland Government.[48]

Despite the convention, there were enough fuzzy areas in the relationship between the Westminster parliament and government and their counterparts in Northern Ireland to encourage an attempt to probe the limits of the convention's restraint on Westminster intervention. The central principle of the convention was one which it was never easy to define. As J. P. Mackintosh pointed out:

> The three Home Rule Bills and the Government of Ireland Act were based on a few, relatively simple, assumptions and they encountered the same intractable problems even at the early stage of passage through Parliament. The first assumption was that certain 'imperial' functions could be isolated and left with the Westminster Parliament while 'internal matters' could be transferred to Dublin or Belfast. This was a more sensible idea eighty years ago, when there was not the vast range of government activity that there is today, but even in 1886 it caused difficulties.[49]

One of the anomalies identified by Wallace was that the 1920 act made Northern Ireland

> a separate financial region, a self-financing region, by separating its revenues from national accounts, but at the same time denying it the power to raise whatever revenues were necessary for the proper government of the six counties . . . It was . . . a strange system which originated not in Northern Ireland's needs but in the British Government's wishful thinking about the relationship it could establish with Southern Ireland.[50]

Changes in the system, especially after 1945, ensured that Northern Ireland would keep in step with social expenditure in the rest of the United Kingdom and that the Stormont government was in advance of Britain in financing new industrial development. The Northern Ireland exchequer was a net beneficiary from the common United Kingdom tax haul, on the same principles which funnelled money to the deprived areas of England, Scotland and Wales. But although MPs at Westminster found themselves voting huge sums of money to Northern Ireland, they did not have the same powers to determine how that money was spent. The CDU MPs homed in on this anomaly and used the debate on the Consolidated Fund Bill of August 1966 to try to break the convention.

Gerry Fitt rose at 4.50 a.m. on 8 August and admitted that 'if I were to abide by the rule book, all I could discuss in this debate would be defence, foreign affairs, Income Tax and the Post Office'.[51] To him this seemed illogical and there was only one interpretation he could put on the words of Section 75:

> I say Sir, that this gives ultimate and overriding responsibility to the Parliament of the United Kingdom, and as the representative of Belfast, West, as the representative of 26,000 people, I stand here to demand of the British Government that they accept the responsibility which they themselves have written into this Act of 1920.

At this point the deputy Speaker, Sir Eric Fletcher, intervened to say that Section 75 did not give responsibility to Westminster ministers 'over matters within the competence of the Northern Ireland Government'. Previous Speakers had ruled repeatedly that 'matters within the competence of the Northern Ireland Government' could not be debated in the House of Commons.

Kevin McNamara and Elystan Morgan, MP for Glamorgan, tried

to argue that Westminster responsibility for finance and the wide-ranging nature of the Consolidated Fund debate were reasons for permitting a discussion, but without success. Michael McGuire, MP for Ince, argued that a minister, using the powers of Section 75, could 'intervene directly in Northern Ireland' and would be

> the supreme authority delegated with powers given to him under Section 75. Your ruling seems to me to suggest that he does not have that power, but I suggest that Section 75, in anybody's clear interpretation, gives the Minister overriding authority over the Parliament at Stormont.

The deputy Speaker suggested that the confusion had arisen because McGuire had 'failed to distinguish between the United Kingdom Parliament and the United Kingdom Government'. The Government of Ireland Act 1920 did give the Westminster parliament supreme authority and enabled it to legislate on matters affecting Northern Ireland, but because there was no ministerial responsibility in the House of Commons, it was not possible to debate Northern Ireland matters.

Elystan Morgan, Liberal MP Eric Lubbock, and Kevin McNamara made further unsuccessful attempts to challenge the ruling before Gerry Fitt finished his speech, firing salvoes off against the Unionist Party and Terence O'Neill and being warned off various lines of argument. He closed with a plea for some way to be found to get round the convention that prevented him from raising at Westminster grievances to which Stormont turned a deaf ear. Shortly after Fitt sat down Edwin Brooks, MP for Bebington, drew a further important clarification of the convention from the deputy Speaker:

> It is perfectly competent for the Parliament to intervene in any legislative sense in Northern Ireland. The competence of the sovereignty of the United Kingdom Parliament has been preserved by Section 75, which would therefore, for example, enable this legislature to revoke or amend that Act; but that would involve legislation. It is not permissible, in debating the Consolidated Fund Bill, to introduce matters which involve legislation.

Reg Freeson asked for guidance on where it was defined that the sovereignty of Westminster was confined to legislative sovereignty and was told that it was inherent in the proposition:

Parliament exercises sovereignty over any part of the United Kingdom by legislation, but it has delegated administrative responsibility in certain matters to the Government of Northern Ireland . . . If hon. Members want to seek an opportunity of suggesting that the Government of Ireland Act should be amended, they should seek appropriate opportunities for doing so, but it cannot be raised here.

After an intensive barrage, the CDU MPs had elicited the information that Section 75 gave the Westminster parliament power to intervene in Northern Ireland by legislation, either through passing bills, which by convention would have to be by agreement with the Stormont government, or by revoking or amending the Government of Ireland Act. Since the Government controls the timetable of the House of Commons, such a step would normally require a government initiative. Private members' legislation was possible, but this would require government support in order to steer it through all of its stages. The ball was firmly in the Government's court.

Alice Bacon, replying to the debate, made it clear that the Government would not contemplate such action. Mention has already been made of her opinion that direct intervention would be harmful to relations between the two governments. She quoted a reply given by Harold Wilson on 28 May 1966 in which he had said that he preferred informal talks with Terence O'Neill as a means of achieving change in Northern Ireland. There had been a working lunch the previous Friday at which a 'profitable discussion' had taken place. She was unable to give the House any details of the discussion, which had included Home Secretary Roy Jenkins, but Wilson expanded on the meeting in his account of his first and second governments:

Captain O'Neill had already made more progress in a matter of three years in attacking problems of discrimination and human rights than all his Stormont predecessors in more than forty years. But this progress had aroused open hostility on the part of his atavistic grass-roots supporters and many of his backbenchers, to say nothing of a black reactionary group in his Cabinet. It was essential that the progress be maintained for, as the world learned three years later, time . . . was not on our side.

Wilson recalls pressing O'Neill about the concern felt on the Labour benches at the lack of progress on constitutional reform and liberal policies, particularly in view of the large sums of money they were being asked to vote for Northern Ireland:

> Captain O'Neill readily took these arguments. He stressed how much had already been done and explained his plans for the future. But he gravely underlined the threats to his position and to the reform movement . . . He had moved so far and so fast by Northern Ireland standards that he felt there must be a period of consolidation, certainly for the rest of the year, or a dangerous and possibly irresistible tide of reaction would set in.

Wilson and Jenkins 'agreed not to press him further for the next few months'.[52]

O'Neill's recollection of the meeting is somewhat different; he stresses the conviviality of the occasion but not the searching questions about the progress he was making with reform. Wilson, he said, did ask him why he was pursuing policies such as meeting with Sean Lemass, when that was unpopular with the Protestants, and both Wilson and Jenkins welcomed the fact that the talks had taken place, so that rather than showing concern about the tardiness of the pace of reform, he claimed, they were mildly surprised at its rapidity.[53]

Whatever actually took place at the meeting, it is clear that Wilson and his government were fundamentally at odds with the CSJ, the CDU and the civil rights movement in Northern Ireland in their assessment of what was happening. The civil rights movement believed that O'Neill was unwilling to make any substantial changes and was a prisoner of the Orange Order and the backwoods members of his party. The Government thought that his progress was commendable and that he must be supported against the threat of an extreme Unionist backlash. While this attitude was maintained, there was no prospect of intervention by Westminster and there was little that could be done to bring it about. It was not just the CSJ and the CDU who tried unsuccessfully to interest the Westminster government; the NILP sent a delegation across within a month of the new Labour administration taking office in October 1964. Its members were received sympathetically but were given no promises. Charles Brett, the main draughtsperson of the NILP's policies on civil rights, considered that the civil service was a major obstacle:

[The ministers'] advisers, like most English politicians, believed (because they preferred to believe) that the state of affairs in Northern Ireland was bound to improve so long as it was left alone, and so long as Captain O'Neill (charming and reasonable man) was left to bring reforms at his own pace. The Home Office officials were not only unhelpful, they were downright obstructive, and we had grounds for believing that they were secretly furnishing Stormont with reports on our private representations to Labour Ministers.[54]

In December 1967, Home Secretary Roy Jenkins replied to a letter from Eddie McAteer, stating his personal conviction that

in Westminster we cannot – and we should not – ignore the constitutional relationship between Northern Ireland and the United Kingdom Government . . . The irritants of which complaint is made relate to matters which lie wholly within the constitutional ambit of the Parliament and Government of Northern Ireland . . . The most fruitful course, I think, would be for you to seek direct discussions with Captain O'Neill.[55]

Less than a week later, number 10 Downing Street was writing in similar terms to the secretary of West Ham trades council in London, noting that the 'allegations of discrimination in Northern Ireland . . . fall within the competence of the Northern Ireland authorities', and that it would 'not be appropriate to set up a Royal Commission'.[56]

The CSJ and the CDU kept trying to find some crack in the stone wall that faced them. Paddy Byrne wrote to the McCluskeys in June 1967: 'The work proceeds, but frustratingly slowly.'[57] The central committee of the CDU discussed a number of initiatives: a proposed 'Ulster Charter' – a mass petition calling for civil rights reforms – was rejected as a good idea but one which was beyond its means at that time; efforts to set up CDU branches in Liverpool, Nottingham, Bristol and St Albans came to nothing; attempts to raise the issue of Northern Ireland at the 1967 and 1968 Labour Party conferences met with no success. The CSJ proposed to print a leaflet for distribution in Britain at the 1968 local elections: 'Irish Voters: First Wilson's promises then none of these promises have been honoured. Please keep this in mind when you come to vote.' Conn McCluskey showed a glimmer of hope in February 1968 when a letter to Wilson 'got a really reasonable and obviously considered reply from Kaufman'.[58] He had hopes that Wilson was vulnerable to threats of losing the Irish vote. 'Green power', he thought, was the only weapon.[59]

However, the CDU was experiencing problems in simply keeping going. In September 1967 the central committee wrote to the treasurer of the now inactive Manchester branch asking for its funds to be transferred to the central CDU account; its printers were getting very impatient for payment of an outstanding bill. In June 1968 the central committee met for a wide-ranging discussion on the CDU's progress. A confidential document submitted by Paddy Byrne listed the successes and failures of the CDU since 1965. The achievements had included: the 'splendid performance' of its MPs; the visit to Northern Ireland by Rose and the others; the January 1968 conference; a call for telegrams to be sent to Wilson about the plight of Derry which had been answered by one hundred organisations; and regular newsletters and contacts made with various groups in Northern Ireland. The list of failures was considerable. Although the central committee had met monthly, 'their efforts appear to be in vain', and only four out of twelve members had attended regularly. There had been a follow-up meeting to the January conference, but only six constituency Labour parties had sent delegates – admittedly at a time of campaigning for the local elections. Only three constituency Labour parties had submitted resolutions on Northern Ireland for the party conference, and despite the efforts of delegates who were CDU supporters, the issue was not put on the agenda. Letters to the Home Secretary had been 'treated with contempt'. A public meeting in Kilburn in London in April 1968 had been attended by only twenty people, although the area had been plastered with posters and the meeting had been advertised in the press – this, despite the fact that up to seven thousand Irish people attended Mass in Kilburn every Sunday. Two thousand copies of the first edition of a newspaper, *Spotlight Ulster*, had been printed, but only seven hundred had been distributed and no further editions had appeared. Only three constituency Labour parties had affiliated to the CDU: 'In short, no mass movement has developed and there is no indication that one will.' The CDU's most likely supporters, the British left, were 'far too concerned to save socialism from extinction than to bother about Ulster, about which the mass of British people know little, care less'.

Byrne was unwilling, however, despite the formidable organisational and financial problems, to abandon the campaign:

> Perhaps therefore the line should be to retain our organisation and bide our time . . . A new start might be made by meeting in the House of Commons in the autumn, similar to the inaugural meeting – having for its object the ending of the CONVENTION. If only this were achieved CDU would not have lived in vain.[60]

There is little evidence that such a renewed attempt would have succeeded, and had developments continued on the course of the first nine months of 1968, the CDU would probably have disappeared. But by the autumn of 1968 the strategy of attempting a fresh start with a meeting at Westminster had been overtaken by events in Northern Ireland. The incidents in Derry on 5 October transformed the situation not only in Northern Ireland but also for the supporters of the civil rights movement in Britain.

4

THE NORTHERN IRELAND CIVIL RIGHTS ASSOCIATION

To Derry we went on October the fifth,
to march for our rights, but oh what a myth!
They beat us with batons, they beat us with fists,
they sprayed us all over with water.

from 'October the Fifth' (civil rights song)

NICRA was the best-known civil rights group but it was neither the first nor the only organisation to agitate on civil rights demands. It was, however, the most important group within the civil rights movement and it initiated the events that led to the creation of a mass movement. For a time it provided an umbrella beneath which the other organisations came together. It began life as a counterpart to the NCCL, but even in this it was not original; in 1962 a Northern Ireland Council for Civil Liberties (NICCL) was set up. In June 1962 the NCCL had adopted a resolution from the Connolly Association calling for an inquiry into civil liberties in Northern Ireland; the NICCL seems to have been set up in response and as its first action, in July, it held a meeting to prepare a memorandum on civil rights to present to Mr Justice Bose of the International Commission of Jurists, who was visiting Belfast.

Martin Ennals of the NCCL visited Northern Ireland in September 1962 to investigate the situation but he was rebuffed by the Nationalist leader, Eddie McAteer, who told journalists that an inquiry at this stage would be inadvisable. This was a considerable about-turn; in March a delegation of Nationalist MPs and councillors had met Home Secretary Rab Butler to present a dossier of complaints about discrimination. But now McAteer said that 'no matter what truths might be revealed by such an investigation they could only be interpreted as weapons of war at this stage'. He was anxious, he said, to create the best possible climate for the Orange – Green talks. Following the visit, Sean Caughey, secretary of the NICCL, issued a statement which said that his council had told

Ennals that an impartial inquiry by an independent body in Britain could do much to redress the grievances of the minority. It said that the Special Powers Act was preventing British standards of justice from prevailing in Northern Ireland, and went on:

> The mass disfranchisement of thousands of citizens in local govern-
> ment, the disgraceful manipulation of constituency boundaries, the
> enforced political tests for government jobs and legislation, such as
> the Flags and Emblems Act, were some of the shackles on individual
> freedom which would never be tolerated in England. Yet the British
> Government was responsible under Clause 75 of the Government of
> Ireland Act for everything that goes on in Northern Ireland.[1]

Caughey's statement paralleled the ideas about 'British standards of justice' and the responsibility of the British government under the Government of Ireland Act which were later put forward by the CSJ and the CDU, but in Caughey's case they were able to coexist with a strong commitment to republicanism. Shortly afterwards the NICCL disappeared from public view and Caughey resurfaced as secretary of the (republican) Political Prisoners Release Commit-tee. He was an example of the contradictory crosscurrents of nationalist and republican politics in this period. Although in 1962 he had appealed to the Government of Ireland Act, in 1963 he described it as a 'constitution of bondage'. In July 1964 he was fined for singing the Irish national anthem, 'A Soldier's Song' (in Irish) at a republican rally in Ballycastle, County Antrim. In 1965 he resigned from Sinn Féin, of which he had been a vice-president, because of its refusal to recognise the legitimacy of both govern-ments in Ireland. In the early 1970s he was editor of the Provisional republican newspaper in the north, *Republican News*.

Following the winding up of the Political Prisoners Release Committee, Caughey became secretary of a small group called Irish Union, which, in its personnel, provided a link between the NICCL and the later Wolfe Tone Societies and NICRA. The chairman was Jack Bennett, a former member of the CPNI; he came from a Protestant background and had led a campaign in the late 1950s to get the CPNI to return to the pro-republican line of the Irish Communists in the 1930s. Another prominent member was Fred Heatley who, like Bennett, was a member of the Belfast Wolfe Tone Society and later of NICRA.

NICRA itself originated at a conference of the Wolfe Tone Societies held in Maghera, County Derry, on the weekend of 13–14 August 1966. The societies had been created in 1964 out of the committees which were set up to organise the 1963 commemorations of the bicentenary of the birth of Wolfe Tone, the leader of the United Irishmen and martyr of the 1798 Rising. Their 'primary objective was a united, independent and democratic Irish Republic in accordance with the principles of the 1916 Proclamation and the Democratic Programme of the First Dáil'. Fred Heatley described them as 'an autonomous adjunct of the Republican Movement', and Roy Johnston called them 'a Fabian Society to the Republican Movement'.

The intellectual leaders of the Wolfe Tone Societies were two Dublin academics, Roy Johnston and Anthony Coughlan. Johnston had been a founder member of the Irish Workers' League (the Communist Party in the Irish Republic), and both were involved with the Connolly Association during periods spent in England. Johnston was important as a systematic thinker who put together a package of ideas on the links between Marxist and republican politics. He had the distinction of being viewed with deep suspicion by Seán Mac Stíofáin and William Craig, who both saw him as being responsible for leading the republican movement in a Communist direction. It is clear, however, from examining some of his writings, that by the mid-1960s his nationalism was far stronger than his Marxism. In an article published in 1966 Johnston identified the failure of Irish governments in the 1920s and 1930s as one of not having acted to 'assume full control over the reinvestment of the economic surplus'. The article advocated a policy of economic autarchy, with the exclusion of foreign investment and legislation to ensure that 'gombeen capital' was invested in Ireland. The state 'could have developed along managed capitalist lines, such as a small nation occasionally can do, for example, as Norway'.[2] In 1968 he advocated a 'national revolutionary programme' which would seek to unite 'workers in industries threatened by "monopolistic rationalisation" ', small farmers, emigrants and 'technically qualified intellectuals'. This programme would have 'social objectives appropriate to the contemporary situation, and quite distinct from the classical European path of nation-building. This programme may be successful in helping a small nation to emerge from the grip of imperialism even though under considerable economic domination'.[3]

Johnston's Communism, therefore, had been transmuted into a nationalism which emphasised economic independence, state planning and the unity of a wide range of social groups in the tasks of nation-building. When Johnston joined the republican movement in 1965, at the invitation of Cathal Goulding, IRA chief of staff, he was probably some distance to the right of some existing members of the movement and he was responsible not so much for leading the movement to the left as for crystallising a more coherent political strategy. Through the Wolfe Tone Societies, Johnston and Coughlan initiated projects such as a Co-operative Development Trust which assisted in the creation of co-operative enterprises along the lines of those started by Father James McDyer of Glencolumbcille in County Donegal. They also agitated against the Anglo-Irish Free Trade Agreement of 1965 and argued for a strategy of building republican support through involvement in agitation on social and economic grievances, as well as by a principled stand for a united and independent Ireland.

The republicans were active in influencing the direction taken by NICRA as well as in its creation. Goulding himself was present at the Wolfe Tone Societies meeting in Maghera in 1966. To understand the significance of their involvement, however, and the direction in which republican influence took the civil rights movement, it is necessary to examine carefully the political strategy of the republicans in the mid-1960s. The abandonment of the 1956–62 IRA military campaign was highly ambiguous and from outward appearances it was possible to interpret republican actions as either preparation for a renewed onslaught or as a delicate operation to keep the movement together while its direction was fundamentally changed. It is clear, however, that important innovations were being made in republican political activity. A document taken by the Garda Síochána (the Irish police force) from a leading republican, Sean Garland, in May 1966, and later published as an appendix to the Scarman Report,[4] contained a good deal of evidence of plans for intensive military training, but it also outlined some of the new political initiatives being taken by the movement. It began by stating the need for an organisational form which could attract trade-unionists and for a 'radical Social and

Economic programme'. Committees should be created to deal with such issues as housing and co-operatives, which would work with other radical groups and with individual members of the Irish Labour Party and trade-unionists.

There would have to be extensive education within the movement: here the document indicated that social and economic agitation would be given a much higher priority than purely military activity:

> The present form of recruit training will be changed. This change will replace the emphasis now placed on arms and battle tactics to a secondary position and be replaced by an emphasis on Social and Economic objectives . . . A recruit . . . finds that there is a lot of unromantic and possibly boring work to be done before he gets a chance to use his military training. This accounts for the high turnover in membership . . . the recruit having seen emphasis laid on military activity is not prepared for the political activity which must come before it.[5]

The document proposed that the basic unit of the movement should be the local *cumann* (branch), with factory-based *cumainn* wherever possible. These should have specialised sections that would agitate on different issues and among different sections of the population. Elections were to be contested up to the level of Dáil Éireann when the movement had built up sufficient support. There was a quixotic suggestion that elected representatives north and south should meet to set up an alternative national parliament which would proceed to 'legislate' for the whole country. This, it was suggested, could lead to a situation of 'dual power', which might come to a head over the 'nationalisation' of some foreign-owned factory which would be 'occupied' on behalf of the Irish nation.

In June 1968 William Craig read out in Stormont lengthy extracts from a document published in the secret IRA journal *An tÓglach* (the volunteer). This contained several passages which gave credence to the idea that the nature of the IRA and its aims were unchanged:

> To re-unify our country. To force the withdrawal of the British Army of Occupation. To abolish the existing Governments of our country, North and South, and replace them with a true Democratic

Republican Government owing but one allegiance to the Irish people.

A commitment to armed force was stated unambiguously:

> For mark this well: our enemies will never concede or surrender their Power, Position or Privileges to anything but armed men who are determined, committed and trained in every field of Revolution.

The main thrust of the document, however, was to point out the lessons drawn by the leadership from the failure of the 1956–62 campaign:

> 1 The fact that the people saw no connection between the fight in the North and the idea of improving the Irish social conditions, etc.
>
> 2 A lack of resources . . . money and the right type of weapons.
>
> 3 The lack of an efficient publicity and propaganda machine.
>
> 4 A dwindling of public support both North and South making it virtually impossible for men to operate on Guerrilla lines – one of the basic ingredients for a successful guerrilla campaign is the support of wide sections of the people. This comes only from an awareness and understanding of the reasons and nature of the struggle.

It was not enough to have modern weapons and 'the best of young Irishmen' if the people did not understand the nature of the freedom for which they were fighting and that

> this freedom we talk about is worthy of their support because it is for them we fight; it is for the establishment of a social system that is going to provide them with the opportunity and the means to develop all that is best in them and the Nation.

Propaganda by itself was insufficient; they must involve themselves in social agitation and make it known that the republicans were involved:

> For instance in one area recently there has been a series of protests and demonstrations regarding poor and inadequate housing conditions, the majority of the members of the committees which were responsible for organising the protests are members of the IRA. They are known publicly as such. Further, an Army section actually helped the occupants of houses threatened with eviction to barricade their homes, and actually stayed with the family for a week to help them resist eviction if need arose.[6]

These documents demonstrate a commitment to developing broadly based, open political agitation, but they contain little about a civil rights strategy in the north; such a strategy could be deduced from the analysis which they contain, but the documents give no indication that it had been proposed in any detail.

The Wolfe Tone Societies, as the section of the republican movement most directly involved in creating NICRA, had the most thoroughly worked-out civil rights strategy. In August 1966 their bulletin *Tuairisc* (information) published a long analysis of the political situation facing Irish republicans. The civil rights initiative was put in the context of a changed situation brought about by the Anglo-Irish Free Trade Agreement and the moves to join the EEC. These were seen as products of a new strategy on the part of Britain to ensure its continued domination of Ireland:

> Britain now hopes to ensnare Lemass back into the United Kingdom. The Free Trade Agreement will do the trick . . . *a situation in which the old-fashioned Unionist intransigence which served Britain so well in the past will also be outdated and no longer so convenient to imperialism.*

The contacts between the Lemass and O'Neill governments were seen as having been brought about by pressure from Britain, and as a result 'O'Neill has got his orders to play down discrimination'.

A liberalisation of the north, particularly in its treatment of Catholics, was a prerequisite for these new methods of domination, which would involve the economic integration of north and south. Concessions from the Unionists were necessary to enable Lemass to sell the new arrangements to public opinion in the south. But this strategy might not work out as the British government hoped; the resultant 'unfreezing [could] release the political energies of the people', and it could lead to a situation in which Protestant workers were weaned away from Orangeism and united with their Catholic fellow workers in the Labour movement:

> How can Unionism possibly survive when Protestant and Catholic are no longer at each other's throats, when discrimination has been dealt a body-blow? . . . This is the most progressive outcome to the present situation . . . the destruction of the machinery of discrimination . . . the unfreezing of bigotry . . . the achievement of the utmost degree of civil liberties possible, freedom of political action,

an end to the bitterness of social life and the divisions among the people fostered by the Unionists . . . They would permanently weaken the basis of Unionism, and towards these objectives the energies of the progressive people in the North should be bent in the coming months.

This would not occur automatically. The Unionist government would try to make the minimum concessions and strong pressure would have to be put on it:

> *There can be no doubt that the policy of Republicans must be to ensure that everything is done to make this demand more strong, vigorously organised, widespread, well-expressed and heard not only in the North but in Britain and throughout the world.* Force O'Neill to CONCEDE MORE THAN HE WANTS TO OR THAN HE THINKS HE CAN DARE GIVE without risking overthrow by the more reactionary elements among the Unionists. Demand more than may be demanded by the compromising elements that exist among the Catholic leadership. Seek to associate as wide a section of the community as possible with these demands, in particular the well-intentioned people in the Protestant population and the trade union movement.
>
> Civil rights, electoral reform, an end to gerrymandering and to discrimination in housing, jobs and appointments, the legal banning of incitement to religious discrimination. These are the essential demands of the present time.

The article went on to disavow the use of violent methods:

> Above all, actions must be avoided which would serve to solidify the disintegrating Unionist ranks – all irresponsible adventures, anything which could be construed as provocation. There may well be people who think, for example, that it may be a good thing to throw a bomb at some orange hall, because Orangemen have thrown bombs at Catholic halls. But this would undoubtedly be playing into the hands of the enemy at the present time. Let us choose our own battlegrounds and not be provoked. At the present time the strength of the Catholic and nationalist forces in the North lies in their political discipline and restraint. Let the Unionists expose themselves and rend one another asunder. Why should we join in and help them to unite against us?

Another document, *Ireland Today*, published by the Republican Education Department in 1969 when the civil rights movement was already an established fact, gives further evidence on republican strategy:

> The achievement of democracy and civil rights will make the way open for linking of the economic demands to the national question. Those who see the former as an end in itself . . . insofar as they comprise the present leadership of the NICRA . . . may be expected to lose interest as rights are gained. They must then be replaced by more consistent people.

It was necessary to work for the 'maximum co-ordination of efforts between the principled radical elements' and to win support from the NILP and the trade unions. It was also

> essential that the civil rights movement include all elements that are deprived, not just republicans, and that unity in action within the civil rights movement be developed towards unity of political objectives to be won, and that ultimately (but not necessarily immediately) the political objective agreed by the organised radical groups be seen within the framework of a movement towards the achievement of a 32-county democratic republic.[7]

The republicans, in other words, were keen to push the civil rights agitation further and to use it to build a radical coalition which would set its sights, eventually, on a united Ireland. But it should be noted that this document envisaged a definite stage of development in which Northern Ireland would be significantly changed as a result of success in achieving the reforms being demanded by the civil rights movement. A further stage of more radical agitation, including the objective of a united Ireland, would follow. It is unclear how quickly this stage would follow the preceding one, but clearly this more radical phase was predicated on a successful achievement of the limited demands of the civil rights movement.

Another Republican Education Department document, published in 1970, offers further clarification. A section, which the editor notes was originally written in 1967, discusses 'Tactical Objectives' in Northern Ireland:

> The major obstacle to the development of radical national ideas in the six counties is the lack of any form of communication between the Movement and the people. There is an extreme need for a paper which would inform the general public of the stand point of the

Movement. The existence of a ban on the legality of the Movement makes the position even more difficult in that it is practically impossible to even get a hall in some areas in which to hold a meeting. Both these facts point to the high priority of the struggle for civil liberties. In taking this up, however, it is necessary to realise that non-Republican people in the North are not disposed to agitate to get full civil rights for Republicans; they have to be involved in their own interests. This means that the civil rights movement in the North will have to involve Catholics on the issue of the local government election register which is weighted against them by property qualifications.[8]

In other words, the republicans saw the civil rights movement, at least in part, as a means of achieving the legalisation of republican political activity. Once this had been achieved they could campaign more openly for a united Ireland on the basis of uniting Catholic and Protestant workers, small farmers and the lower rungs of the business community for an independent, democratic, united and self-sufficient Irish Republic. Military action, although retained as an option for the future, did not figure as part of this strategy. Exactly when, where, how and if it would be resurrected was extremely vague. It is clear, however, that it was not regarded as a useful adjunct to the civil rights agitation. For all practical purposes the republican leadership saw its movement as being in a phase of activity which would concentrate on non-violent, political agitation.

The initiative of setting up NICRA was very much that of Johnston, Coughlan and the Dublin Wolfe Tone Society. The Belfast Wolfe Tone Society 'had always maintained a sturdy independence, but somehow lacked the interconnection necessary to become an effective ideas forum. Contact with the Belfast Republican and Labour Movements was tenuous, there was no link with Queen's at such a level as to influence student ideas'.[9] Among the people most prominent in Belfast were: Jack Bennett; Fred Heatley; Liam Burke, a veteran Belfast republican and adjutant general of the IRA from 1942 to 1943; Alec Foster, a former headmaster of the Royal Belfast Academical Institution and a rugby international; and Frank Gogarty, a Belfast dentist who was a chairman of NICRA in later years.

One of the achievements of the Belfast Wolfe Tone Society was the publication in 1967 of a pamphlet by Fred Heatley on Henry Joy McCracken, a Protestant and a hero of the United Irishmen and the 1798 rebellion in the north. This had prompted the Ulster Museum to put on an exhibition about McCracken and BBC Northern Ireland and Ulster Television to feature the bicentenary of his birth. The following year the Belfast society promoted the commemoration of another Irish patriot, James Connolly. A meeting in February 1968 brought together representatives of the Wolfe Tone Society, the Communist Youth League, the CPNI, the QUB Republican Club, the Republican Clubs, the NDP and Dúchas, Council of Irish Tradition. A series of lectures was arranged, as well as a *céilí* and film show. On 9 June there was a parade down the Falls Road to the house in which Connolly had lived while he was in Belfast. There a commemorative plaque was unveiled by Connolly's son, Roddy Connolly. The event was marred, however, by the refusal of the Young Socialists to march behind the Irish tricolour, which they described as a 'bourgeois flag'. It had been included in the first place on the insistence of the republicans, who refused to march without it. The following weekend a similar parade in Derry was called off when its route through the city centre was banned; an alternative route through a Catholic area was not acceptable. In June 1969 a proposed Connolly commemoration parade through Belfast city centre was bitterly opposed by loyalists. John McKeague of the Shankill Defence Association forecast that thousands of loyalists would gather in Royal Avenue to prevent it marching. The police restricted the parade to the Falls area and the organising committee then called it off so as to avoid compromising the principle of working-class unity. However, four members of the organising committee tried to hold a silent protest march over the proscribed route but were chased by loyalists.

The events surrounding the Connolly commemorations were an important indicator of the difficulty of reconciling Ulster Protestants to nationalist pageantry, no matter how much it was stressed that the traditions being commemorated included the Protestants. Since most of those involved in organising these commemorations were also involved in NICRA, and both were initiated by the Wolfe Tone Societies, the events illustrate how deep-rooted was their belief that it was possible to bring about unity between workers in both communities in Northern Ireland, provided the right political formula could be found.

It was the Dublin Wolfe Tone Society which suggested a civil rights campaign. Roy Johnston recalled: 'The August 1966 Maghera conference of the Wolfe Tone Societies . . . discussed a memorandum on civil rights prepared by the Dublin Society . . . with some of the Republican leadership present, convincing the latter that this constituted a valid way forward.'[10] The meeting was attended by representatives of Wolfe Tone Societies in Dublin, Cork, Belfast, Derry and County Tyrone. The first political business was to denounce the Unionist Party, following a UVF attack in Malvern Street in Belfast, which, they said, had shown the 'rapid moral disintegration of Unionist ideology'. In something of an afterthought the *Irish News* of 15 August 1966 recorded that 'a discussion took place on the desirability of holding a convention on civil rights for the purpose of drawing up a civil rights charter'. According to Fred Heatley, a letter was read from the Dublin Wolfe Tone Society which outlined the proposed civil rights strategy.[11] It was a long document which took about forty minutes to read and it was not greeted with warm enthusiasm. Michael Dolley and Jack Bennett were severely critical; Fred Heatley and Billy McMillen were doubtful about the emphasis given to the trade-union movement – McMillen pointed out the vast difference between trade unions in the north and in the south. Cathal Goulding was generally in favour but agreed that some of the phraseology could be altered. However, the broad strategy was accepted and the Belfast Wolfe Tone Society began discussions on the proposal with other interested people.[12]

After these discussions it was decided to drop the Wolfe Tone Societies tag, and an ad hoc body was formed which organised a seminar on civil rights on 28 November 1966 in Belfast. The main speakers were the president of the Irish Anti-Apartheid Movement, Kadar Asmal, who was a South African-born lecturer in law at Trinity College Dublin, and Ciarán Mac an Áilí, a Derry-born Dublin solicitor who was a member of the International Federation of Jurists and president of the Irish Pacifist Association. It was agreed that another meeting should be called to launch a civil rights body and this took place on 29 January 1967. Tony Smythe and James Shepherd from the NCCL in London were present and there were over one hundred delegates from a variety of organisations, including all the Northern Ireland political parties. However, Senator Nelson Elder of the Unionist Party walked out after an argument over capital punishment for the murder of policemen. A thirteen-person steering committee was elected to draw up a draft constitution and a programme of activities. Its membership was drawn from the Amalgamated Union of Engineering Workers Technical and Administrative Staffs Section (AUEW TASS), the CSJ, the CPNI, the Belfast Wolfe Tone Society, the Belfast trades council, the Republican Clubs, the Ulster Liberal Party, the NDP, the RLP, the Ardoyne Tenants' Association and the NILP. The committee subsequently co-opted Robin Cole, who was one of the most liberal of the Young Unionists and chairman of the QUB Conservative and Unionist Association.

In February the committee issued a statement deploring Ian Paisley's campaign against the visit of the Church of England Bishop of Ripon. It convened another meeting on 9 April to present the draft constitution and this meeting officially brought NICRA into existence. The new constitution, which was based on that of the NCCL, emphasised the association's character as a body which would make representations on the broad issues of civil liberties and would also take up individual cases of discrimination and ill-treatment. The five objectives of the association were:

1 To defend the basic freedoms of all citizens.
2 To protect the rights of the individual.
3 To highlight all possible abuses of power.
4 To demand guarantees for freedom of speech, assembly and association.
5 To inform the public of their lawful rights.[13]

These objectives said nothing about concrete grievances over discrimination in housing, employment and the electoral franchise. They underline the character of NICRA at this stage as an organisation which, like the NCCL, was concerned with the defence of legal and constitutional rights and the grievances of individuals, not with militant protest.

This phase was to last a year and a half and it was a period of general ineffectuality. As Fred Heatley described it:

The first eighteen months was a time of frustration. William Craig, to whom most of our complaints were directed, usually delayed in replying. When he did he usually denied that the complaints were justified – even when a civil rights officer (myself) was physically thrown out of Hastings Street [RUC] Station! Yet we did detect an easing off in harassment of Republicans and of itinerants. But the most annoying aspect of the early period was the lack of real interest shown by our first council members – at times we couldn't muster up the required six members for a quorum at the monthly meetings.[14]

The work of documenting abuses, which had been begun by the CSJ, was continued and the association intervened on behalf of a group of travelling people who were camped on Belfast's Shore Road. But although in December a national opinion poll in Northern Ireland found that 43 per cent of those interviewed thought that there should be legislation to outlaw discrimination, NICRA seemed incapable of tapping the support of this large, sympathetic minority.

In February 1968 the first annual general meeting of the association saw some changes of officers and in the membership of the executive committee, but no change of direction nor any indication of a breakthrough. It was probably inevitable, therefore, that as one committee member, Ann Hope, put it:

In the spring of 1968 there was much rethinking within the CRA [Civil Rights Association] leadership; the tactics of Martin Luther King in America had been absorbed inasmuch that it was felt by some that only public marches could draw wide attention to what we were trying to achieve by normal democratic means. But there were members on the EC [executive committee] who didn't relish either the trouble this would create or were too constitutional in their thinking.[15]

To some extent NICRA had already become involved in public protest action. In March 1967 Craig had announced a ban on the forthcoming commemorations of the 1867 Fenian Rising and had proscribed the Republican Clubs. NICRA denounced these measures as a violation of the rights of freedom of speech, assembly and association and was represented at protest rallies over the Republican Clubs ban and the banning of the 1968 Easter Rising commemoration in Armagh. NICRA's official history records that the association 'was slowly coming to realise that a ban on demonstrations was an effective Government weapon against political protest and that although letter writing to Stormont was a fine form of occupational therapy, it was unlikely to bring any worthwhile results'.[16]

By the summer of 1968, therefore, the leadership of NICRA was open to proposals for protest action. On 19 June, Austin Currie raised the question in Stormont of the allocation of a house in Caledon, outside Dungannon, to a nineteen-year-old unmarried Protestant woman, the secretary of a solicitor who was a Unionist parliamentary candidate. A Catholic family who had squatted in the house was evicted to make room for her, and a number of other Catholic families in the area were also denied houses. Currie himself squatted in the house to draw attention to the case. Fred Heatley, on behalf of NICRA, addressed a protest meeting in Dungannon on Saturday 22 June. In July, NICRA's executive committee was meeting in Kevin Agnew's house in Maghera; Currie had phoned Fred Heatley and asked to be allowed to put an idea to the committee, and he was invited to address the meeting. He proposed a march from Coalisland to Dungannon, ending with a rally in the town's Market Square. The committee was at first divided over the proposal, with Betty Sinclair opposing the whole idea of protest marches, and a decision was deferred to a later meeting, which agreed to go ahead and fixed the date for 24 August. An important factor was the support given to the proposal from both the republicans and the CSJ, which as a Dungannon-based group was particularly important.

A statement issued prior to the march claimed that there was support from the Nationalist Party, the RLP, the NILP, the NDP, the CSJ, the Irish National Foresters, the GAA, the AOH, the Derry Housing Action Committee (DHAC) and the Wolfe Tone Societies. The RUC initially agreed to the proposed route and to the meeting in Market Square. But Senator William Stewart, the Unionist chairman of Dungannon Urban District Council, intervened and forecast that there would be trouble if the march was allowed to proceed to the centre of Dungannon. John Taylor, the Unionist MP for South Tyrone, also made representations and the Ulster Protestant Volunteers, a body led by Ian Paisley, announced a meeting for the same time and place as the civil rights rally. The police responded by re-routing the march to the Catholic sector of the town but NICRA refused to accept this, since it would have implied that theirs was a sectarian march.

Some two thousand people assembled in Coalisland and proceeded, accompanied by nationalist bands, to Thomas Street in Dungannon. There they were met by a cordon of police, standing in front of a barrier of police tenders. A group of about 1,500 loyalists, including Ian Paisley and Unionist members of Dungannon council, were gathered behind the police tenders, with a gap of about fifty yards separating the rival groups. A platform and public address system were set up by NICRA stewards in front of the police cordon. But before the meeting could commence a group of young demonstrators attempted to break through the police lines to get at the counter-demonstrators, who were jeering, shouting slogans and singing party songs. This onslaught was driven back by a police baton charge in the course of which four youths were slightly hurt. But appeals from the platform succeeded in dissuading the civil rights supporters from making any further attempt to breach the police cordon, and the trouble was contained.

The meeting was chaired by Betty Sinclair, who reminded the supporters that their objective was to demonstrate for civil rights, for jobs and for houses: 'We are asking you to listen to the speakers, and what we have done today will go down in history and in this way we will be more effective in showing the world that we are a peaceful people asking for our civil rights in an orderly manner.'[17]

Austin Currie condemned the police action in blocking their route, and said that NICRA would be organising more parades, which would not stop at Thomas Street: 'O'Neill and those Orange bigots behind him [will] realise once and for all that we are on our way forward. We will keep going with disobedience and anything else that is necessary to achieve our aims.'[18] He said that looking out from the platform towards the town reminded him of the late President Kennedy looking out over the Berlin Wall. The regimes in Czechoslovakia and other Eastern European countries were no different from the regime in Dungannon.

Gerry Fitt reiterated the point about Czechoslovakia (the Soviet invasion had occurred a few days before). What had happened in Dungannon, he suggested, was no different from what had happened in Prague: 'We ordinary people have been walked over by a militant force.' They were there to demand fair play in the allocation of housing and jobs; he was not the enemy of the counter-demonstrators and NICRA had people of all religions demanding the same social justice. He promised to draw the attention of the government at Westminster to what was happening in Dungannon. He ended by saying that the lights would not go out until they had achieved civil rights and a thirty-two-county republic.

Jack Hassard, an NILP member of Dungannon Council, condemned the ban on the Market Square meeting, which had only been notified by the police at twelve o'clock the previous night. Pleas for housing made at council meetings, he said, had fallen on deaf ears. Many Protestants, like himself, were in favour of civil rights. Joe McCann, secretary of the NDP, said that the meeting bore witness to the failure of the Unionist Party to keep faith with the British traditions it professed to admire. In return for the money received by Northern Ireland from the British taxpayer, the Unionists had turned the British flag into a party-political symbol and had made a mockery of the British tradition of social justice. Other speakers were Erskine Holmes of the NILP and T. O'Connor of the Republican Clubs. After the meeting was over and the main demonstration had dispersed, some civil rights supporters succeeded in infiltrating to Market Square by a roundabout route. There they staged a sit-down and were batoned by the police.

In a press statement issued afterwards, NICRA said that the events in Dungannon had proved the need for a civil rights body in Northern Ireland. It condemned the police for failing to control the counter-demonstration and for not ensuring the right of the NICRA marchers to demonstrate peacefully. It praised the stewards who had kept order on its side. However, its supporters were not unanimous; a statement issued by the Belfast Young Socialists condemned the police and also accused NICRA of selling its principles by not leading the demonstration into Dungannon.

The Cameron Report's judgement on the march was that

it is significant that this first civil rights march, unaccompanied by any provocative display of weapons, banners or symbol was carried out without any breach of the peace. It attracted considerable public attention and was also regarded as proof in certain circles that many elements in the society of Northern Ireland whose ultimate political purposes differed in very marked degree could co-operate in peaceful and lawful demonstration in favour of certain common and limited objectives.[19]

As we have seen, there were in fact two minor clashes with the police and the presence of bands playing nationalist tunes could be interpreted as provocative. The organisers kept control of some of their supporters only with great difficulty. Bernadette Devlin recalled that in its early stages 'the whole thing had a sort of good-natured holiday atmosphere', but when they realised that the police had re-routed the march

> the whole atmosphere changed. Most of the people . . . hadn't really thought about civil rights; they had come, with a sort of friendly curiosity, to hear something. I do believe that then for the first time it dawned on people that Northern Ireland was a series of Catholic and Protestant ghettoes. The meeting got very angry, though it was still a passive anger, with very little pushing and shoving of the police. Some men were calling out that we should force our way through, and the lines of the march were breaking formation and crowding the police.[20]

The trouble was kept to a minimum as much because of the novelty of the situation as anything else. No significant section of the marchers had formed a determination to defy the police, and the RUC, for its part, seems to have behaved in a generally good-natured way. It was clear, however, that such restraint could not survive a serious clash between civil rights demonstrators and the police or counter-demonstrators.

Shortly after the Coalisland–Dungannon march, NICRA was approached by the DHAC with a proposal for a march in Derry. The DHAC was a coalition of radicals from the local Republican Clubs and the left wing of the NILP; they had organised a series of imaginative protests in Derry to draw attention to bad conditions and discrimination in housing. Since NICRA had already targeted Derry for a march, there was ready agreement and a delegation from NICRA travelled to Derry to discuss arrangements with the DHAC. According to Eamonn McCann, who was a prominent member of the DHAC:

> It was immediately clear that the CRA knew nothing of Derry. We had resolved to press for a route which would take the march into

the walled centre of the city and expected opposition from the
moderate members of the CRA. But there was none. No one in the
CRA delegation understood that it was unheard of for a non-Unionist
procession to enter that area.[21]

This seems highly unlikely. There had been violent clashes
between police and nationalist demonstrators in the mid-1950s in
Derry city centre and only the previous June the Connolly commemoration had been banned. A more credible explanation is that the
NICRA leadership was unwilling to accept that its marches should be
treated as sectarian and provocative. Adoption of this route,
however, did not necessarily mean that the association would defy
the police in order to march on it. NICRA probably meant to register
its protest but to stop short of an actual confrontation, as it had
done in Dungannon. This interpretation is supported by a letter
written by McCann, before the march, to Michael Farrell, leader of
the Young Socialists in Belfast, in which he gave an account of the
meeting between NICRA and the DHAC:

> The police are more than likely to ban the march. [Betty] Sinclair
> adopted a 'cross that bridge when we come to it' attitude, which
> means that she wants the back door left open for a sell-out. I think
> one would have to push for a 'we are marching and that's that'
> position. The DHAC and the Republican Clubs will push for that but
> I can't see anyone else.[22]

In the event, the more fateful decision was not the proposal of a
route within the walled city but making the starting point for the
march the railway station on the Protestant Waterside. This meant
that the entire route was prohibited and there was little scope, as in
Dungannon, to march peacefully to a token, non-violent confrontation with the police. The ban was imposed by Minister of Home
Affairs William Craig after the Apprentice Boys of Derry had
announced a procession at the same time and over the same route as
the civil rights march. They claimed that this was an annual event
and it does seem that the date coincided with a regular initiation
ceremony for new members of their organisation. But the ceremony was usually held in the morning and would not, therefore,
have clashed with the NICRA demonstration. Fergus Pyle of the
Irish Times was at the station when the expected delegation from
Liverpool arrived on the morning train. He was told that they were

unaware of any plan to switch the ceremony to the afternoon and that arrangements were the same as in previous years.[23]

After Craig had announced on Thursday 3 October that the Apprentice Boys march was to be banned and that the civil rights march would not be permitted to take place within the walled city or in the Waterside ward, an emergency meeting of the NICRA executive committee was called. The committee was divided over whether or not to proceed with the march but it agreed to send a delegation to Derry to consult the local people; this meeting began on the evening of Friday 4 October and went on until 1 a.m. on Saturday. Conn McCluskey of the CSJ held out strongly against defying the ban but the DHAC representatives made it clear that they would go ahead in any case, and this seems to have swayed the NICRA members. Eddie McAteer made a public call for the march to be postponed, but Fred Heatley, John McAnerney and Betty Sinclair visited him at home to persuade him not to pull out. He told them that he did not like the company they were keeping – presumably the DHAC – but he did participate.

The parade formed up outside Waterside railway station, on the opposite bank of the River Foyle to the city centre. There was police intervention almost immediately; an NILP loudspeaker van, which was making announcements, was stopped and its three occupants were taken to Victoria RUC station where, one of them later told the *Belfast Telegraph*, they were charged with incitement to defy the ban on the march. At the head of the parade was a blue banner bearing the words 'Civil Rights March', which had been carried on the Coalisland–Dungannon march. In the front rank were Ivan Cooper, Eddie McAteer and Gerry Fitt. Behind them were Austin Currie, Proinsias Mac Aonghusa and David Green of Citizens for PR in the Irish Republic,[24] and three Westminster Labour MPs, Russell Kerr, Ann Kerr and John Ryan, who had travelled directly from the Labour Party conference with Gerry Fitt. Placards proclaimed such slogans as 'Police State Here', 'The Proper Place for Politics is in the Streets', 'Class not Creed', and '*A Dhia Saor Éire*' (God free Ireland). The turnout was much smaller than for the Coalisland–Dungannon march, at about four hundred. County Inspector William Meharg of the RUC warned the crowd that no march was permitted in 'this part of the Maiden City'. He advised them, for their own safety and that of the women and children present, to leave the area. He later reiterated the warning and told them that the police would have to see that the prohibition order was enforced. Ivan Cooper asked the crowd to behave responsibly and stressed that NICRA did not want any violence or bloodshed.

The original route would have taken the march up the steep slopes of Simpson's Brae and Distillery Brae to Spencer Road and then to the upper tier of Craigavon Bridge. The police had blocked this way and the marchers set off along Duke Street, trying to find another way onto the bridge. The police hastily threw a cordon across the end of Duke Street and here the first clashes occurred. Fred Heatley believes that he was the first marcher to be arrested. He had arrived late with other NICRA leaders from Belfast, and seeing the march moving off, he ran to its head. On reaching the front, he claims, he was kneed in the groin by a policeman, dragged behind police lines and ordered into a Black Maria. Fergus Pyle saw a Young Socialist being hit on the head by a baton and a 'girl in a mini skirt carrying the Plough and Stars [flag] wrestling with a constable, and a few men grabbing and fighting with policemen'. It was at this point that Gerry Fitt, Eddie McAteer and Austin Currie were injured. Paddy Kennedy, an RLP councillor who was himself taken to hospital with suspected broken ribs, said that he had seen Fitt fall to the ground and he had appeared to be on his knees when he was struck by a baton. During these first scuffles the blue civil rights banner was seized and ripped by the police.

There was a brief attempt at a sit-down in front of the police lines, and a ragged snatch of 'We shall overcome' was sung. Then an impromptu meeting, on the model of what had happened in Dungannon, was held. Michael Farrell of the Young Socialists said that the protest was over housing, gerrymandering and discrimination: 'We are met by police with batons in their hands. Is that democracy?' Betty Sinclair said

> it had to be made clear that the Civil Rights Movement was not anti-constitutional. In all the negotiations for the march and the meeting the police had been co-operative. The Association would have changed the day if the Minister had consulted them, but he had banned it without enabling them to change their plans. However, she declared, 'We want to make our case that, for certain people in Northern Ireland there are no civil rights. Have we made that clear?'

There were cheers when she added, 'There may be people here who think you have to spill blood for this. That would mean you are playing Mr Craig's game.'

Eddie McAteer repeated Betty Sinclair's plea for restraint: 'Join with me in wishing that no one should be exposed to hurt here today. I advise you to make your way in a wee walk to the Diamond.' Eamonn McCann said that events had shown that the old policies would get no one anywhere: 'I don't advise anyone to charge that barricade,' he said. 'I also want to make it clear as a private individual that I can do nothing to stop them.' Ivan Cooper and other speakers were less ambiguous in calling for restraint and Betty Sinclair came back to ask the crowd to disperse quietly. But almost immediately violence broke out again.

Some of the crowd attempted to strike up with 'We shall overcome' but they were interrupted by a police loudspeaker announcement, which was shouted down; this was probably an order to disperse but very few could have heard it. At this point some of the protesters started to throw their placards over the heads of those in front at the police. Then the police, with batons drawn, advanced on the crowd. Retreat for marchers fleeing them was blocked by a cordon at the other end of Duke Street, where police also charged the demonstrators. After the action had lasted for a few minutes, County Inspector Meharg, through a loud-hailer, ordered: 'The police will hold their hands, please.' Fergus Pyle reported:

> Instead of a pause, this announcement was the prelude to a methodi-cal and efficient movement forward by the police, hitting everything in front of them. Some people in the crowd tackled them back and poles from the placards were flying through the air. From my vantage point I saw nothing in the few seconds between the County Inspector's announcement to have incited what appeared to be a concerted start by the police.

The police carried on down Duke Street, clearing the crowd in front of them as demonstrators screamed hysterically. Detach-ments of police went after individuals and when the street was nearly clear, water cannon were brought in. Later it was alleged that the RUC sprayed not only those who remained on the road but also groups sheltering in shop doorways and the first-floor windows of houses, some of which were open. Passers-by, and others who had taken no part in the demonstration, were also soaked. Kenneth Orbinson, an Ulster Television cameraman, gave evidence at the trial of those arrested on 5 October: he said that he had been sprayed while filming from the window of a flat in Duke Street; but his film was not admitted as evidence.

A small number of demonstrators followed McAteer's advice and took a 'wee walk' to the Diamond on the city side of the river, infiltrating in groups of two or three. A Campaign for Nuclear Disarmament banner was unfurled and carried round the war memorial before one of those carrying it was arrested. A crowd gathered and shouted at the police, provoking another baton charge which forced them down towards Butcher Gate and the Bogside. Stones were thrown at the police and a number of shop windows were broken. By this time the original confrontation between marchers and police had given way to a general battle between the police and young residents of the Bogside, most of whom had taken no part in the march. A barricade was built in Fahan Street and set on fire and a continuous fusillade of stones was thrown at the police sheltering behind Butcher Gate. Attempts were made to disperse the stone throwers with a water cannon, but its progress was halted by a barricade; police trying to clear the obstruction returned fire with stones which had been thrown at them. The battle lasted for several hours and at about 10.30 p.m. there was a further clash as a crowd charged the police and was dispersed by a counter-charge. After this a section of the crowd marched to the Guildhall, from where they were driven back up Shipquay Street towards the Diamond, where two baton charges were needed to disperse them. Violence continued into the following afternoon and evening; petrol bombs were thrown and shops looted.

There were many stories afterwards of what appeared to be gratuitous police violence. A young Derry woman was walking past a group of police who were pushing and kicking a man. As she passed, she said, a policeman had struck her in the face with a baton, 'and I hadn't opened my mouth to him'. John Ryan MP claimed to have seen a policeman remove a woman's glasses and then strike her on the head; she had appeared, to him, to be over sixty years of age and a bystander. Other stories of bystanders who suffered included that of a man going home from his work in a bookmaker's shop in the Waterside when he was set upon and batoned. A railway worker, also making his way home, was caught up in the riot and, as a result of baton blows, was deafened in one ear and had to have sixteen stitches to his head.[25] Martin Cowley, a reporter with the local nationalist newspaper, the *Derry Journal*, was put into the police van beside Fred Heatley, his head streaming with blood. He told Heatley that he had been walking along the footpath when the police had made a baton charge. He had shouted that he was a reporter but he was struck several blows on the head and shoved into the police tender.

The *Irish News* reported that the police had struck at the testicles of male demonstrators but none of the other papers reported this. However, a medical certificate was read out in Stormont some days later, which reported that a medical examination of Eddie McAteer had found an oval bruise below his right groin, about one inch away from the scrotum. McAteer could not remember having been struck there and made no claim as to how the injury had been caused.[26] A famous film clip, which has been shown countless times, shows a NICRA supporter in front of the police line, appealing for restraint before suddenly doubling up, apparently in agony. At his trial in December, Eamonn Melaugh, a prominent Derry republican, testified that he had seen a demonstrator struck in the groin.[27]

The most bizarre story concerned Margaret Healy of Anne Street, Derry. She was a polio victim and only four feet nine inches tall, with curvature of the spine. She was running down Duke Street, away from the baton charge, when she was arrested. Both the nationalist *Irish News* and the middle-of-the-road *Sunday News* reported what happened. She told the former:

> I lifted a broken placard that was lying in the centre of the road to throw it into the side when two policemen pounced on me. They accused me of going to hit one of them with it . . . they put me in a police van and took me to Victoria Barracks where they kept me for two hours.

At the police station, she said, she was told first that she would be charged with assault and then that she would be charged with disorderly behaviour. But eventually she was released without a charge being made. Later, relatives of another polio victim told the *Derry Journal* that he had been beaten up by a group of policemen when he went to buy cigarettes on the evening of Sunday 6 October.

Not all policemen behaved brutally. Fergus Pyle reported that 'many of the officers, probably local men, went no further than duty required. I heard one man say "bastards" as a group of policemen went past him. One of them rounded on him, grabbed him by the arm, but only asked him for his name and address.' A QUB woman student, a member of the NDP, recalled having told a group of policemen early in the events that their conditions were as bad as those the demonstrators were protesting about. Some had been hostile but others were quite friendly. Later, after a friend had been batoned, she approached a group of policemen and remonstrated with them. One had raised his baton but the others opened a gap for her and let her through. After the first clash, when the crowd was halted in front of the police cordon, some of the women had argued with the police and told them that they too were victims of the 'system'. This was either ignored or taken with good humour. According to Fred Heatley, the demonstrators who were detained in Victoria RUC station were well treated.

The Cameron Report found that four policemen were injured during the clashes in Duke Street and a further seven during the later clashes at the Diamond and on the fringes of the Bogside. The total number of civilian casualties was seventy-seven, most of whom had suffered bruises or lacerations to the head. Only four people – two policemen and two civilians – were detained in hospital. The report suggested that there were severe shortcomings in police tactics. Lord Cameron came to the conclusion that there had not been a baton charge in Duke Street but that many policemen had drawn their batons individually and when ordered to disperse the march, had then used them indiscriminately. The situation was made worse by the fact that the officers who had originally been blocking Simpson's Brae moved down to the rear of the march and then, unaware that their colleagues were dispersing the head of the demonstration, were confronted by protesters running towards them. Here too, the report found, there was indiscriminate use of batons. The use of water cannon was criticised as having been unnecessary and for affecting members of the public who had not been involved in the march.

The march organisers can also be criticised. The choice of the Waterside railway station as an assembly point only made sense if the sole criterion was the convenience of demonstrators coming from other parts of Northern Ireland. The Coalisland–Dungannon march had given everyone a good day out and had used up a lot of their energy by the time the moment of confrontation arrived. The confrontation was predictable and planned, therefore relatively easily controlled. The organisers were well prepared and able to maintain their authority. In Derry things were very different.

The incipient differences between NICRA and the DHAC had never been resolved and the Derry radicals and their allies in the Belfast Young Socialists were determined to provoke a more drastic challenge to authority than had occurred in Dungannon. Gerry Fitt, too, seems to have had aims at variance with those of NICRA. He had brought three British Labour MPs to Derry and may have thought that the opportunity to expose the RUC should not be wasted. The key leaders of NICRA arrived late, after the march had already started; if they had any plans for preventing a clash with the police, they were unable to put them into operation. The demonstrators' tactic of walking into the police lines, while it was a principled assertion of their right to march, invited the violent response that followed and made further violence much more likely. The throwing of placards by the Young Socialists provoked the RUC without damaging its capacity to inflict punishment on the crowd. McCann's speech, with its suggestion that the police lines ought to be charged, while refusing to actually call for such action, seems to have typified the confused militancy of the radicals, who were suddenly precipitated into a conflict for which they were quite unprepared. In later years the events of 5 October were to be polished into simplified and incompatible propaganda versions; it has to be stressed that the whole affair was a series of blunders and the violence resulted from a breakdown of control by the leaders of the march and the controllers of the police, and not from any pre-existing plan.

However, the judgement of the London *Times* of 7 October on the affair was probably widely shared by political and public opinion in Britain:

The refusal of Mr William Craig . . . to hold an inquiry into police methods in Londonderry cannot be the last word. His assurance that the police used no undue force echoes exactly that of Mayor Daley in Chicago last month. Nonetheless Mayor Daley had to submit to an inquiry and the Prime Minister of Northern Ireland should now persuade his colleagues to agree. The reports of police brutality to individuals and loss of self-control in general are too uncomfortably convincing to be waved away by Mr Craig.

The *Guardian* asked: 'If the police practice is to strike obstructive demonstrators on the legs, as Mr Craig claims, how did heads happen to be bleeding?'

In the aftermath of the events in Derry, Craig, members of the Government and other Unionists strenuously defended both the ban on the march and the actions of the RUC. In an interview with William Hardcastle on BBC Radio 4's 'The World This Weekend', the text of which was published in the *Irish News* on 7 October, Craig introduced two themes which were to be repeated over and over during the next few days. Challenged about the ban, he claimed:

> 'The civil rights march was banned because they were proposing to march through areas that would provoke serious riot.' He said that in Derry, down through the years, it had been established that Loyalists could parade in certain places, Republicans in certain places.
>
> Mr Hardcastle: 'But they don't regard themselves as a sectarian group either?' Mr Craig: 'This absolutely astonishes me. We can see little or no difference, and indeed yesterday we unfortunately failed to arrest some very prominent IRA men, including Cathal Goulding from Dublin.[28] There is little doubt in police circles that it is, in fact, a Republican front.'

The *Irish Times* quoted Craig as claiming that a reason for banning the march had been that it posed a threat to the United States military base in Derry:

> 'The authorities in Northern Ireland were quite satisfied that a substantial amount of explosives was in the area, and it might only be a matter of time until this sort of activity was renewed.' The Minister said that all of the activities of the civil rights movement had indicated that it was predominantly a Republican body, and activities in Derry did not disprove that. Genuine supporters of civil

rights in principle were extremely ill-advised to associate as they were doing with the IRA and Communism.

In the Stormont debate on the events of 5 October, Craig referred to NICRA as 'an *omnium gatherum* made up of members of the Londonderry Housing Action Committee, the majority of whom are also members of the Connolly Association, of the Republican Party which includes well-known members of the IRA and Sinn Féin, of the Young Socialists and of the Communist Party'.[29] He went on to stress the likelihood of sectarian clashes had the procession followed the original route and he defended the actions of the RUC as necessary to avoid even worse violence. Other Unionist speakers – the debate was boycotted by the opposition parties – who supported his judgement on the ban included the liberal Phelim O'Neill. Several speakers also repeated Craig's claims about links between NICRA and both republicanism and Communism.

Many commentators pointed out later that there was, in fact, no trouble between the demonstrators and the Protestant residents of the Waterside. The only confrontation in Duke Street, or later at the Diamond, was between police and civil rights marchers or their supporters. It should also be noted that on this occasion the march was not accompanied by nationalist bands. This is not proof, of course, that there was no reasonable expectation of trouble; the late announcement of the ban, however, gave credence to the assumption that it had only been prompted by the Apprentice Boys march, and that the Government, as in Dungannon, was allowing a loyalist organisation to manipulate the situation so that an opposition demonstration would be banned. NICRA also had a reasonable complaint that the lateness of the ban gave them no time to negotiate any alternative date or route.

Craig and other ministers were at pains afterwards to make it clear that irrespective of the likelihood of a rival parade, the march would not have been allowed to proceed through the Waterside or the walled city. This cut little ice with NICRA, which rejected the claim that the march was in any way provocative and accused the Government of suppressing free expression. Craig seems to have been determined to undermine the association's credibility and to brand its members as troublemakers. The accusations of republican and Communist links were significant, and Craig obviously believed that it was reasonable to assume that the motives of NICRA were subversive. It is important, therefore, to examine the nature of republican and Communist involvement in NICRA, and their motives, strategy and tactics within the association.

The Cameron Report found evidence of republican involvement in NICRA, but in a famous passage praised the way in which IRA stewards had kept order on demonstrations. But the report missed the fact that the republicans, through the Wolfe Tone Societies, had been largely responsible for creating NICRA in the first place and some commentators have accused Cameron of naïveté about republican influence. One of these, Patrick Riddell, asks:

> If the sole intention of the Association were to secure civil rights for Ulster Catholics while accepting and loyally supporting the consti-
> tution of the Ulster state . . . why has it admitted to its counsels and
> membership, as it undoubtedly has, a number of men from an
> organisation pledged to the destruction of that state?[30]

Riddell partly overstates the extent to which NICRA claimed to accept the constitution of Northern Ireland. There is a difference between 'accepting and loyally supporting' the constitution and acting within legal boundaries to press demands for reform within the existing constitutional framework. Riddell verges on suggesting that an organisation may be deemed subversive not simply if it works to undermine the state, but if its members have any mental reservations about the constitution. Nevertheless, it is reasonable to question the motives of IRA members and supporters in NICRA, and whether their influence might, at some future date, have led the association into subversive activities.

Cathal Goulding gave an interview to the *Belfast Telegraph* of 10 February 1969 in which he readily admitted that republicans were involved in the civil rights movement. However, he was anxious to stress that

> we have not organised the civil rights movement and we have not
> infiltrated it . . . We have issued no directive about it. But we have
> encouraged Republicans to be active in it, always accepting the
> directives of the CR [civil rights] committees. We have emphasised
> . . . that peaceful demonstration along the lines of CR is the true way
> to support its aims. The Republicans are in the civil rights

movement the same as they are in the trade unions. They are members of the community being denied civil rights. It is not a specific IRA assignment. Our attitude is that we want to see everyone in the six counties, whether Protestant or Catholic, active in the movement to attain civil rights for the people there.

The republican documents quoted show that the republican movement was much more centrally involved in the creation of NICRA than Goulding suggests. They also show that political activity had by no means ousted the republicans' commitment to armed force; indeed it was seen as a necessary preliminary to the resumption of the military campaign. But they do not prove that NICRA was a front for the preparation of such a campaign or that it was reasonable or wise to treat it as such. Quite simply, the concept of agitation on civil rights, far less the creation of a movement to carry out such agitation, is missing from the documents. They propose broadly based agitation on social and economic issues but nowhere do they contain blueprints that correspond with the objectives, structure or activities of NICRA. There is also clear evidence that the republicans were not actually in control of NICRA in the period up to and including the 5 October march. This can be adduced from the fact that their internal document, *Ireland Today*, speculated about the replacement of some of the leadership of the association at a future date. This would hardly have been necessary if at that time they were in a position to dictate the policy and actions of the association.

It is also necessary to distinguish between different sections and levels of the republican movement. Although the civil rights strategy could not have been adopted by republicans without the approval of the leadership of the IRA – and Roy Johnston stressed the importance of its involvement in the Maghera meeting of 1966 – this does not mean that the army council initiated the setting up of NICRA or that it paid any detailed attention to the work being done by republicans within the association. Seán Mac Stíofáin indicates that the first time the leadership discussed the civil rights movement was when

a proposal arrived at Dublin HQ from the Tyrone unit of the IRA. It asked that members of the Republican Movement be permitted to take part in a civil rights march to Dungannon from Coalisland . . . The leadership unanimously gave permission and word was sent out to all Republican units in the North to encourage as many people as possible to participate. I emphasise 'encourage' because the leadership did not make it compulsory. It was also decided that no known members of the IRA from the South would participate.[31]

Even the Wolfe Tone Societies, the one section of the republican movement which had a well-worked-out strategy for the civil rights movement, were unable to implement their plans exactly as they had intended. NICRA, in its early stages, differed in two important respects from the model proposed by the societies in August 1966. They had emphasised agitation on the concrete issues of electoral reform and discrimination in housing and employment, but NICRA originally operated as a body which made representations on the broad issues of civil liberties and took up individual cases of infringement of rights. Undoubtedly the republicans were influential in steering the association towards public marches but they had to persuade others within NICRA; they could not determine the matter in advance. The other difference was in the way in which the association was organised. *Tuairisc* proposed the creation of

> local committees and groups . . . on the widest possible basis throughout the towns and villages of the North . . . Civil Rights committees, electoral reform groups, community development associations, friendship clubs, it matters not what they are called, or how diverse they are in structure and organisation. They should seek to organise the maximum number of people at local level to bring pressure to bear on local authorities, on Stormont, but particularly on Westminster.

This was a proposal for a loose federation of locally based groups; NICRA, however, was a centralised organisation based mainly in Belfast. Had the *Tuairisc* model been adopted, there would have been no question of NICRA initiating demonstrations in Dungannon or Derry; this would have been the responsibility of purely local groups. The form which NICRA took, therefore, was determined by the coalition of forces which actually came together to create it, of which the republicans were only one element. Since a number of different initiatives on the issue of civil rights took place between 1962 and 1966, it was probably fortuitous that the one which led to the creation of an organisation was the Wolfe Tone Societies conference, and even without their intervention, something very like NICRA would probably have emerged in any case.

The CPNI was involved in NICRA from the start. From the early 1960s the party had seen the issue of civil liberties as a key area of agitation. Its 1962 programme, *Ireland's Path to Socialism*, said:

> In no other aspect of public affairs has the authority of the Executive been abused as much as in Civil, Religious and Democratic Liberties. This is the outstanding feature which has enabled the Unionist Party to create divisions and govern unchallenged since the foundation of the Northern Ireland Parliament . . .
>
> Abolition of all anti-democratic laws, an end to civil and religious discrimination, and an end to the rigging of electoral areas in the interests of the wealthy, can be accomplished by the united action of the people. The organised Labour Movement is the force to lead the struggle for democracy and the rights of the individual to participate with equality in public affairs. The Communist Party has this struggle as its foremost aim.[32]

The 1966 congress of the CPNI adopted a 'Democratic Programme for Unity', which included demands for the electoral law in Northern Ireland to be brought into line with that in Britain, except for the reintroduction of proportional representation and the abolition of cash deposits by candidates.

The CPNI was not instrumental in creating NICRA but it was well represented on its first executive committee: Noel Harris of AUEW TASS, a CPNI member, was the first chairman; Derek Peters of the CPNI was secretary; and Betty Sinclair of the Belfast trades council was elected to the committee. At the meeting which adopted the constitution, Ken Banks of AUEW TASS was added to the executive committee; he was close to the CPNI, although not actually a member. However, at the first annual general meeting in February 1968, Banks and Harris were not returned to the executive committee and although Sinclair replaced Harris in the chair, Peters was replaced as secretary by John McAnerney of the CSJ. Banks, Harris and Sinclair were probably elected because of their trade-union connections, but precisely because of these existing responsibilities, the first two could not devote much time and effort to what appeared to be a marginal group making little impact. There is not much evidence of a determined drive by the Communists to control NICRA and even less that they had a great deal of influence.

The one member of the CPNI who was centrally involved in NICRA was Betty Sinclair; as secretary of the Belfast trades council she had more time to devote to it than trade-union officials like Banks and Harris. Her involvement led one Unionist MP to comment after the events in Derry:

> Last but not least we have the Communist Party led by that veteran Miss Sinclair, who is the chairman of the whole civil rights movement. When we hear of the Communist Party appealing for law and order it seems to me that it is a matter of Satan rebuking sin. There is no doubt about it that this programme is an Irish Republican Army programme sponsored and inspired by Communism.[33]

In fact, Sinclair was a strong advocate of caution and moderation. Her opposition to what she regarded as adventurism and ultra-leftism was shown in 1969 when she resigned from the executive together with Conn McCluskey, John McAnerney and Fred Heatley in protest at NICRA involvement with the People's Democracy (PD). Eamonn McCann, in his letter to Michael Farrell describing the joint DHAC–NICRA meeting of September 1968, said:

> The meeting was chaired by Betty Sinclair. I brought up the question of bans and proscriptions and Sinclair finally stated that no red flags or 'unauthorised' slogans will be permitted. I said, to push the point, that having talked to some of the YS [Young Socialists] . . . I had no doubt that there would be a YS contingent with a red flag and that I would 'react physically' to any attempt to remove it. Sinclair steered the discussion away into safer waters, but not before herself and McAnerney had agreed that 'the Young Socialists are the biggest problem'.

An article based on interviews with Betty Sinclair shortly before her death in 1981 discussed her attitudes during the early months of NICRA:

> During this time she wanted to exploit all the constitutional possibilities and consolidate a broad-based support around the civil rights demands. This was why she initially opposed the first march from Coalisland to Dungannon, but the arguments of the Nationalists and the Republicans on direct action tactics had become dominant and she was outvoted.[34]

She may actually have pressed her case with less vigour than is indicated above, since by mid-1968 it was abundantly clear that 'broad-based support' was not emerging and she may have suspended her earlier judgement in view of the success of the first march. But in any case, her prominence in the preparations for the 5 October march, and her leading part in it, did not mean that she intended that it should lead to a violent outcome, and the mere fact of her CPNI membership cannot be taken as evidence for the existence of a violent conspiracy.

Accusations of republican and Communist domination of NICRA and attempts to link the civil rights movement to subversion and violence were to some extent understandable responses by Unionists to the events in Derry. But they were a gross oversimplification. Craig had been monitoring developments within the republican movement since 1966, when he had obtained intelligence from RUC, Garda Síochána and British sources about the IRA's turn to agitation on social and economic issues. He had, correctly, seen the civil rights movement as a realisation of one aspect of the new republican strategy and he had observed that the turn to legal and open political work had not resulted in an elimination of the IRA's military capacity. He had concluded that the new strategy would eventually lead to a resumption of the armed struggle, but, more dubiously, had gone on to suppose that civil rights activities could be treated as if they were an armed insurrection.

Twenty years later Craig was still convinced that he had been right. In a BBC Radio 4 programme about the civil rights movement he said:

> It gives me some satisfaction that those who laughed at me and poked fun at me now have evidence in front of their very eyes. It's a pity it had to happen that way. If people had taken me as a sincere, genuine man who was worried, I think we could have avoided all that has happened. We've created in Ulster and Ireland a monster that will terrify the island for a good many years to come.[35]

This is a typical conspiracy theory, which adduces the fact that something *did* happen as evidence that someone *meant* it to happen. It also supposes that vigorous enough action in the early stages of the civil rights movement would have nipped it in the bud and restored Northern Ireland to stability.

In fact, Craig's actions contributed significantly to destabilising the situation. His response was predicated on the idea that he was dealing with an IRA insurrection when he was actually faced with a group of unarmed demonstrators who posed nothing more than a difficult public order problem. The chaotic and often brutal policing of the march contributed to the very problem which the RUC was supposed to control. At the trial of those arrested on 5 October the police gave confused evidence about whether or not stones, as well as placards, had been thrown. No coherent explanation was given as to why demonstrators, running away from the confrontation at one end of Duke Street, were met by a line of police barring their way at the other. It also emerged that the police assumption that it was an offence to begin marching in the prohibited area was wrong. No law had been broken until the demonstrators disobeyed the order to disperse, following the meeting in Duke Street. This was a warning which, as Fergus Pyle reported, very few of them could have heard. The result of all this was that the Government's claims about the march and its defence of the actions of the police carried very little conviction outside the ranks of its own supporters. The events discredited the Government and fuelled the discontent that had created the civil rights movement in the first place.

Proof of republican involvement in NICRA prior to 5 October 1968 actually says very little about the civil rights *movement*. NICRA was a small, self-selected group of activists, not a movement. In theory, members of the executive committee were representatives of affiliated organisations and the committee was supposed to co-ordinate the efforts of the groups which supported it. In fact, the executive *was* the association. Executive members did all the organising work and very largely constituted the activists within NICRA. Members of the CSJ, the NILP, the CPNI, the Belfast Wolfe Tone Society, the Republican Clubs and private individuals worked together because they had developed a personal commitment to the association, and not because they were directed by any outside agency.

Before the events in Derry on 5 October, the civil rights movement did not exist; there was only a small, isolated group of activists. In the wake of 5 October, NICRA mushroomed into a movement with branches in most towns in Northern Ireland in which there was a significant Catholic population. Contacts were established with supporting organisations in the Irish Republic, Britain, North America, Australia, New Zealand and various countries in Europe. Two other important civil rights groups emerged – the DCAC and the PD. NICRA was the largest and most representative civil rights organisation but it was only one part of the civil rights *movement* and the original, pre-October NICRA was swamped by hundreds of new activists and thousands of supporters.

The emergence of this new movement transformed the political situation in Northern Ireland, producing sectarian tensions, instability, conflict and violence. But responsibility for this should not, retrospectively, be fixed on the small group which initiated these events. It is manifest that they were too weak and uninfluential to produce such a major upheaval by their own efforts. In fact it was the television and newspaper pictures of police batoning demonstrators which proved to be the catalyst in transforming the situation. The events in Derry crystallised the feelings of frustration and discontent among Catholics and the dissatisfaction with the lack of progress towards reform felt by a wide range of opposition groups. They also put Unionists on the defensive, prompting them to make accusations about a republican and Communist conspiracy which stoked fears among their own rank-and-file supporters. The civil rights marches created an opportunity for Ian Paisley to put himself at the head of plebeian Protestant resistance to the civil rights movement.

The use of the term 'civil rights' by NICRA inevitably invites comparisons with the Black civil rights movement in the United States. The adoption of street marches, sit-downs, passive resistance and songs like 'We shall not be moved' and 'We shall overcome' are evidence that the civil rights movement in Northern Ireland saw a close parallel between its activities and the struggle of Blacks in the Deep South. However, on closer examination the parallel proves illusory, as Frank Wright points out:

> Blacks were subject to far more drastic inequalities than were Catholics, therefore civil rights made far more difference to blacks than to Catholics. Integration – meaning equal access to public facilities, political participation and equal citizen rights – was a coherent objective for blacks because most of the denials of equality were sustained by segregation.

However, where blacks had no viable method of expressing nationalism when disillusion with the achievements of civil rights set in, Catholics could revert to a nationalism which already shaped much of their previous experience.[36]

Steve Bruce makes a similar point:

> American blacks were always assimilationists because they had nowhere else to go. There was never a time when any more than a handful of eccentrics advocated the establishment of a separate black nation-state. The issue in America was, and still is, the relationship between two populations *within* a nation-state. Concessions to blacks, while they did amount to debits from poor whites, were not major threats to the continued existence of the state . . .
>
> The Ulster situation has always been quite different. Perhaps some parts of the civil rights movement were genuinely, rather than tactically, assimilationist . . . However, the speed with which many of its leaders shifted to more traditional nationalist and republican positions suggests that a large part of the movement was always ultimately interested in dismantling Northern Ireland.[37]

These passages highlight some of the strategic and tactical problems involved in transferring the model of the Black movement in the United States to Northern Ireland. But their flaw – and this is particularly true of Bruce – is that they telescope the development of the Northern Ireland civil rights movement and retrospectively ascribe to it a coherence and a level of strategic thinking which it never had. After 5 October 1968 a poorly organised and deeply divided movement attempted to apply some of the methods used in the Deep South. But the situation had already run out of their – or anyone else's – control. By then the extent to which the Black movement was an appropriate model was irrelevant. Before 5 October 1968 the handful of NICRA activists had a very simple and extremely limited impression of what was happening across the Atlantic. Given the absence of any mass movement, the only activity which they could propose was street marches. This was risky and proved to be an extremely ill-advised tactic. But it was precisely the kind of initiative which could be expected from a small, isolated and frustrated group of political activists. It showed that they were ill-fitted to become the leaders of a mass movement, but no more than that. They were not in control of all the factors. They did not determine the actions of the

Ministry of Home Affairs nor of the RUC in Duke Street. Nor were they in control of the young hooligans of the Bogside or the Paisleyite counter-demonstrators. They were not, in other words, the leaders of a conspiracy to overthrow the Northern Ireland state.

5

DERRY AND ITS ACTION COMMITTEES

The gentle rainfall drifting down
Over Colmcille's town
Could not refresh, only distill,
In silent grief from hill to hill.

from 'Butcher's Dozen' by Thomas Kinsella

'An Old City Faces a New Sorrow'
headline over *Irish Times* report of events in Derry on 5 October 1968

Derry was the crucible of the civil rights movement. It was of enormous symbolic importance as the second city of Northern Ireland, as the site of the legendary siege of 1689 in which the Protestants resisted the forces of James II, and as the town in which a Nationalist majority was denied control of local government by a particularly flagrant gerrymander of the electoral boundaries. It was in Derry on 5 October 1968 that Northern Ireland crossed its Rubicon, and on the streets of the city in subsequent months Northern Ireland was, again and again, ratcheted nearer to crisis. The events of August 1969 in Derry brought Northern Ireland close to civil war and the killing of thirteen anti-internment demonstrators in the city on 30 January 1972 precipitated the imposition of direct rule and the end of the Stormont parliament.

The first gerrymander of the city occurred in 1896, with the Londonderry Improvement Bill; this created five electoral wards, one of which held the bulk of the city's Catholics, and enabled the Unionists to have a majority in the others. In 1922, following a brief period of Home Rule Party–Sinn Féin rule, the abolition of proportional representation in Northern Ireland in local government elections and a readjustment of the ward boundaries enabled the Unionists to regain control of the corporation. In 1929 the Northern Ireland parliamentary boundaries were drawn up so as to attach areas of the surrounding countryside to the city centre, creating the safe Unionist seat of City of Londonderry, while the mainly Catholic areas were put into the Nationalist seat of Foyle. In 1936 the city was divided into three local government electoral wards, two of which elected eight councillors whilst the third ward elected four. In the North and Waterside wards nearly eight thousand Unionist electors sent twelve representatives to the council, while the huge South ward returned eight Nationalist councillors on a poll of over ten thousand.

Unionist control of local government was resented because it represented minority control and the resentment was kept alive by accusations of discrimination in the allocation of council jobs and housing. But there was resentment also at the lack of industrial development in the city and its surrounding areas. A British visitor, Ian Nairn, described the state of the city in 1961:

> This is one of the most unexpected and paradoxical of our cities. It is one of the remotest places in the British Isles . . . For forty years it has been the victim of a real topographical tragedy . . . a manufac- turing town of 50,000 people where a rural centre of 20,000 would have been sufficient. Partition made comparatively little difference to its position as a market town for Donegal, but inevitably the industrial goods of Derry have to get to the mainland. And for this it is as remote as Inverness . . . So whenever a recession or squeeze begins, Derry is likely to feel it first. It is like being attached to the free end of a rope; a gentle pull at one end means a vicious kick at the other.[1]

In the postwar era, government stimulus to industrial devel- opment failed to rescue the city. Derry's first 'advance' factory was completed in 1951, but by that time sixty-seven new industries had been established in Northern Ireland. The fragility of much of the industry attracted to Derry by government aid was shown by the Birmingham Sound Reproducers factory which was opened in the summer of 1967, employing 1,800 of the abundant supply of cheap young labour; by January 1968 it had closed down. The more successful Du Pont synthetic rubber factory could never mop up the ever-growing pool of surplus labour.

Unemployment was a clear example of Derry's less-favoured status within Northern Ireland. As Alan Robinson points out:

> Before the . . . recession in March 1966, 5.9% of the insured population of Northern Ireland were registered as unemployed, but

in Derry no less than 10.1% were unemployed (23.3% males and 4.8% females). In February 1967, during the recession, unemployment in the province increased by 2.2% to 8.1% but in Derry unemployment increased by as much as 10% to reach 20.1% (23.3% males and 15.2% females). Thus in discouraging industrial development, Derry's marginal situation results not only in high levels of unemployment but is responsible for relatively high levels of increase in unemployment during periods of national recession.

Derry's inequitable share of misery was also reflected in housing. During the ten-year period from 1951 to 1961, 1,640 houses were built:

This number more than met the 1,119 houses that were needed in 1951 to eradicate undesirable overcrowding and subtenancy. But, in the same ten-year period, no less than 1,278 new families came into being in the city, with the result that the number of houses built fell short of the number required.[2]

This unequal share of wretchedness was itself unequally distributed within Derry. The percentage of persons living at densities of more than two per room in 1961 was 5.7 per cent in the North ward, 7.9 per cent in Waterside and 21.1 per cent in the mainly Catholic South ward. The contours of working-class Catholic life in Derry were marked out by unemployment, bad housing, emigration and close family and community life. Nell McCafferty, the Derry-born writer and civil rights activist, poignantly remembered family prayers from the 1950s: 'God send John a job; God send Jackie and Rosaleen a house; Holy Mother of God look down on Peggy in America and Leo in England; Jesus and His Blessed Mother protect Mary that's going out with a sailor.'[3] There was, of course, similar deprivation among Protestants in Derry but their numbers were fewer and a smaller proportion of the total Protestant population suffered such conditions.

Population remained static during the 1960s; the 1966 census showed a total of 55,681 living in the Londonderry County Borough. At 3.8 per cent of the total population of Northern Ireland, this was the same as the 1961 percentage; it compared with a modest increase of 0.86 per cent in the three counties east of the Bann (Antrim, Armagh and Down) and a small decline of 0.23 per cent west of the Bann (counties Derry, Tyrone and Fermanagh).

Belfast had declined by 2.3 per cent, but this is largely explained by government policies of funnelling population to other areas, policies which did not apply to Derry.

One reason for organising the 5 October 1968 march in Derry was that NICRA had always considered the city to be a natural focus for its attempts to raise the question of civil rights, but the demonstration was not the first attempt to organise around the issue in Derry. In April 1964 the working committee on civil rights, which had been established at QUB in March 1963, carried out a survey based on interviews with four hundred people; an earlier survey had been made in Newry. Among those involved were Bowes Egan and Eamonn McCann, later to become prominent civil rights activists. The exercise led to a bizarre episode in 1967, when the mayor of Londonderry, Councillor Albert Anderson, produced a letter which he claimed had come from the working committee. The text was reproduced in the local Unionist newspaper, the *Londonderry Sentinel*, on 22 February. It said that as a result of these investigations the committee was satisfied that there was no evidence of Londonderry Corporation being guilty of discrimination. Unfortunately for the mayor, the *Londonderry Sentinel* also reproduced the signature on the letter – 'Eamonn McCann, Secretary'. There was no resemblance between this and McCann's real signature. He commented:

> I have not at any time or in any capacity written to Cllr Anderson. The letter . . . is a forgery. Moreover I can reveal that the findings of the Committee were certainly not those indicated in this letter; we found that Derry Corporation had for many years been carrying out a policy of anti-Roman Catholic discrimination in employment and rigid segregation in housing.[4]

The local nationalist paper, the *Derry Journal*, gleefully published McCann's statement on 2 May, but there was no response from the mayor or the *Londonderry Sentinel*. Nor was there an explanation as to why the letter, which was dated 10 June 1965, had waited for over a year and a half before being revealed.

The first involvement with Derry by NICRA was a visit by its secretary, Derek Peters, in August 1967. He discussed prospects for activity in the city with Terence O'Brien, a Magee College lecturer who was a member of the executive committee of NICRA. In

September, O'Brien called a meeting in an attempt to establish a Derry branch of the association but it never got off the ground; indeed even at the height of the civil rights movement NICRA had branches in north and south County Derry but in the city itself the principal civil rights organisation was the DCAC, which although affiliated to NICRA, was completely autonomous. In 1967 no one in Derry showed much interest in the civil libertarian work of NICRA. The city was dominated by material problems like unemployment and housing, which although related to the issue of discrimination, were more obviously tackled by campaigns that focused on the issues themselves. In addition, Derry was a provincial town, distant from the corridors of power where lobbying could be carried out and it was not a natural locus for a pressure group like NICRA. Another factor, however, was related to the city itself; the entrenched and static nature of politics in the city did not encourage activities which assumed that there was at least a little capacity for the political system to respond to popular campaigning. Derry politics aroused nothing but distaste for working within the system among the few people who were interested in politics but who were not already involved in one of the two main parties.

The political leadership of the majority Catholic community was in the hands of the Nationalist Party and Derry's best-known Nationalist politician, Eddie McAteer, was party leader at Stormont from 1964 until the loss of his seat in 1969. He had represented the rural seat of Mid-Londonderry for eight years when, in 1953, he challenged the incumbent MP for Foyle for the nomination. The first Nationalist nominating convention resulted in a tied vote but McAteer won the second by a short lead. He went on to win the seat, despite the fact that the former MP, Paddy Maxwell, stood as an Independent.

Although the Nationalists were almost unchallenged in the Catholic community, by the early 1960s their position was more vulnerable than it appeared. For one thing they were a rural party in an urban environment. Since the 1950s and the failure of the APL to gain a foothold in Belfast, the Nationalist Party had been mainly a rural phenomenon. In Derry its elected representatives were, as in rural areas, mainly drawn from the ranks of small businessmen. In the countryside this was natural since this social grouping was the focus of local communication and leadership, but in Derry it meant that the Nationalist leadership was drawn too heavily from one social group. And since the party was principally an election machine, it did not offer channels for new young talent. Moreover, educated young Catholics were likely to be put off by the party's style of opposition, which could often appear even more obsessed with sectarian symbolism than the Unionists were. For example, in August 1962 Alderman James Hegarty objected to the corporation paying its contribution to the equivalent of the arts council because, at sponsored plays and concerts, nationalists 'were invariably insulted by the playing of a foreign [British] national anthem'. In September he announced that the Nationalist councillors would not be attending a Battle of Britain commemoration service in St Columb's Cathedral: 'We simply had no part in this,' he said. 'Our Government in Dublin declared its neutrality.' The following June, Eddie McAteer said that the Nationalists would not be attending a ceremony conferring the freedom of the city on The Honourable The Irish Society. They had accepted their invitations only in order to disrupt the proceedings, as they had done on a previous occasion in 1953. But due to the death of Pope John XXIII they had dropped their plans. In August they objected to a Battle of Britain parade, which they regarded as a recruiting drive for the 'occupying armed forces'. The following month they made a similar objection to the Royal Inniskilling Fusiliers beating the retreat in Shipquay Street. In May 1964, McAteer criticised his Nationalist colleague, Patrick Gormley MP, for saying that he had no qualms about rising for 'God Save the Queen', or the loyal toast.

Even assaults on the Unionists over alleged cases of discrimination could rebound. In January 1964, when Hegarty complained about imbalance in corporation employment, Alderman Gerald Glover, for the Unionists, was able to point out that according to the records, ninety-nine appointments out of one hundred were agreed by all members of the corporation. In July, when Nationalists protested at the failure of the corporation to appoint Nationalists to committee chairs, the mayor pointed out that fifteen or sixteen years ago the Nationalists had said that they would refuse to take such chairs and that they would only take part in corporation affairs in order to disrupt them.

In the early 1960s, however, changes within Northern Ireland were beginning to create a degree of common interest between

Unionists and Nationalists in Derry, and they were brought closer together in resistance to the industrial and commercial decline of the city. The priority for the O'Neill government was development in the area east of the Bann; the proposed new town of Craigavon underlined what was seen in Derry as neglect of the north-west. In quick succession the city was faced with plans to cut the last of its rail links to Belfast and the closure of the ferry services to Heysham and Glasgow. Then, in 1965, Derry was confronted with the Government's decision to accept the recommendation of the Lockwood Report and site the proposed second university for Northern Ireland in Coleraine – despite the fact that Derry already had a focus for third-level education in Magee College. This created an unprecedented degree of unity across the sectarian divide. The University for Derry Action Committee, formed under the chairmanship of John Hume, agitated for a reversal of the decision. At a mass rally in the Guildhall, where McAteer shared the platform with Major Gerald Glover of the Unionist Party, Hume roused the crowd with a speech which made no reference to partition or traditional nationalist grievances, but emphasised the common heritage and common interests of all the citizens of Derry.

There was no doubt about the anger felt in the city. Glover recalled in later years that 'ninety per cent of the population was bitterly disappointed, and this became a tremendous grievance shared by both Protestants and Roman Catholics'.[5] Hume organised a motorcade from Derry to Stormont in which both Unionist and Nationalist politicians took part. The annual meeting of the City of Londonderry and Foyle Unionist Party called on the Government to change its mind and site the new university in Derry. Seventeen Stormont MPs were taken on a tour of inspection by the University for Derry Action Committee and one of them, Dr Robert Nixon, the Stormont Unionist MP for North Down, declared that they had been misled by the Lockwood Report and that there was no shortage of suitable land or amenities in the city.

The unanimity did not last long; E. W. Jones QC, Stormont MP for City of Londonderry and Northern Ireland attorney general, came under fire for supporting the Government on the issue and Dr Nixon was rebuked by Terence O'Neill for alleging that 'nameless and faceless men' from the city had conspired against the siting of the university in Derry. Shortly afterwards Patrick Gormley MP announced the names of seven Derry Unionists whom, he alleged, had opposed the location of the university in the city. A petition calling for an inquiry into the allegations was signed by 15,118 people and a delegation headed by Raymond Wolseley of the Junior Chamber of Commerce went to Stormont to plead, vainly, for a change of policy.

The campaign petered out when it became obvious that the Government was not going to budge. But it had established three important points: first, that there was potential to cut across established Green–Orange divisions in pursuing the interests of Derry; second, that some educated young Catholics who were uninspired by the Nationalist Party would work enthusiastically on a campaign which challenged traditional sectarian prejudices; and third, many people came to believe that a section, at least, of Derry Unionists was prepared to sacrifice the interests of the city to those of its party. This reinforced distaste for party politics and the tendency to work along lines which challenged established political practices and institutions.

During the next three years, however, the initiative was seized by the radical left and not by moderate, cautious leaders in the John Hume mould. This was a surprising development; Derry had a relatively weak Labour movement and had too small a population to create a sizeable pool of individuals who were prepared to stand out against the political and social attitudes of the majority. In fact, the number of left-wing activists was never large but their impact was out of all proportion to their numbers because they found new methods of protest which caught the imagination of much larger numbers. They were able to be original in their methods precisely because the Labour movement was weak and did not trap them in the confines of established institutions and procedures. The state of Labour politics in Derry was described by a veteran, John Sharkey, writing to a friend in Dublin on 1 October 1962: 'Labour in Derry has become a dirty joke. It is an actual fact that eventually membership whittled down to about three or four.' He had worked in Belfast in the late 1940s, and compared the Labour scene in Derry unfavourably with that of the larger city: 'We may pride ourselves on being a city but politically we are still a small Ulster town.' There was no branch of the NILP in Derry, 'just a group that [Stephen] McGonagle mobilises at election time. There is no other forward movement, nor does there appear to be any prospect for the future.' The trade-union leaders and the 'occasional professional man' who would be the natural leaders elsewhere were too interested in being 'respectable'.[6]

The NILP branch in Derry had collapsed in 1949 under the twin blows of the party's electoral losses and its split over partition. In 1962 the only focus for the local Labour movement was the trades council. This was beginning to revive, with new affiliations like the Amalgamated Engineering Union and the Irish Transport and General Workers' Union (ITGWU). In December 1963 it discussed whether or not it should contest the next local government elections but no decision was taken. Almost certainly it felt that its position was still too weak. In January it decided not to revive the May Day parade in Derry; there was not enough interest and most of the trade-unionists who would be likely to take part would be attending the Belfast parade.

The dominant figure in local Labour politics was Stephen McGonagle.[7] He was district secretary of the ITGWU and had stood on the NILP ticket a number of times before the split of 1949, when he went over to the Irish Labour Party. He had been local organiser for the National Union of Tailors and Garment Workers but in 1952 he led a breakaway which two years later merged with the ITGWU. The Irish Labour Party in Derry quickly collapsed, leaving McGonagle at the head of his own small Independent Labour group, which was little more than a personal election machine. In the 1962 election he stood against McAteer, making it clear that he was just as committed a nationalist but criticising the MP for the narrowness of his appeal and calling on him to send his election literature to all voters, not just to Catholics. He was defeated by 8,720 votes to 5,476. At 38.5 per cent of the vote, this was a respectable result for a candidate who was only supported by a loose group of associates. In 1965 a permanent Independent Labour group was formed, which ran McGonagle's ITGWU colleague, Seamus Quinn, secretary of the trades council. The decision to contest the election was taken against McGonagle's advice, but the percentage result was almost a re-run of 1962, with 7,825 votes for McAteer and 4,371 for Quinn, a percentage of 35.8 for Independent Labour.

In the meantime the NILP had reappeared on the scene. At a

meeting in April 1965 a Londonderry branch of the NILP was formed. The meeting was addressed by Charles Gallagher, who was elected chairman of the branch, and by David Bleakley, Charles Brett and Vivian Simpson of the NILP administrative council. Gallagher spoke about local problems and Bleakley and Simpson produced standard NILP denunciations of 'Blue' and 'Green' Tories. Brett spoke out firmly on the question of discrimination in housing, electoral laws and public employment. This was not an opportunist concession to Derry's Catholic majority, since he also stressed that any weakening of the link with the United Kingdom was unacceptable to the NILP and that the constitutional issue should not become 'a party shuttlecock'. The secretary of the new NILP branch was Ivan Cooper, who had come to public attention the previous year when he resigned from the Bond's Glen and Claudy Young Unionist Association and had stood as an Independent candidate for the Londonderry Rural District Council. He had become dissatisfied with the council's record on housing and its bias in favour of the farmers who composed its membership. He polled 32 per cent of the total vote.

In March 1967 the NILP announced that it would contest all the council seats in the May elections. The party stood on a detailed manifesto which addressed local issues but stressed that the NILP had 'new ideas free from the old sectarian catch cries'. It linked this to the economic problems of the city, claiming that employment was affected by the 'sectarian image projected by the city fathers'. A number of demands which were to be raised by the civil rights movement were taken up by the manifesto. The NILP pledged an extension of the city boundary and the extension of the local government franchise to all citizens over the age of twenty-one, the abolition of the company vote, the realignment of electoral boundaries and the allocation of houses 'solely on the basis of need'. These objectives were wrapped up in a programme that included pledges on road safety, home helps for the elderly, bus shelters, a more comprehensive library system and the encouragement of tourism. Many of them were possible only if the NILP got control of Stormont and were propaganda points in its ideological war against the doctrines of Orange and Green.

In the Catholic South ward the NILP polled 34.5 per cent, a similar proportion to that of McGonagle and Quinn in Foyle and an indication that the existing political mould was not going to be broken easily. In the Protestant North and Waterside wards it won 30 per cent and 27.5 per cent respectively. Here the Unionists were challenged for the first time in many years but the NILP shared the anti-Unionist vote with Independents, who polled 4.5 per cent in North and 2 per cent in Waterside. There was, therefore, a vote of about one-third of the Derry electorate which was being deployed against the established parties.

In the three years between its foundation in 1965 and the summer of 1968 the Londonderry branch of the NILP underwent a significant swing to the left. Of the officers and committee elected in May 1965 only two names remained after the annual general meeting of 1968. A majority of those elected in 1968 were later active in the civil rights movement and a number were involved in the DHAC at the time of their election. Tensions between right and left flared up in a dispute over the May 1968 by-election in the City of Londonderry constituency, and this helps to illuminate some of the characteristics of the Derry Labour left. In the 1965 Stormont general election Claude Wilton of the Ulster Liberal Party had polled 47 per cent, and some members of the NILP thought that he should be given a clear run in the 1968 by-election, in the hope of defeating the Unionist candidate. He was a Protestant lawyer who had enormous prestige among Derry Catholics for his work in combating injustices against them in the courts. The Liberals, in fact, had a much more substantial record of fighting sectarianism and discrimination in Derry than the NILP had. However, the NILP candidate, Janet Willcock, supported by the younger members of the party, insisted on standing. She was at this time secretary of the Londonderry branch of the NILP. A former schoolteacher and the wife of a Magee College lecturer, she was of pronounced left-wing sympathies and in later years she became Bernadette Devlin's secretary in London. She rejected all ideas of agreements with other parties and pledged Labour to fight Orange and Green until Derry was 'rid of Toryism once and for all. Anti-Unionism is not enough. We reject the idea that it doesn't matter which anti-Unionist force opposes the Tory candidate.'[8] Her programme included electoral reform, housing allocation according to need and based on a points system, the extension of the Race Relations Act to Northern Ireland, and the provision of employment through state investment. Apart from the final point, these were no different from the policies being advocated by the Liberals. The result was 9,122 for the Unionist candidate and 3,944 for the NILP. Willcock had polled 30 per cent of the vote, 17 per cent short of Claude Wilton's result in 1965.

Writing about the episode later, Eamonn McCann, one of the leaders of the Derry Labour left, saw the result as a 'glaring indictment of the continuing failure of the Northern Ireland Labour Party to make any impact on the electorate'. He did not see the failure as a consequence of the refusal to unite all opponents of Unionism, but of the NILP's willingness to compromise in order to achieve such unity:

> Labour needs a clear idea of its own *raison d'être*. It must reject an analysis of Northern politics which consists of a simple division of people into Unionists and anti-Unionists. Such an analysis, beloved of silly clerics like Albert McElroy, is an acceptance of sectarianism, and as such, can never lead to its defeat.[9]

Too many NILP members, he asserted, were 'unable to distinguish between the social force represented by Labour and that represented by Liberalism'. He also insisted that 'every compromise with the existing system leaves us less capable of changing that system'. McCann was advancing a traditional Marxist view which insisted on the importance of economic and social class divisions as the basis of politics: but his analysis ignored the extent to which, in the intimate context of Derry politics, such divisions were blurred by local and personal factors. He also ignored the extent to which the concrete policies of Derry Labour, as distinct from its rhetoric, were the common currency of all opponents of the Unionist Party, including the Nationalists, for whom he had boundless contempt.

McCann had returned to Derry in February 1968 after some years' absence. He had studied psychology at QUB from 1961 and made a reputation there as a debater, winning the Orator of the Year award in 1963. He was expelled from QUB after a conviction which resulted from a too-well-celebrated student society dinner. He moved to London where he worked as a gardener with the Greater London Council and became editor of the *Irish Militant*. This fringe left-wing newspaper was produced by the Irish Workers' Group, a Trotskyist *groupuscule* which had a scattering of supporters in Ireland but was strongest among Irish exiles in London. McCann happened to be at home in Derry on a visit when he was invited to take part in a DHAC demonstration. He stayed on, joined the NILP and became one of the leaders of the DHAC. A highly talented writer and a compelling public speaker, he quickly became the best-known left-wing agitator in Derry.

The pioneers of left-wing protest in Derry, however, were the republicans, who also experienced an influx of young radicals during the 1960s, following the turn to left-wing political agitation by the new leadership of the movement. Republicanism in Derry was weak – one activist has estimated that the total number of republicans of all shades of opinion in the city in 1968 was less than one hundred.[10] This was to the advantage of the young radicals; like the leftists in the NILP, they were not hampered by tradition and did not have to placate their seniors before or after embracing heresy.

The link with the Labour left was useful to both sides. Especially after McCann's return to Derry, the NILP contained a number of talented writers and speakers. The republicans, for their part, provided muscle, discipline and willingness to undertake risky tasks – it was the republicans who smuggled placards and banners out of the Bogside and across Craigavon Bridge to the Waterside, under the eyes of the RUC, on 5 October 1968. The division of work between themselves and the Labour left put the latter into the public eye as spokespeople, and the republican contribution to developments has tended to be downplayed in consequence. Without the republicans the Labour left would have remained abstract propagandists; without the Labour left, the republicans would have been less able to communicate to people in Derry and beyond. It was a close partnership, made all the closer by the small numbers involved and the intimacy of Derry.

The Derry republicans had organised a Release the Prisoners Committee in 1962, but they then retired into obscurity until 1966, when six members were arrested for taking part in an illegal Easter Rising commemoration. One of those charged was George Finbar O'Doherty, who was alleged to have given a command in Irish to the colour party. Finbar O'Doherty was to appear in the pages of the *Derry Journal* numerous times over the next few years, under a variety of names, including George Doherty, George O'Doherty,

George F. O'Doherty, Finbar Doherty, Finbar O'Doherty and Fionnbarra Ó Dochartaigh. Eamonn McCann described him as a 'passionate Republican, much given to violent rhetoric'.[11] Other prominent left-wing republican activists were Eamonn Melaugh and John White. All were later to be intensely involved in the civil rights movement.

In October 1966 the Derry Young Republican Association held an open-air meeting to protest at the eviction of a family from a house in Creggan. It denounced the corporation's housing record and claimed that 'Rachmanism [is] rife in Derry'. The Nationalist councillors, it declared, would be better taking up such issues than 'attending functions behind closed doors at which toasts to the Queen are drunk'. During the same month the Young Republicans barricaded themselves into a house in Harvey Street to resist the eviction of a family that had been on the housing list for eighteen years. They left when they were assured that no eviction would take place until alternative accommodation had been found for the family. In December they picketed the Guildhall and the local Unionist Party headquarters, and called on the unemployed to become more militant. In July 1967 they were, once again, barricaded into a house in Harvey Street, this time to resist the eviction of a widow and her two teenage children. The family was all that the Young Republicans could have wished for: the mother threw crockery at police and bailiffs and the son offered physical resistance when police broke through the barricades. The eviction was successful but the family was quickly offered accommodation in Creggan. It was this episode which occasioned Derek Peters's visit to Derry in August 1967 on behalf of NICRA.

In August the Young Republicans set up a front organisation, the People's Action League, which planned to campaign on the issue of high-rise flats, and picketed the Guildhall, calling for an extension of the city boundary and, on another occasion, at the siting of a new Michelin factory at Ballymena in County Antrim instead of Derry. But the league made little impact and there was more success with the Derry Unemployed Action Committee (DUAC) which involved NILP leftists as well as republicans. It was set up by about thirty young unemployed men in January 1965. The DUAC quickly achieved considerable publicity when four of its members disrupted a corporation meeting. The mayor was in the process of proposing a motion of sympathy with Lady Churchill, following the death of Sir Winston, when James Gallagher of Creggan Heights rose in the public gallery to read a short statement on behalf of the DUAC calling on the councillors to sink their political differences and to unite in efforts to press the Government to establish new industries in Derry. Further interruptions came from Eamonn Melaugh and Robert Campbell, but they desisted when the mayor offered to receive a deputation following the close of business.

In February 1965 the DUAC picketed a dinner in the Guildhall which was being addressed by Minister of Commerce Brian Faulkner. At this dinner Faulkner claimed that only one in ten of Derry's unemployed had any previous industrial experience; the DUAC carried out a survey at the Bishop Street Labour Exchange which, they claimed, showed that 50 per cent of those interviewed did have such experience. In May the DUAC called for a special 'industries for Derry' drive, with an office in the city as its focal point. It wrote to a number of firms pointing out Derry's potential for industrial development. In October it demanded to know what had happened to the seventy-acre industrial site and the industrial training centre promised by Faulkner and Minister of Development William Craig, and in February 1966 the DUAC lobbied the House of Commons at Westminster, led by Finbar O'Doherty, who was at this time its London representative.[12]

The DUAC disappeared from view shortly after this, although it was revived in November 1968 in the wake of the 5 October demonstration. It should be noted that while the style, rhetoric and actions of the DUAC were militant, its demands were not. It called for greater and more concentrated effort along lines which the Government already accepted as the basis for solving the problem of unemployment. It demanded development, investment, planning and greater government intervention, not an assault on the capitalist system. It appealed for sympathy with the unemployed in a way which did not challenge the consensus about the problem. It was characteristic of the radical agitational movements in Derry to echo ideas which were already widely accepted, but to put them forward in a more aggressive, combative and militant style.

The next action committee to be formed was the DHAC. It was the most important of these groupings as it was directly responsible for bringing NICRA to Derry for the 5 October 1968 march and thus was the catalyst which turned the civil rights movement into a mass campaign. It developed the direct-action methods of earlier campaigns into new and more dramatic forms and it took up an issue which was the central and most widely felt grievance of Derry Catholics – housing. In Derry housing was a scarce resource; the city's house-building record was dismal, even compared with other Northern Ireland towns. Between 1946 and 1967 Coleraine had built 109 new houses per 1,000 of population, Newry 144, Portadown 109, Larne 140 and Limavady 137; Derry's figure was 70.[13]

Needless to say, the issue was the subject of regular battles across the floor of the Guildhall and in the Stormont House of Commons. In February 1962, Eddie McAteer asked Minister of Health and Local Government W. J. Morgan for the numbers of houses which the corporation and the NIHT expected to finish in Derry that year. When told that the total would be about 170, he asked if this was not 'pitifully inadequate as compared with an annual enrolment of housing applicants of 400-odd, not to mention a backlog of 2,000'.[14] The minister had, in fact, outlined a programme of some 1,828 new houses, including corporation, NIHT and private developments, but 1,300 of these were to replace houses which were to be demolished in redevelopment, so that the plans did not envisage wiping out the existing demand for houses. Even these plans were subject to delay; in November 1962, at a special corporation meeting, Alderman James Hegarty moved a vote of censure over delays which meant that 300 out of 500 houses planned in the autumn of 1960 had been delayed. The 144 which were in progress included 18 high-rented flats at Deanfield and a redevelopment scheme of 50 houses. The Unionists accepted that this was unsatisfactory and after the deletion of the reference to Deanfield, Hegarty's motion was passed unanimously. Hegarty also attacked the NIHT for the letting policy on its Belmont estate where, of 185 families, 48 were from outside the Derry area, 25 were policemen and 71 had made applications after 1 January 1959: 'That makes 144 families who should never have been considered for housing at all,' he said.[15]

In January 1964, Councillor Patrick Friel (father of playwright Brian Friel), addressing a Nationalist protest meeting, said that 212 houses announced by the corporation included luxury flats and other specialist accommodation, leaving only 22 of these houses for occupation by ordinary applicants. The corporation had agreed to let houses to ten families from the local Springtown Camp; this left twelve houses. In January there had been twenty-six fresh applications; the marriage rate in Derry was 420 per year and there were at least one thousand applicants on the waiting list. He did not explain how this latter figure squared with McAteer's figure of two thousand; Nationalists and Unionists often threw figures at each other in this way but it was not always clear exactly what they meant. In May 1964, Councillor T. J. McCabe compared Derry's housing record unfavourably with that of Lisburn in County Antrim which had built 1,556 corporation and NIHT houses since World War II. On a comparison of populations there should have been 4,500 houses built in Derry but only 3,000 had, in fact, been built. Alderman Glover said that the corporation's record would have been better had they not handed over some of their schemes ready-made to the NIHT. Alderman Hegarty claimed that of 250 houses in the Belmont estate, only 17 had been let to Catholics. He quoted the case of a man who, he claimed, had sold a house in Omagh, County Tyrone, for £3,000 in order to move into a house in Belmont. There were corporation employees whose first child was born in Belmont while other people were living in 'dog boxes'. The argument usually switched in this way from overall comparisons to individual cases, which was one reason why the dispute was so difficult to resolve.

However, in December 1967 a review of housing in Derry showed that a total of 4,420 'units of accommodation' had been provided – 2,170 by the corporation, 1,745 by the NIHT, and 505 by private enterprise. During 1967, 258 families had been provided with subsidised dwellings, 43 by the corporation and 215 by the NIHT; this included 169 families rehoused from condemned properties, so that only 89 of these households represented an overall addition to the housing stock. In the year ending May 1967 only seven corporation houses had actually been completed. The last monthly housing report to be issued before the abolition of the corporation in November 1968 showed that only four corporation houses had been built.

In September 1968 the executive sanitary officer in his annual report for 1967 said that over one thousand houses were occupied by more than one family and in several cases seven or eight families occupied what was originally a single dwelling. Rented accommodation other than corporation or NIHT houses was rapidly diminishing, since it was uneconomic for landlords to maintain rent-controlled housing. Virtually all empty dwellings were now sold with vacant possession, at extremely high prices. Many larger houses were being split up into 'so-called flats', and he called for protection for such families. There were cases of families being made to leave by conditions being rendered difficult for them after they had made complaints to the corporation housing department. Councillors received many heart-rending pleas from families who were being forced into emigration as the only alternative to their miserable and expensive accommodation; complaints about rat infestation were not infrequent.

The argument over housing in Derry soon came to be focused on an important issue of corporation policy – the question of extending the city boundary so as to include more land for housing and industrial development. In November 1963, Councillor T. J. McCabe challenged the Unionists on the issue. Between 1951 and 1961, he said, population had increased by 10,000, but 6,500 had left the city because they were unable to find accommodation. In 1962 the increase in population had been 1,172 but in the same year only nineteen new houses had been built; land had to be found for new housing. In September 1964 a special meeting of the corporation finance committee, which included all councillors, adopted an amended motion which gave the boundary extension sub-committee the power to include in its remit the progressive expansion of Derry, so as to maintain its position as the second city in Northern Ireland. By the end of 1965 there was an accumulation of evidence supporting a boundary extension. The city accountant had compared Derry's acreage, which had not changed for a century, with other Northern Ireland towns. Derry had an average population density of twenty-five per acre, compared with towns that had extended their boundaries which had average densities of twelve per acre or less. Reports from the city's sanitary officer, director of education, and city surveyor also supported an extension. Nevertheless, the Unionist majority on the council voted not to submit these reports to the Ministry of Development, Londonderry County Council, or Londonderry Rural District Council, whose co-operation would be needed to extend the boundary. In May 1967 the mayor ridiculed a Nationalist proposal to submit a draft memorial to the Ministry of Development asking for an extension. He proposed instead that

> we should build more intensively in some areas and build higher in many cases . . . We could only acquire areas outside our own boundary with the consent of the two other local authorities. We would need their agreement to build houses outside the city boundary and you know that this is part of what the Steering Committee will propose . . . I therefore think that [the] motion is out of place at this time and that it is proposed for a certain purpose.[16]

The most acute of Derry's housing problems was the Springtown Camp. This former United States military base had been occupied by homeless families when the American forces left at the end of World War II. The corporation had assumed responsibility for the site in 1945 and had purchased the land in 1957, although technically it was in the rural district area. When the corporation took control, all the families living there had moved in from the city area. In 1964, when the problem again came under scrutiny, there was a total of ninety-two families living in the camp but some of these had moved in subsequently from the rural area. The corporation and the rural district council were in dispute about who should rehouse them. The rural district council relied on the assumption of responsibility by the corporation in 1945, while the corporation denied responsibility for the former rural district families and claimed that the 1956 Housing Act had made the rural district council responsible for all the families in the camp.

Conditions in the camp were deplorable; the temporary buildings had deteriorated considerably and the site had few amenities. In addition to the squalor, residents suffered from prejudice when they had to give a Springtown address. Early in 1964 the Springtown Residents' Association staged a protest march to the Guildhall, which was reported in the *Derry Journal* of 31 January under the headline 'Derry's Little Rock Calls for Fair Play'. During a corporation debate the Nationalists pressed the Unionists to give greater priority to rehousing Springtown residents and to increase the total number of houses available for let. They were told that consideration would be given to allocating houses which became vacant to Springtown residents and that discussions had taken place with the rural district council and the NIHT about allocations of houses by them. In June the Springtown residents launched a petition calling for the families living there to be rehoused before the winter and for the camp to be closed. Later that month it was presented at Stormont with 21,428 signatures. The mayor and the chairman of the rural district council met the Minister of Health and Local Government on the issue, and Eddie McAteer also raised with the minister the additional problem of thirty-one subtenants, mostly the sons and daughters of Springtown residents, who had not been mentioned in the statement issued following his meeting with the two local authority leaders.

In July 1964 the corporation, the NIHT and the rural district council came to an agreement to share responsibility for housing Springtown families over a period of time, but this did not end the problem. Two weeks later Springtown residents staged a demonstration in the public gallery of the Guildhall, a tactic which was becoming a regular resort of protest groups. A delegation of the residents complained that they were not getting the priority in rehousing which had been promised them and demanded to know whether or not they would be moved before the winter. The mayor told them that he could not add to what had been said in the statement about the agreement between the three housing authorities. The corporation meeting proceeded with Nationalist protests and barracking and interjections from the protesters, until the mayor ordered the gallery to be cleared. Thereafter controversy over the issue subsided until June 1967, when eviction proceedings were taken against eleven families who had refused accommodation offered to them by the rural district council because it was at some distance from the city. In the end the matter was resolved amicably and Springtown was cleared of residents and demolished. It had, however, served to draw attention to the acute housing problem in Derry and like the HCL in Dungannon, it gave an example of effective protest and direct action.

A different form of direct action was taken by the Derry Housing Association, set up in October 1965. The association was chaired by John Hume and drew on the self-help traditions of the credit unions. It was inspired and created by Father Anthony Mulvey; he had been influenced by Father Eamonn Casey, later to become

Bishop of Galway, who had experience of setting up a housing association for Irish people in London. The association provided flats for young couples who after two years were given a return of half the rent they had paid to be used as a deposit on the purchase of a house. In the first year one hundred families were housed through the scheme. Another project resulted in the erection of twenty-seven houses on the Buncrana Road, in the South ward. But the association was frustrated in its attempts to build larger schemes in the Waterside and in the North ward on the site of the old Birmingham Sound Reproducers factory. The corporation cited planning and zoning regulations for refusing these applications but it was generally assumed that the real reason was that the new houses would have been built in Unionist-controlled wards but would have been inhabited by Catholics.

Underpinning all of these disputes was a suspicion, amounting to a certainty in the minds of most Catholics, that the Unionists were unwilling to provide substantial new housing and to extend the city boundary because that would upset the existing political balance. Because of overcrowding in the South ward, any major new development would have to take place in the other two wards. This in turn would mean shifting Catholics into these wards. A boundary extension would require new electoral boundaries and these could not easily be adjusted so as to retain Unionist minority control. In addition, better housing conditions, more industrial development, and the fillip for the city that would result from siting the new university there would reduce the flow of Catholics from Derry. By the mid-1960s opponents of the Unionists were firmly convinced that the party, both in the Guildhall and in Stormont, made a simple equation that what was good for Derry was bad for the Unionists and vice versa.

The bitterness created by these disputes and the importance of housing as an issue not only in Derry but in the United Kingdom as a whole in this period helps to explain the choice of this issue as a focus for agitation by the radical leftists of the DHAC. The general bitterness also helps to explain why the DHAC was tolerated within the Catholic community. The intensely provincial, Catholic and Nationalist environment within which the DHAC operated was not conducive to its kind of class-based, quasi-Marxist political rhetoric which would, ten years earlier, probably have unleashed a backlash that it would have found difficult to survive; even the mild leftism of Stephen McGonagle had in the past made him an object of suspicion among Derry Catholics. The DHAC did, in fact, provoke a backlash but it was by no means as intense as the persecution which many earlier Irish leftists had to suffer. By the mid-1960s the influence of Irish McCarthyism was beginning to wane and there was a generally more tolerant atmosphere, which even Derry shared. But what was probably more significant was the fact that the target of the DHAC, the Unionist administration at the Guildhall, was so widely execrated and the fact that the ammunition it fired had already been prepared by more traditional anti-Unionists.

The DHAC originated in the abortive attempt to set up a branch of NICRA in Derry. One of those who had attended the initial meeting in September 1967, an independent radical Matt O'Leary, had been dissatisfied with the aims of NICRA. He wanted a campaign of direct action and mass protest, not an organisation which would take up individual cases of discrimination. He organised a meeting of some of the more militant people who had attended the NICRA meeting and about two months later the DHAC was launched. It attracted some of the activists of the DUAC and leftists from both the NILP and the republican movement. O'Leary was elected chairman and he immediately drew criticism on the committee. During a DHAC demonstration in the Guildhall, Alderman Hegarty of the Nationalist Party called out to the demonstrators: 'It is just unfortunate that you have come under the influence of card-bearing members of the Communist committee.' In July 1968, O'Leary resigned from the chair because, he said, he had 'become the target of agents of the establishment and their many Judases'. In November he called a press conference to deny that he was a member of the CPNI. He was a Marxist and might be called a 'Christian Communist', but he could not answer the question 'was he a communist?' directly, he could only state his beliefs.[17]

The first DHAC demonstration took place when its members turned up, uninvited, to the March 1968 meeting of the council. Despite the efforts of the mayor to stop him, one of its number read out a statement:

[The DHAC] regarded the Corporation as representing primarily the interests of property owners and business speculators and not the interests of the working class of Derry. They demanded that the Corporation immediately extend the city boundary and embark on a crash housing programme. They demanded the immediate appointment of a rent assessment officer and a halt to all rent increases. Tenants . . . were no longer prepared to accept the appalling housing conditions and would take whatever action was necessary . . . 'Finally we believe that the only long-term solution to the social cancers which beset Derry lies in the establishment of workers' power and public ownership of all land, banks and industries. The formation of this committee marks the beginning of a mass movement away from the false political leaders and against the exploiting capitalist class who have in their wake a trail of human misery, degradation and decay.'[18]

During the reading of the statement the Unionists withdrew; the Nationalists stayed but Alderman Hegarty made his accusation about Communists. Eventually the police were called and the protesters left quietly. The language of their statement was more extreme and militant than that of earlier protest groups but the concrete demands were already the common currency of anti-Unionists in the city and, as such, were neither new nor especially radical. An indication of the tension between these moderate demands and the DHAC's extreme rhetoric was the fact that almost immediately after this first demonstration there was a split. Nine of the seventeen original members resigned, claiming that the DHAC was being used to further the aims of a 'political group'. They set up a new organisation called the Sub-Tenants' Committee, which would campaign 'not on political but on humanitarian grounds'. However, it quickly disappeared from sight and was never an effective rival to the DHAC.

In May the DHAC was back at the Guildhall, where Matt O'Leary told the corporation that its members 'filled him with nauseation'. Members of the DHAC showed their distaste for the Nationalists when Councillor James Doherty and some Nationalist supporters in the gallery created a disturbance. The DHAC withdrew from the chamber and said that it 'did not wish to become involved in another pseudo-sectarian Puck Fair'. The DHAC's policy was to 'go through all the existing channels before taking extreme action'.[19] It had made its final appeal to the corporation and the response had been unsatisfactory.

Its next action was much more original. One DHAC member had discovered John Wilson, his wife and two children living in a small caravan in the Brandywell. Although one of the children suffered from tuberculosis, the corporation housing department had told them that they were unlikely to be housed. According to Eamonn McCann:

> Mr Wilson's case was tailor-made. On 22 June, a Saturday, about ten of us manhandled the Wilsons' caravan on to the Lecky Road, the main artery through the Bogside, and parked it broadside in the middle of the road, stopping all the traffic. We distributed leaflets in the surrounding streets explaining that we intended to keep the caravan there for twenty-four hours as a protest against the Wilsons' living conditions and calling for support. We then phoned the police, the mayor and the newspapers, inviting each to come and see.[20]

The mayor did not respond, but the police did, although they took no action and the caravan stayed put for twenty-four hours. The DHAC announced that the exercise would be repeated the following weekend; although the police warned that they would have to intervene this time, the demonstration went ahead and was extended to forty-eight hours. It was decided to block the city centre the next weekend, but during the week the Wilsons were given a house and eleven DHAC members and supporters were summonsed.

Among those brought to trial were Finbar O'Doherty, Eamonn McCann, Matt O'Leary, Eamonn Melaugh, Jerry Mallett and Janet Willcock. All the defendants were bound over for two years on a personal bail of £350 and some were also fined. After the hearing Willcock issued a statement saying that the action had been symbolic: 'They could not move the hovels in which hundreds of decent men and women were forced to live in deprivation and degradation, or they would.'[21] She forecast that if nothing were done, violence would erupt. That was why they had taken non-violent direct action. The members of the DHAC were delighted with the outcome:

> It had very publicly been made clear that outrageous tactics worked, that blocking roads worked better than MPs' intervention . . . The court proceedings provided us with a platform; fines and suspended

sentences conferred on us an aura of minor martyrdom . . . We really began to believe that we had the Nationalist Party on the run.[22]

The next demonstration was on 3 July 1968 at the opening of a new carriageway of the Craigavon Bridge. No sooner had the mayor cut the tape than five DHAC members ran to the centre of the road and sat down, holding up placards. Finbar O'Doherty, John Lafferty, John Anthony Doherty, Neil O'Donnell, Roderick Carlin and John McGettigan were charged in connection with the event. O'Doherty, who had not taken part in the obstruction, was fined £5 for allegedly leading the singing of 'We shall overcome' (a charge he denied), and the others were bound over for two years on £50 personal bail. Two Young Republicans, Carlin and O'Donnell, refused to enter bail and were sent to Belfast's Crumlin Road jail for one month, receiving a hero's welcome on their return.

In July, DHAC members accompanied three women and their seven children to the corporation housing manager's office to protest at the allocation of a house to a former Belfast prison officer. The women complained that the officer could only have been on the housing list for a few weeks, while they had waited for periods of between eighteen months and four years. In August the DHAC announced a public meeting at the Diamond with a list of invited speakers which included the Catholic Bishop of Derry, the mayor, three Nationalist councillors, a curate from St Eugene's Catholic Cathedral, the city's medical officer of health and John Hume. As they had expected, none of the invited speakers turned up, but Eamonn Melaugh, who did speak, forecast violence if houses were not built. The following week the DHAC picketed the house of a landlord who, they alleged, charged exorbitant rents and refused to supply rent books.

At the August meeting John White said that the DHAC intended to organise tenants' associations. During that summer, tenants' associations which had been formed in Rossville Flats, Meenan Park, Shantallow, Rossville Street, Lecky Road and Foyle Hill set up a central council to co-ordinate their activities. However, there is no evidence of any link with the DHAC. Among the issues which they pursued were proposed NIHT rent increases, resettlement grants, poor soundproofing and finishing in their accommodation and the refusal of the NIHT to provide a communal television aerial for Rossville Flats which would enable the tenants to receive Radio Telefís Éireann (the Irish television network). The methods adopted by these tenants' associations were those of lobbying and persuasion and the issues they took up were specific grievances affecting their own members, not the problem of housing as it related to the political system in Northern Ireland. The DHAC was concerned with homelessness and the poor quality of housing as part of an assault on the capitalist system. It also contrasted with the tenants' associations in that it was not directly representative of those whose cause it espoused. It was a loose group of freewheeling radicals who had chosen a particularly acute social problem as a vehicle for broader political aims.

By the summer of 1968 the DHAC had achieved, according to its lights, considerable success in attracting publicity and in embarrassing the political establishment in Derry. But there was a problem about what to do next. It would be difficult to keep up the momentum of its campaign and in addition it had created tensions within the two organisations from which most of its members came, the NILP and the republican movement. It was under pressure, therefore, to find new issues and new methods of campaigning. According to McCann:

> By this time our conscious, if unspoken, strategy was to provoke the police into over-reaction and thus spark off a mass reaction against the authorities. We assumed that we would be in control of the reaction, that we were strong enough to channel it. The one certain way to ensure a head-on clash . . . was to organise a non-Unionist march through the city centre.[23]

The summer of 1968 saw the centenary of the birth of James Connolly, the man who epitomised both socialism and republicanism in Ireland. McCann suggests that the idea of having a march through the city centre to commemorate him was inspired by this desire to provoke the authorities; but given the importance of the centenary, it is likely that some kind of parade would have been organised in any case. McCann throws doubt on his own assertion when he reveals that the Connolly commemoration committee, which had been initiated by the DHAC radicals, was thrown into a 'welter of recrimination' when the planned march was abandoned.

He suggests that this was because of a dispute over the carrying of the Irish tricolour; the NILP would not march with it and the republicans would not march without it. He does not mention the fact that the police banned the parade from the city centre, thus testing to destruction the resolve of the radicals to confront them. Janet Willcock accused the RUC of 'trying to make a sectarian event out of an occasion which was intended to symbolise the non-sectarian nature of the ideals of Connolly'.[24] And it was this concern to avoid any sectarian connotations which seems to have been uppermost in the minds of the organisers. When the police tried to get them to accept a re-route through an entirely Catholic area, they abandoned the march altogether and confined the event to a rally which was held in the open air in a car park in Foyle Street.

This rally was addressed by Gerry Fitt, Betty Sinclair, Roddy Connolly, Sean Nolan of the Irish Workers' Party (the name of the Communist Party in the south), and three of the Young Turks from the Derry Labour and republican left. Janet Willcock called for the unity of all radical opinion in Derry; Eamonn McCann said that Terence O'Neill could not be distinguished from Lord Brooke-borough and that reference to liberal unionism was double talk. The recently formed Council of Labour should summon a rank-and-file conference of all the radical political movements in Ireland and call on them to discuss the creation of an all-Ireland socialist party. In Derry they should take their politics out on to the streets and he urged an extension of direct action. Finbar O'Doherty presided and denounced the RUC ban on the original route: 'On future occasions the question of a police ban at the dictates of their Orange masters would be a matter for meeting in a different manner.'[25]

Despite the débâcle over the march, the rally had been a success and the DHAC returned to the Guildhall in late August for its largest and most successful demonstration so far, in the council chamber. The *Derry Journal* of 30 August reported that shortly before the beginning of the corporation's monthly meeting, 'the Guildhall foyer was crowded with men, women and children waiting to voice their protest'. The NILP was represented by a strong contingent which carried the party banner and for the first time Ivan Cooper took a prominent part in the proceedings. When the mayor ordered the lobbyists standing round the side of the chamber to move into the public gallery, Cooper protested that they had every right to be there: 'They are not peasants to be roped in.' Eamonn Melaugh told the mayor that he would have to take the consequences of any violence caused in trying to clear the chamber. In the event the crowd left quietly when the police arrived.

An impromptu meeting was held in the foyer, which began with the crowd singing 'We shall not be moved'. Finbar O'Doherty was cheered loudly when he mounted the stairway to address the crowd. He called for working-class unity across the sectarian divide and accused both Unionist and Nationalist members of the council of not representing the interests of the working class. Ivan Cooper called on the people of Derry to fight for their rights, 'as the Blacks in America were fighting'. Councillors were jeered and heckled as they emerged and the mayor was given the Nazi salute as he drove off. While the meeting in the foyer was going on, the corporation gave a clear indication that it felt under pressure. It adopted a motion from Councillor Doherty of the Nationalist Party, instructing the city architect to publish target dates for the completion of seven housing schemes and for all possible steps to be taken to press on with other housing projects. However, a Nationalist motion calling for the setting up of a small committee to be responsible for housing allocations was rejected. This would have abolished the system under which such allocations were the individual prerogative of the mayor. Eamonn McCann later scorned this proposal as evidence of 'political nappy-rash', since such a committee would have a built-in Unionist majority. The Nationalists, he said, had no idea of how to rectify Derry's social ills and alternated between 'semi-hysterical outbursts of militancy [and] silly moderate suggestions . . . building and burning bridges simultaneously'. The party's problem was that it was a Catholic organisation and could not see the class basis of the problems. It could, therefore, only operate as a 'movement of middle-class protest'.[26]

However, McCann's assumption that because the DHAC espoused a theory of fundamental class antagonisms, this was accepted by all who applauded their actions, was not borne out by events. The DHAC had proved that new and imaginative methods of protest could make an impact on the Unionist administration at the Guildhall, but for most opponents of the Unionist Party in Derry this was a reason for achieving a greater degree of anti-Unionist unity in order to press home their advantage, not to become equally hostile to the Nationalist Party. This was shown by the first major DHAC protest following the 5 October 1968 demonstration, when the committee supported an NILP delegation to the council on the housing issue. There was uproar when the council refused to hear the delegation and the meeting was adjourned, the Unionists withdrawing but the Nationalists remaining in their seats. Eamonn Melaugh went over to the mayor's chair and sat down. He shouted to the protesters: 'I ask you citizens of Derry, do you approve of a crash programme of 2,000 houses?' There were cries of 'yes'. They also approved his call for an extension of the boundary and he commented, 'This is democracy.' He then vacated the chair saying, 'on second thoughts, it is not a decent chair for a man to be seen in'.[27] When the Unionists returned they approved a motion for the council to go into committee, which would require the gallery to be cleared. At this point a protester shouted to Alderman Hegarty, 'I do not agree with your personal politics, but take the chair.' There were cries of 'take the chair' and Hegarty walked up to the mayor's chair. There was a minor scuffle between Hegarty and a Unionist councillor and before desisting, Hegarty shouted to the gallery: 'Whom do you want to see in the chair?' There were cries of 'Hegarty'. There was further confusion during which Hegarty told the Unionists, 'You were the cause of October Fifth', and Councillor Anderson called the protesters a 'rabble'. The protesters withdrew, but were angered by news that the council had again refused to meet the deputation, although accepting an amendment that the next general purposes committee would receive it. The DHAC and NILP supporters sought to get back into the chamber; finding the doors locked, they got in through the mayor's parlour and were joined in the gallery by Alderman Hegarty and Councillor Friel. Finally a police sergeant was called and the demonstrators withdrew.

What had occurred was precisely the sort of 'semi-hysterical outburst of militancy' which McCann had criticised, and far from exposing and isolating the Nationalists, an informal united front had been struck up and the politicians were being allowed to clamber onto the DHAC's bandwagon. This was hardly surprising since the differences were ones of style and rhetoric, not of fundamental demands. A week later, when the NILP delegation was received, the Nationalists were able to achieve concrete results by having six important motions accepted, including acceptance of a points system and a committee for the allocation of houses. The DHAC had softened up the Unionists by publicising the housing situation in Derry and causing embarrassment for the Stormont government, but it was the Nationalists, as elected representatives, who were able to press home the advantage and force the concessions. The mayor also outlined plans which, if implemented, would have gone a long way towards mopping up the demand for houses in Derry. It is a matter for speculation whether or not this would have been enough to cut the ground from underneath the feet of the DHAC, but in any case the situation had been radically transformed by the 5 October march and by the prorogation of Londonderry Corporation announced on 22 November 1968 by the O'Neill government.

Even before 5 October 1968 it was clear that the radicals around the DHAC were beginning to lose the initiative and would be unable to consolidate themselves as an alternative leadership for anti-Unionists in the city. Eamonn McCann is frank about the lack of perspectives and the frenetic activity which characterised the Derry left. 'Often,' he notes, 'we resembled a rather violent community welfare body rather than a group of revolutionaries.'[28] In so far as they were looking forward, it was with a much more gradual pace of development in mind. McCann reveals parts of a 'perspectives document' which was circulated within the left of the NILP prior to 5 October. This was realistic about the difficulties of achieving anything substantial within the conservative and sectarian environment of Derry. It advocated action on housing and unemployment as a way in which Labour could begin to communicate with workers on both sides of the sectarian divide. The NILP should 'assume a quasi-educational function in tracing the connection between the political system and bad housing, unemployment and the negation of democracy'.[29] The Labour and republican radicals were essentially propagandists, not mass leaders. Their direct-action tactics did not aim at involving large numbers of people in militant action; they were propaganda stunts designed to attract an audience. They then harangued their audience with long and complex arguments about the exploitative nature of capitalism and the need for working-class unity which no one, apart from themselves, wanted to hear. It was not surprising that after 5 October, leadership of the mass movement which they had evoked was gently, but firmly, taken out of their hands.

The 5 October march was very much outside the mainstream of Derry politics. The members of the DHAC represented only themselves and NICRA was a group of well-meaning outsiders. The smallness of the demonstration, compared with the Dungannon march, showed the modest scale of the organisers' influence, although McCann is probably right in saying that they made a mistake in starting it in hostile territory. But the events of 5 October traumatised the city as a whole and the rioting which followed showed that there was serious danger of a major sectarian conflict. The more respectable leaders of the Catholic community could not possibly sit back and leave things to the radicals of the DHAC.

An independent oppositional movement like the DHAC had emerged in Derry because of the narrowness of the Nationalist Party's politics. But because it already occupied the existing space for electoral politics, the layer of educated and professional younger community leaders who might have become involved in politics was atomised. John Hume is an example; he had become prominent in the credit union movement and from this had taken the leadership of the University for Derry Action Committee. But when that failed, he retired from public activity in order to pursue his own business interests. The events of 5 October convinced him of the need to get involved again. Other leaders, like McAteer, McGonagle, Wilton and Cooper, also saw the need to unite in order to provide responsible and moderate leadership.

On Tuesday 8 October there was a meeting in the City Hotel of fifteen of the left activists, and it was agreed to call another demonstration on Saturday, 12 October, over the same route. However, on the evening of Wednesday 9 October another meeting was called, also in the City Hotel. This time about 120 people turned up, mainly business and professional people, clergy, trade-unionists and political leaders. Their motives were later explained by the editor of the *Derry Journal*:

> The new situation presented all the leaders of nationalist [sic] protest with a large and looming problem – how to harness the energies and enthusiasm of the people in a disciplined manner. Unless the growing spirit of the movement could be harnessed

coherently, mob rule would replace Unionist minority rule. Clear leadership was essential, and quickly.[30]

Eamonn McCann was invited to take the chair and in *War and an Irish Town* he relates:

> We, the organisers of the march, would be interested in what they had to say. Various speakers congratulated us on the marvellous work we had done over the past few months. A few expressed their regrets, apologies etc. that they had not 'been as active in the past as I would have liked'. All now urged that we now all work together. Finally it was proposed that the meeting elect a number of people who, together with the original organisers, would constitute a new committee. I explained that the meeting could elect anything it wished so long as it understood that the 'original organisers' . . . would make up their own minds what status, if any, to accord those elected.[31]

Eleven people were then elected from the floor. McCann refused to be nominated; he took the quite accurate view that the meeting had been called in order to incorporate the militants, attach the lustre of their achievements to a new, more moderate group of leaders and thus deny them any significant influence. But McCann found himself alone in his hostility to the new committee. The other radicals who were present argued that they should join with the eleven newly elected people, 'reasoning that since we held the initiative we would be able to force the pace, drag some of them along in our wake and force the others quickly to resign'.[32] McCann 'stomped out', denouncing the new group as 'middle-aged, middle-class and middle-of-the-road'. He thus denied himself any further influence, but the radicals who did join what was now called the Derry Citizens' Action Committee did not dictate the pace of events and had little which was distinctive to say or propose within the new body. The strength of the DCAC was not simply that it had the backing of the existing leadership of anti-Unionist opinion in Derry, but also that it succeeded in attracting new people who had not previously been involved in any kind of political activity but who found unsuspected reservoirs of energy and initiative.

One such person was Dr Raymond McClean, medical officer of the local Du Pont factory. A man of sincere, but unformed, liberal political convictions, he had been angered by the events of

5 October and had given medical treatment to some of those injured on that day. Like many others, he attended the founding meeting out of a conviction that 'something had to be done'. He was bewildered by McCann's behaviour and felt too inexperienced to accept nomination to the committee. He was, however, appointed as one of the leaders of the stewards who were to control the DCAC's first demonstration, which was to be held on 19 October:

> I didn't say much at those early stewards' meetings, but realised very quickly that many of the very excellent people present were somewhat lacking in the ordinary muscle a steward requires to carry out his job quietly and efficiently. As a result, during the next week, Micky McGuinness and myself toured the boxing clubs, the wrestling clubs and the youth clubs in the city, gathering as many new stewards as possible.[33]

This demonstrated the advantages which the DCAC derived from its ability to attract fresh minds like McClean's and the good will it had from the Catholic community in general. It also showed that the DCAC, unlike the DHAC, took seriously the likely outcome of its actions and prepared carefully in order to give effect to its determination to avoid violence. This further increased its authority and enabled it to keep control over events, at least for the next few months. Its authority was quickly established when it called off the demonstration called by the meeting of radicals on 8 October. No one, not even McCann, challenged what was a fairly high-handed decision, given that the event had been called by a different body.

The first DCAC-organised protest took place on 19 October and consisted of a mass sit-down in Guildhall Square.[34] Between four thousand and five thousand people took part and the demands of the rally were for a crash housing programme, a fair points system for the allocation of houses and legal control over the letting of furnished acccommodation. John Hume, addressing the protesters, stressed that 'we are a peaceful and dignified people, but . . . we are a determined people and we will stand for these social, economic and political injustices no longer'. He went on to deny that they had any political ends other than an end to discrimination: 'It has been said against this movement that its purpose is to unite Ireland and to unite the working class . . . We are not dealing with political issues, civil rights is not a political issue but a moral issue.'[35]

The speeches of Finbar O'Doherty and Eamonn Melaugh were more militant in tone but they did not demur from Hume's denial of what had been the central purpose of the DHAC – the unity of the working class around a material grievance. Moreover, they were outstripped in militancy by Ivan Cooper, who pointed to the city walls and said: 'We are denied the right to walk within these walls which are loved by every citizen . . . In a peaceful civil rights march we will walk within the walls of this city . . . We mean business.'[36] There had been a morning of heavy rain before the event and this must have reduced the expected numbers present and made it more subdued than it might otherwise have been. Loyalist opposition was minimal; Major Ronald Bunting's Loyal Citizens of Ulster had threatened a counter-demonstration but this was banned by Minister of Home Affairs William Craig, and the RUC sealed off the stairways to the top of the walls and erected barriers which would prevent any clash. In the event the Loyal Citizens failed to appear and the only incident occurred when a small group began to sing 'God Save the Queen' as the demonstrators struck up with 'We shall overcome'. The counter-demonstrators were quickly surrounded by stewards and they dispersed quietly. Not long afterwards the protesters also dispersed, obeying the order of the chief steward to take with them the newspapers on which they had been sitting.

Good organisation, popular support and tacit collaboration from the police had enabled the DCAC to protest peacefully and responsibly. The next event was just as successful, although it sailed closer to the wind. On 2 November the ban on the 5 October route was challenged by fifteen DCAC members who walked it, accompanied by a large crowd who followed them on the footpaths. On reaching Carlisle Square, at the city end of Craigavon Bridge, they were jeered by a crowd of loyalists, but stewards lining the square prevented any clash. At Ferryquay Gate they were met by a blockade of loyalists which was being addressed by Bunting. There was a brief sit-down by some DCAC supporters but stewards quickly cleared a path. By this time the crowd following the marchers had spilled out across the roadway, effectively breaking the ban on a march within the city walls. They gathered in the Diamond where Eamonn Melaugh's eleven-year-old-son Martin read the Universal

Declaration of Human Rights and the crowd sang 'We shall overcome'. Shortly before the end of the rally, Bunting and his followers made their way up Ferryquay Street towards the Diamond but they were blocked by the police and the rally ended peacefully. Once it had dispersed, Bunting was allowed to hold a meeting in the Diamond and for a short time afterwards there was tension as rival groups of teenagers faced each other, but police and DCAC stewards persuaded them to disperse before any trouble broke out.

On 16 November the 5 October route was traversed again, this time by a mass demonstration. The police imposed a change of route which involved marching to Craigavon Bridge via Duke Street, instead of Distillery Brae and Spencer Road, and to the Diamond via John Street and Foyle Street instead of Carlisle Road. The DCAC accepted the change to Duke Street but rejected any further re-routing. A crowd, which the *Derry Journal* estimated at 15,000, set off across the bridge, to be brought to a halt by the stewards thirty yards from the police barriers at Carlisle Square. A delegation asked the police to clear the way and when this was refused, four DCAC members made a token protest by leaping over the barriers. John Hume returned to the head of the march to ask the demonstrators to accept this as the limit of their defiance. At this point a Union flag was waved by loyalists at the foot of Carlisle Road and there was a surge forward by DCAC supporters, but the stewards restrained them. Eventually the crowd dispersed down John Street; any enthusiasm for the original route was dampened by the presence of a large crowd of loyalists who were being restrained by the police behind the barriers. As it was, marchers approaching John Street had to dodge a fusillade of missiles thrown by the loyalists. The crowd made its way to the Diamond where there were some minor brushes with the police before stewards restored order. Some of the demonstrators were denied access to the Diamond by police tenders drawn up across Shipquay Street but after a time the RUC withdrew altogether and the Diamond was filled by the vast crowd. Some loyalists who approached the Diamond from Bishop Street were restrained by the police and the rally ended peacefully.

Once again the DCAC had shown its ability to mount a peaceful protest and to maintain discipline over its followers. But the committee's rank-and-file supporters were becoming increasingly militant and ready to respond to provocation by loyalists. Peace hung by the slender thread of the DCAC's moral authority. Ray McClean describes his mild surprise on several occasions, when demonstrators accepted the authority of his steward's armband and obeyed his orders. Had the crowd not been prepared to accept the directions of the stewards at Carlisle Square and had they made an attempt to follow the original route, there would have been a major clash with the RUC and the loyalists and large-scale violence. It was in the course of these protests that the civil rights movement realised most fully its aims of defying authority without provoking violence or a direct sectarian confrontation. But the increasing activism of its supporters, particularly young Catholics living in ghetto areas, made it more and more difficult to exercise restraint. Following the 16 November demonstration, the DCAC was drawn into a series of fire-brigade operations, rushing around trying to prevent minor flare-ups. There had been a foretaste of this the previous Saturday, when a loyalist march and rally, led by Ian Paisley, was held in Derry. During a meeting at the Diamond police restrained attempts by loyalist and Catholic youths to break through their lines. Several smoke bombs were thrown by Catholic youngsters who had gathered at Shipquay Street, stones were thrown and a policeman was knocked unconscious. The police moved the youths down Shipquay Street, despite a brief sit-down which ended after an appeal by Paul Grace, chief steward of the DCAC. A few teenagers refused to leave with the others, but after about ten minutes they joined the crowd in Guildhall Square where the recently revived DUAC was holding a teach-in.

On Monday 18 November the DCAC was faced by a number of spontaneous demonstrations which could have resulted in trouble. The defendants arrested on 5 October were appearing at Derry courthouse and by the time the hearing was in progress, a crowd of about one hundred had gathered outside. About fifty people attempted to gain entrance, but were held back by the police. Paul Grace and Councillor James Doherty came out of the court and appealed for restraint, and after negotiations with the police about a dozen relatives of defendants were allowed in. After the short hearing, the crowd, by this time about three hundred strong, carried Gerry Fitt and Ivan Cooper shoulder high down Bishop Street, through the Diamond and down Shipquay Street to Guildhall

Square, where there was an impromptu meeting. There was a short scuffle with police, who thought the demonstrators were trying to get into the Guildhall, but Cooper successfully diffused the situation. They marched back to the Diamond and down Butcher Street, where they dispersed.

Some thirty minutes later a crowd of about four hundred dockers left work and marched through the city centre to their trade-union headquarters in Orchard Street. They told reporters that they were protesting at a police attack on the demonstrators at the Guildhall. They were addressed by their branch secretary, George Hamill, and by Vincent Coyle and John Hume on behalf of the DCAC. Hamill assured them that he had sent telegrams on their behalf to Terence O'Neill and Harold Wilson protesting about the incident at the Guildhall. They marched back to the docks and resumed work after another address by Hume. The DCAC had earlier called off a proposed token strike by shirt-factory workers, but at about 3 p.m. about one thousand workers, mostly young women from some half-dozen factories, left work and marched up Strand Road, through Guildhall Square and via Shipquay Street to the Diamond. They were addressed by Hume and McCann, who congratulated them on breaking the ban on city-centre marches. They marched back to Great James Street, where they dispersed. A group of about fifty teenagers who had followed them then set off on their own march through the banned area. They dispersed quietly after a short meeting on top of the city wall, over Magazine Gate, which again was addressed by Hume.

The following day Ivan Cooper appealed for an end to unplanned marches; clearly the leaders of the DCAC were aware of the large amount of good luck, as well as careful planning, which had enabled them to avoid any major violent incidents. On 9 December they responded to O'Neill's 'crossroads' address by announcing a moratorium on marches until 11 January 1969. In the meantime there had been a major change in the political landscape of Derry, with the announcement on 22 November of the imminent abolition of Londonderry Corporation and the appointment of a Development Commission to run the city's affairs. This fell far short of the change which the Catholic majority wanted – which was the transfer of power to their elected representatives – but the DCAC could afford to take a sanguine view of the change. The clear implication was that, eventually, their full demands would be met and in the meantime the Unionists had been obliged to accept that they could no longer rule with total disregard for the feelings and aspirations of Derry's Catholics.

There was, therefore, something of a ritual character to the DCAC's statement on the appointment of the commission. It expressed resentment at the failure of the Government to concede majority rule, but welcomed the commission in principle, reserving judgement until full details were available. It pledged to continue the struggle for democratic representation but appealed to its supporters to continue to exercise restraint. John Patton, press officer of the DCAC, refused to comment on plans for a fresh campaign but it was clear that the committee was extremely cautious about getting involved in further large-scale demonstrations. Early in December it channelled its supporters' energies into a mass petition calling for the implementation of the Universal Declaration of Human Rights in Northern Ireland, obtaining the signatures of nearly half the population of the city. After the Queen's Speech at the opening of the new session of the Stormont parliament, it criticised the failure of the Government to give any commitment on a universal franchise and the Special Powers Act, but the only action it proposed was a low-key educational programme.

The year 1968 drew to a close and with it the life of Londonderry Corporation. It was entirely fitting that it should end with a sit-in at the Guildhall by a number of homeless families and with a dispute over the allocation of houses. The new year would see a disintegration of the unanimity of the DCAC's supporters; the committee had grave doubts about the wisdom of the PD march from Belfast to Derry, although it arranged material support and a welcoming rally for the marchers. These doubts were confirmed when the march was savagely assaulted at Burntollet Bridge and again on entering Derry. A Paisleyite rally in the Guildhall, and the DCAC rally to greet the marchers, led to serious rioting, and in the aftermath there were ugly incidents in which the police used violent and provocative tactics. By March things had settled down sufficiently for the DCAC to mount a mass demonstration which successfully traversed the original 5 October route – this time without diversions, but this was the last occasion on which the DCAC was able to organise a peaceful mass demonstration. Already, by February, the unity of the committee had been disrupted by disputes over the incursion of some of its leading members into politics during the Stormont general election. In August violence, which began in Derry, spread to Belfast where it led to serious sectarian clashes and resulted in the intervention of the Westminster government and the arrival of British troops. In Derry the civil rights movement achieved its greatest moral authority and it was in the city that its authority first began to crumble.

6

THE PEOPLE'S DEMOCRACY

It was on the first day of the year in 1969
We gathered at the City Hall, the weather being fine.
With McCann in front to lead us, Michael Farrell in the van,
Off on the long march to Derry . . .

They ambushed us at Irish Street and at Burntollet too,
And the air was thick with stones and bricks, and the missiles fairly
    flew.
But we got up and struggled on, though battered black and blue,
To finish the long march to Derry.

from 'The long march to Derry' (civil rights song)

The events of 5 October 1968 created a mass movement but they
also initiated the processes which were to lead to its dissolution.
Over the next year the civil rights movement was riven by bitter
disputes as irreconcilable differences emerged. At the centre of
these disputes was the group of young radicals known as the
People's Democracy. To some extent it is misleading to see this
group as a dissident section of the civil rights movement. The PD
was distinctive in its student origins, its predominant youth and its
international links and influences. NICRA came to be predominantly
made up of branches in the provincial towns, which were strongly
rooted in traditional nationalism and republicanism. In Derry the
DCAC was dominated by established community leaders. The PD
was almost as hostile to these strands of the civil rights movement
as it was to the Unionist government. The PD affiliated to NICRA and
worked within it for a time, but as a deliberate tactical ploy. The
two groups met at many points but they never really mingled.

QUB students of the 1960s shared the tendency of students
elsewhere in the United Kingdom to support radical and humanitarian causes, but as Paul Arthur has pointed out:

By 1968 there was very little indication that Belfast undergraduates
were part of the world-wide wave of student protest. There were a

few demonstrations protesting at American involvement in South East Asia but . . . the largest anti-Vietnam march in Belfast attracted only about fifty participants.[1]

The Conservative and Unionist Association at QUB told the Cameron Commission that 'apartheid, CND and other *causes célèbres* of the fifties never made much impact . . . Outbursts of student enthusiasm were frequent but seldom political.'[2] Bernadette Devlin remembered the profoundly unserious nature of university politics. In 1965 the main debating forum, the Literific Society, 'had degenerated into nothing more than student obscenity'.[3] In fact the 'Lit' was suspended by the university authorities in 1964 after a guest speaker had stripped off in front of the audience. Devlin sampled the offerings of the main political societies but found that they 'weren't *real*'[4] and that there were more genuine political ideas in the Folk Music Society. Ciaran McKeown suggested that a deterioration in the quality of debate and discussion was due to the 'oppressive level' of the pressures arising from an enhanced importance of qualifications, brought about by the expansion of the university in line with developments in higher education elsewhere in the United Kingdom.[5]

McKeown was the initiator of a movement of 'like minded people' which opposed the domination of the Student Representative Council (SRC) by sectarian blocs and worked to get control of the SRC. By 1966, he claims, there was 'no longer a sectarian majority' on the council.[6] This, however, did not necessarily have any profound political significance; McKeown was a skilful organiser and one student leader reckoned that 'SRC elections are decided 60% by personality, 10% by politics, 10% by religion and 20% by apathy'.[7]

The first organisation to use the term 'civil rights' was the Working Committee on Civil Rights in Northern Ireland, set up at QUB in 1964. It was an ad hoc and self-financed student group which carried out surveys in Newry and Derry. According to Eamonn McCann, in Derry they

interviewed Unionist and Nationalist members of the Corporation . . . We spoke to local union leaders and employers and the Catholic and Church of Ireland Bishops. We heard oral evidence from members of the public and gathered considerable data from official and unofficial sources. We carried out a public opinion poll. It was our intention to publish the results . . . together with the results of a similar study of Newry.[8]

But by the time the work was completed the committee was heavily in debt and could not raise the necessary funds to publish its findings.

The driving force behind the committee was Bowes Egan. Kevin Boyle remembers him as 'young, bright, anarchistic, totally intolerant of anybody's opinion but his own . . . He organised an empire . . . and seemed to control all the various debating societies'.[9] A number of the more radical students were grouped around Egan at this time, including Michael Farrell, but the latter's increasing interest in Marxism drove them apart. Farrell claims that Egan was a cynic who was opposed to any ideology, of left or right, and by 1967 they had little to do with each other. Egan reappeared after the mushrooming of the civil rights movement; he co-authored a widely distributed pamphlet on the ambush of the PD march at Burntollet in early 1969 and was the PD candidate for Enniskillen in the February 1969 Stormont general election. Subsequently he returned to London, where he was a law lecturer. He was active in the Anti-Internment League there in 1971 and 1972, before dropping out of politics to pursue a lucrative practice as a consultant on industrial relations law. He shunned the limelight and scarcely figures in any of the published reminiscences but he seems to have been highly innovative and imaginative and will probably never be given his full due as an influence on events in Northern Ireland in the 1960s.[10]

In the early to mid 1960s one of the most energetic groups at QUB was the New Ireland Society. Its aims were 'to bring together all those interested in the eventual re-unification of Ireland; and the political, social, cultural and economic advancement of the country, and to foster and encourage . . . debate, discussion, lectures, etc.'. Its patrons included a number of literary and political luminaries and it published a high-quality review, *New Ireland*. Its debates and lectures attracted considerable attention outside the university and it also initiated a prestigious award for people in public life who had made an outstanding contribution to good community relations.

There was some overlap between the New Ireland Society and one of the most effective political organisations in the university, the National Democratic Group, founded in 1966, which was affiliated to the NDP. Its first president was Ciaran McKeown and he was followed by Fred Taggart, a member of the Church of Ireland and Brian Turner, a Methodist. Its officers and committee included Denis Haughey, later to be prominent in the SDLP, and Peter Rowan and Peter Cush, who were active members of the early PD. Among the group's activities was a scholarly seminar on the Easter Rising in 1966 and a survey of the Suffolk–Andersonstown area of west Belfast to determine the size of the future labour force and the likely availability of employment.

The moderate approach of the New Ireland Society and the National Democratic Group was shared by the Conservative and Unionist Association, which was firmly on the O'Neill wing of the party. One of the most remarkable events of these years was the election of a Catholic, Louis Boyle, to the chair of the Conservative and Unionist Association, at the same time as the National Democratic Group had elected a Protestant as its president. Boyle had some difficulty within the association when he was falsely accused of trying to recruit anti-Unionists to disrupt the organisation, but he was reinstated with a full apology. His experience with the party outside was less happy, and in July 1969 he resigned, blaming Orange influences which had blocked his nomination as Unionist candidate for South Down. His brother, Kevin Boyle, later became a prominent member of the PD.

There was an active Liberal Association which was formed in March 1962. However, it was not as effective as the New Ireland Society, the National Democratic Group and the Unionists, probably because its politics tended to overlap with theirs. The Labour Group was the largest political society and it did not try to compete for the middle ground. It was affiliated to the NILP but some, at least, of its members were not enthusiastic about the party. One of them, Michael Dowling, castigated it for not proposing a 'distinctive socialist alternative to Unionist policies' and for being 'too timid in its advocacy of the proposals it does support'. Nevertheless, the NILP had to be supported because it was the 'only party possessing organic links with the organised working-class movement'.[11]

The other important radical group at QUB was significant not so much for its activities as for its existence. On 8 March 1967, the day after Minister of Home Affairs William Craig had announced a ban on commemorations of the 1867 Fenian Rising and proscribed the Republican Clubs, a meeting of about sixty students set up a Republican Club at QUB. This had no associations with the illegal organisations and Ciaran McKeown, who was at this time president of the Students' Union, estimated that there were no more than four or five genuine republicans at Queen's. At the same time a Joint Action Committee Against the Suppression of Liberties was set up to organise protests against the ban. It linked all the political groups with the exception of the Unionists (although its chairman was an honorary life member of the Unionist Association). The other officers were drawn from the Labour Group, the National Democratic Group, the Republican Club and the Liberal Association. Two days later about eighty students took part in a demonstration from the Students' Union to the city hall. Officially this was not a student march since there had not been enough time to clear it with the Academic Council of the university. The following day many of the same people were on a Young Socialists march against the ban, through the city centre. Despite police fears of conflict with a loyalist flute band which was parading in Sandy Row, this event, like the first, passed off peacefully. Towards the end of April the National Democratic Group and the Labour group, together with the Republican Club, picketed Armagh courthouse in protest at the prosecution of twelve republicans for their part in an Easter Rising commemoration in the town. They had been refused the use of the Students' Union minibus, an indication that those involved were part of an active, but small, minority of the student body.

In May 1967 the SRC recognised the Republican Club as a student society by a vote of thirty-three to six, after a strong intervention in favour of the motion by the president, Ciaran McKeown. The executive of the SRC had obtained an assurance in advance from the club that it had no links with any proscribed organisation and had no intention of forming such links. The decision was taken despite a statement made in Stormont a few days earlier by William Craig:

In view of the ban it would not only be unwise, but illegal, for clubs, even though constitutional in character, to adopt the title 'Republican Clubs', which is that of an unlawful association. They should choose some other, appropriate, title and provided their objects are . . . lawful, there would not be any objection to their formation.[12]

However, on this occasion, and in one or two later exchanges, Craig avoided any direct reference to the QUB Republican Club. On 14 November Harry Diamond MP asked him to place in the library the evidence on which he had acted to ban the QUB Republican Club. The Minister replied: 'I did not place a specific ban on the club to which the hon. Member refers.'[13] He denied having ordered a police investigation of the club, but added that they did not need to have his sanction to investigate any possible breach of the law. A little later he commented that the students, 'if they act as hon. Members say they are acting, could have so arranged the constitution and organisation of the club as to leave no doubt how it stood as regards the law'.[14] To which Eddie McAteer replied: 'The Minister does not know students.'

The SRC's recognition of the Republican Club was required to be ratified by the Academic Council. Ciaran McKeown had informed the secretary to the council of the SRC decision and had approached the vice-chancellor, Dr Arthur Vick, to suggest that the matter be referred to the university's legal advisers and there the matter rested until the new academic year. Early in November 1967 the Academic Council wrote to the SRC: 'After having advice from the Legal Advisory Committee, which stated that the Republican Club is an unlawful association . . . the Academic Council on November 3rd resolved that the Council and the SRC are prevented from recognising the club while the Government order remains in force.'[15] This revived the issue. The secretary of the Republican Club made it clear that it would remain in existence and the Labour, National Democratic and Liberal societies reiterated their support for the right of the Republican Club to operate as a recognised student group; the New Ireland Society passed a resolution deploring the ban and Louis Boyle, chairman of the Conservative and Unionist Association, stated his personal support for the right of the club to be recognised.

The Joint Action Committee Against the Suppression of

Liberties was revived; over one thousand students and staff had signed a petition supporting the Republican Club and the committee organised a march to hand this in to Unionist Party headquarters in Glengall Street in Belfast. Shortly after the announcement of the march William Clulow, described as 'Secretary of the Unionist Trade Unionist Association', called on all loyalist trade-unionists to join a counter-demonstration in Glengall Street to 'help educate these so-called intellectuals a little further'. Then Ian Paisley announced that he would organise a counter-demonstration in Shaftesbury Square, on the students' route to Glengall Street. This was a sensitive area because of its proximity to the loyalist Sandy Row area. When the march assembled on the afternoon of 15 November 1967, the police proposed a change of objective. Instead of Glengall Street, the students marched to William Craig's house by a route which took them well away from the city centre. There the permanent secretary to the Ministry of Home Affairs received the petition and promised to pass it on to the minister. About 1,500 people took part, a significant growth in support compared with the earlier marches. The marchers included Austin Currie MP and a delegation from University College Dublin.

Two weeks later a deputation consisting of Rory McShane, Brian Patterson and Brian Turner of the joint action committee, together with the Students' Union president Ian Brick, met Craig at Stormont. He told them that he was satisfied that the QUB Republican Club was constitutional and only infringed the law by using the name 'Republican Club', and suggested that they should call themselves the 'Republican Society' or 'Republican Association'. Needless to say the club rejected this advice; commenting on its refusal, Craig said that 'they will, of course, be in breach of the law and the matter becomes one entirely for the police'. The police, as might have been forecast, did not get around to prosecuting anyone and the club continued to operate, using the name of a sympathetic society, such as the Labour Group, to book facilities in the Students' Union. It organised one or two meetings and debates, but it was largely symbolic and not a major force within student politics.

The affair raised some important issues and it is significant that Craig thought it a straightforward matter to prosecute citizens who had infringed a prohibition which, clearly, was never meant to cover their activities. He also made it clear that their illegal act had been to use the word 'club' in conjunction with the word 'republican'. This raised some nice points of jurisprudence and about the obligations of citizens in a democratic society. But the implications were fairly direct; had it not been for his explicit statement in parliament that the QUB Republican Club was in breach of the law, the university authorities might have been able to find some way of recognising the club, while not adverting to the fact that they had been advised that it was, technically, illegal. Craig closed that option and what had been a passing enthusiasm for a few score of radicals then became an issue which was of concern to hundreds. It created an alliance between a tiny group of revolutionaries, a minority of liberals and a large number of students who were vaguely worried about civil liberties. The students did not direct their protest at the university authorities, but at the Government, as personified by William Craig, whose statements and whose accessibility made him a more obvious target. This turned the protest outwards, away from the university, and contributed to the later evolution of the PD. While this was helpful to the university authorities, it meant that student radicalism was a further complicating factor in the developing political crisis. The joint action committee was a nucleus which was used to mobilise the students after 5 October and the earlier demonstrations had alerted extreme loyalists to the existence of a vigorous anti-Unionist opposition at QUB, which was all the more objectionable because it contained a large number of 'Lundys' from a Protestant background. Moreover, because of the location of Queen's, student protests took place outside traditional nationalist areas. This compounded the public order problems arising from the civil rights movement.

The 5 October march in Derry took place before the beginning of the new academic year and the first response of students was a small picket of William Craig's house on Sunday 6 October (the RUC having obligingly let them know its location eleven months earlier). On the first day of term, Tuesday 8 October, the joint action committee held a meeting in the Students' Union which was attended by seven hundred to eight hundred students. They agreed on a march from the university to the city hall to take place the next day. The proposed route would have taken the marchers through Shaftesbury Square and, predictably, Ian Paisley announced a counter-demonstration. About three thousand marchers gathered at 2 p.m. on Wednesday 9 October in Elmwood Avenue, beside the Students' Union. At first they voted to maintain the original route but the police served an order banning them from Shaftesbury Square and they accepted an alternative route which would have avoided any contentious areas. While the march proceeded, Paisley's meeting in Shaftesbury Square broke up and he and his supporters made their way to the city hall, arriving before the students did. After addressing his followers, Paisley asked them to go home quietly, but about two hundred remained and were waiting in May Street at the back of the city hall when the students reached Linenhall Street, which leads directly on to the rear entrance of the building. The police cordoned off the end of the street, leaving a space of about fifty yards between the students and the jeering, singing Paisleyites.

The marchers obeyed the instructions of the joint action committee and sat down in the street with their backs to the police and the Paisleyites. After consultations with the march organisers and with university chaplains who were present, Sheelagh Murnaghan MP phoned the cabinet office at Stormont and asked that a minister come to meet the students and discuss their demands. They were invited to send a deputation of five or six to Stormont but this was rejected by the demonstrators who remained sitting on the street. At about 6 p.m. a further vote was taken and a majority favoured trying to reach the front of the city hall. As the marchers began to stand up, the police prepared for a confrontation, but Fred Taggart of the joint action committee and Peter Rowan, the chief marshal, successfully persuaded the students to sit down again. After another half-hour only about 150 demonstrators remained and Taggart successfully persuaded them, over the police loudspeaker, to march back to the university.

It was a classic case of the police restricting a legal civil rights demonstration because they had not been quick enough to prevent an illegal loyalist counter-demonstration. This highlighted the students' moderation and restraint. Ciaran McKeown recalled that 'they seemed to be discussing among themselves as they might have done on any afternoon in the Students' Union coffee bar'.[16] Seamus Heaney saw them as 'embarrassed indignant young Ulstermen and women whose deep-grained conservatism of behaviour was outweighed by a reluctant recognition of injustice'.[17] Bernadette Devlin remembered that 'our behaviour on that day earned us a great deal of respect in the community'. [18]

On returning to the university the marchers crowded into a mass meeting which lasted until the early hours of the morning and which resulted in the emergence of the PD. This was the first of the open unstructured meetings which were the chief distinguishing characteristic of the early PD. One commentator described them as 'a cross between a Quaker meeting and a Pentecostalist service. Enthusiasm was high, commitment was strong and idealism pervasive.'[19] The Cameron Report described the form and structure of the new movement:

> People's Democracy has no accepted constitution and no recorded membership. At any meeting any person attending is entitled both to speak and to vote; decisions taken at one meeting may be reviewed at the next – indeed during the currency of any given meeting. No subscription, entrance fee or membership qualification is required of members . . . and the requisite finance is obtained from collections at meetings, subscriptions or contributions from well-wishers or supporters.[20]

The mass meeting elected a Faceless Committee, so called because it was deliberately selected from people who were unknown and who were not likely to act in the interests of their career or a political faction. The committee had purely executive functions. It was to carry out the decisions of the mass meetings and was not to be a leadership nor to substitute itself for the 'people's democracy'. The committee's first job was to arrange another march. This was to have been on Saturday 12 October, but two days beforehand a mass meeting agreed to postpone it to avoid a clash with a Paisleyite march which had been called as a spoiling tactic. The march eventually took place on 16 October and it was, once more, re-routed away from Shaftesbury Square but permitted to reach the front of the city hall. About 150 Paisleyites heckled the meeting but declined a polite offer of the microphone to put their point of view to the students. Again there was praise for the responsibility shown by the marchers. The vice-chancellor wrote to Kevin Boyle saying that the arrangements had been 'excellent', but he suggested that marches should be used cautiously, 'if at all', in the future.[21]

The praise was not unanimous. Almost from the start there were dissenting voices among the students. At the original meeting on 8 October the president of the Students' Union, Ian Brick, had strongly counselled against marching. He organised an alternative rally in the Whitla Hall at QUB to coincide with the march. A leaflet issued by his Action Committee for a Peaceful Protest claimed that the march was being 'organised by various political groups in the University and others outside'. In the current atmosphere of Belfast, it claimed, the march could end in 'bloodshed'.[22] Less than one hundred students attended this rally; it did not oppose the aims of the marchers, only their tactics and the presence among them of 'agitators'. It passed a motion calling for greater efforts by the Government to achieve reconciliation.

There were no reports of similar actions at any of the other institutions of higher education in Belfast. Undoubtedly a number of staff and students, particularly QUB graduates, from other colleges supported the QUB students, but it was in Queen's alone that most of the university community was caught up in what was happening. The other institutions were smaller and more narrowly vocational; also their students lacked the social prestige and self-confidence which being a student at QUB conferred.

The New University of Ulster did not have its official opening until 25 October 1968, but teaching had already started and a student community of about four hundred had been established on its Coleraine campus. Shortly after the Derry events, the RUC in Coleraine received notice of a march from the university to the Diamond in the town centre. But almost before they had time to consider the implications, the students had cancelled it, 'as they had no desire . . . to cause any local ill-feeling should any irresponsibly minded person from outside seek to attach themselves and cause trouble'.[23] There had, in fact, been local opposition which was led by the Reverend John Wylie, a Free Presbyterian minister and at that time a close colleague of Ian Paisley. There was also opposition within the student body, with pro-civil rights posters being torn down from campus notice boards. Above all, the students did not have any neutral territory, other than their isolated campus, through which to march. These pressures effectively stifled solidarity with the civil rights cause. Even when given an opportunity to demonstrate away from the university, in Derry on 2 November, there was not enough support to justify organising transport. Geoffrey Bell and Inez McCormack, who were students at Magee College in Derry at the time, recall involvement in the civil rights activities in the town but not any specific movement among the college's small student body.[24]

There was, however, an attempt to set up a PD branch in the Royal Belfast Academical Institution, the prestigious boys' school founded in 1810. About twenty senior boys were involved and a friend of Kevin Boyle's, who was teaching there, wrote that they included: 'the best material in the school . . . they are light years ahead of their parents (and 85% of them Protestant)'. However, 'as they are shitting on their own doorstep it will have to be unofficial'.[25] The group seems to have been formed in about early December 1968; after that, increasing communal tension as well as pressure from families and the school authorities would have made it impossible to continue. The historian and feminist Margaret Ward recalls attending the first PD march with classmates from her convent school but found that she and other school students were initially shunted off into a junior group called the 'Young Democrats'.[26] The consequence of all this was that it was at QUB alone that the PD emerged and the lack of any broader student-based movement increased the PD's tendency to look on itself as a civil rights, rather than a student, organisation.

Following the 16 October march there was another mass meeting of the QUB students' new movement, now officially called the People's Democracy.[27] The report in the *Irish News* of 17 October conveyed the early PD's tone of earnest well-meaning:

> Marches are now secondary. Future action will mainly concentrate on what the PD can do to help Northern Ireland's future. This will involve intensive fact-finding activities . . . on such factors as company votes and the number of people with no voting voice in their local government affairs, or the number of families living in unfit and overcrowded conditions in Belfast.

An independent inquiry into the events in Derry was also mooted, along with woolly proposals about helping couples to find the deposit for new homes, helping voluntary agencies and converting old property into flats for the homeless and waste ground into children's playgrounds. Most of these proposals either duplicated work already done or would have diverted the student protest into charitable or community work.

By November strategy was being sharpened up. A document entitled *People's Democracy Agenda* was circulated. Among the proposals being considered were: a lobby of Stormont; picketing William Craig's house and 'irrigating' his garden; a challenge to the ban on Shaftesbury Square by a continuous circuit on the pavement by PD members giving out leaflets; Sunday-evening meetings at the city hall; a 'monster teach-in' at the Ulster Hall; and 'infiltration' of local civic weeks. They would disseminate information by 'infiltrating' the Citizens' Advice Bureaux or alternatively by setting up a PD advice bureau near the city centre. A major 'fact-finding inquiry' was to be set up, utilising social scientists. The university was to be asked to donate a house to the PD; in the event of a refusal, 'we move in and take over'. The proceeds of the rag week were to be 'earmarked for the Derry homeless'. There was to be a march and rally in Trafalgar Square, with a petition to be presented at Downing Street on Christmas Day. The sheer unreality of much of this was highlighted by the proposal to ask for the support of British students for a march at Christmas. Apparently no one appreciated the fact that most British universities simply cease to exist during vacations.

Some action did emerge. There was a very effective protest at Stormont parliament buildings on 24 October. Students demonstrated in the gallery before occupying the central lobby for a number of hours. At this stage they were still being treated with kid gloves and not only was their sit-in tolerated, but the Minister of Education, William Long, discussed with them. There were peaceful pickets of O'Neill on 28 October, of Lord Grey, the Governor of Northern Ireland, on 3 December, of Unionist Party headquarters on 6 December and of William Craig's house on 7 December.

During these activities the mood of the PD was becoming more militant and less 'responsible'. On 4 November another attempt was made to march to the city hall and once more the police insisted on a re-route to avoid a Paisleyite counter-demonstration in Shaftesbury Square; this time the PD refused. A march of about three hundred assembled in Elmwood Avenue and set off down University Road, only to be stopped at the junction with University

Street, the point at which previous marches had been diverted. They sat down as stewards attempted to negotiate, but while the attention of the police was distracted some students filtered round the cordon. On seeing this, some police broke ranks, scuffles ensued and there were some arrests. The main body of the march remained blocked off by the police and by this time some loyalist counter-demonstrators had arrived. After sitting for a time the students agreed to disperse and make their way individually to the city hall. Meanwhile about two dozen PD members had been waiting inside the building, trying to keep out of sight until it was clear whether or not the march would get through. When their presence was discovered they were ejected, but not before laughing students had dodged police and corporation officials all round the corridors. When caught they offered no resistance and were dragged bodily from the building. Outside the affair became less light-hearted when they were attacked by Paisleyites. A meeting was held outside the city hall, where the marchers had gathered after their frustrated attempt to get through the police cordon. After the meeting they sat down across Donegall Square West, blocking the traffic on one of the city's busiest thoroughfares. Police forcibly removed some of them and there were further attacks by loyalists. Eventually the marchers agreed to cease obstructing the road on being promised that they would be allowed to march back through Shaftesbury Square. In fact they were again re-routed, but the return march had swollen to twice the size of the original one from Elmwood Avenue.

The arrests showed that the PD was no longer a purely student movement. Only four of the nine arrested were students and of the others only one, a research assistant, had any connection with the university. Those arrested included a caravan salesman, a barman and an unemployed statistics clerk. The new spirit of militancy was shown again when the PD picketed a prize-giving by Terence O'Neill in the Whitla Hall at QUB on 13 November. Although the PD had decided that the protest should be silent, members of a far left group, the Revolutionary Socialist Students' Federation (RSSF) chanted slogans on the steps of the hall. A number of demonstrators tried to get through the police cordon round the prime minister and mobbed and pounded his car. The PD issued a statement denouncing the federation as 'revolutionary infants'.

O'Neill was given a formal apology but the incident did dispropor-
tionate damage to the moderate image of the PD and of students
generally.

During November the situation in Northern Ireland was becoming more and more polarised and fears of an outbreak of sectarian
violence were growing. As early as 26 October a small civil rights
march from Strabane to Derry was attacked at Magheramason and
some participants injured. This trend coincided with a turn by the
PD to agitation outside the university. They launched a 'Programme to Inform the People' in response to O'Neill's 'Programme to Enlist the People'. Branches of the PD were set up in
Newry on 9 November and in Omagh and Dungannon on 23
November. The Dungannon meeting illustrated the problems now
emerging for civil rights activities. An attempted public meeting in
Market Square had to be abandoned after scuffles with a hostile
crowd and local civil rights supporters and journalists were threatened by loyalists. There was a meeting of about three hundred in a
local restaurant, which elected a standing committee to form a local
PD branch. But they were besieged by a crowd of loyalists, about
thirty of whom broke through the front door and assaulted the
proprietor and his pregnant wife. The police succeeded in getting
the people attending the meeting out of the building safely, but
they were harassed going to their cars. There was tension between
rival gangs of youths in Market Square until the early hours of the
morning.

Concern about this trend of events was crystallised by what
happened in Armagh on 30 November. Loyalists, led by Ian
Paisley, had failed in their tactic of calling a counter-demonstration
to get a civil rights march banned, but they occupied the centre of
the town, armed with cudgels and sticks, and effectively prevented
it from traversing its intended route. Serious violence was averted
but the resources of the RUC were stretched to their limits and there
was good reason to fear that on another occasion they would be
unable to prevent a major outbreak of sectarian conflict.

This was the background to O'Neill's 'crossroads' speech of
9 December. 'As matters stand today,' he warned, 'we are on the
brink of chaos, where neighbour could be set against neighbour.'
He appealed for the civil rights movement to call off demonstrations and to 'allow an atmosphere favourable to change to

develop'.[28] He pledged that there would be no watering down of the changes the Government had already announced – the abolition of Londonderry Corporation, an ombudsman and a new system of housing allocation. NICRA and the DCAC responded by calling a truce, but on 20 December the PD defied the Government, liberal public opinion and the mainstream of the civil rights movement by announcing a march from Belfast to Derry in the first four days of 1969.

At 9 a.m. on Wednesday 1 January about forty PD supporters gathered at the city hall and after a minor fracas with some loyalist women, set off on their march. By mid-afternoon they had reached Antrim, where there was minor scuffling as the police tried to get them through a crowd of loyalists. Eventually they agreed to detour the town in police vehicles, an offer made by the RUC after the intervention of the local Unionist MP, Nat Minford. They reached Whitehall, their overnight stopping place, where the police told them that loyalists were blocking the bridge into their next objective, Randalstown. They were disturbed by a bomb scare at 3 a.m. and next morning agreed to go on to Randalstown and not to insist on going back to try to march through Antrim. Again they had to detour the town, this time in the cars of local supporters, and they marched into the friendly territory of Toome-bridge where, during the previous night, a statue of the local hero of a nationalist ballad, Roddy McCorley, had been blown up. Their next objective was Maghera but the police imposed a triangular detour through Bellaghy. Despite the fact that this was supposed to help them avoid trouble, the march was met by another hostile crowd, with Major Ronald Bunting prominent among them. At this point the march was supported by a large number of civil rights adherents from Toomebridge and, for the first time, the police took determined action to clear the opposing crowd, which dispersed without much resistance.

The marchers were welcomed in Gulladuff, where they agreed, once more, to avoid a confrontation by going round Maghera in supporters' cars to Brackaghreilly, their stopping place for the night. Next day they made another attempt to march through Maghera, where there had been violence during the night, but the RUC blocked their way, and after a token show of resistance they proceeded to Dungiven. The police warned them of a hostile crowd

213

at Feeny, about four miles ahead, but PD members reconnoitred the road and found it clear and they passed through Feeny, reaching Claudy without opposition.

That evening there was serious trouble in Derry when Paisley held a meeting in the Guildhall. Despite pleas from leaders of the DCAC, local youths clashed with police in an attempt to attack the building. The marchers were informed of what had happened and spent a troubled night in Claudy, where opponents yelled threats outside the hall which they were occupying for the night. Next morning there was a long discussion about whether or not the march should be called off: it was now clear to everyone that there was a definite danger of encountering serious violence. But in face of the determination of a number of the marchers, and considering the distance already covered and the short distance which remained, they agreed to proceed.

When the march reached the junction with the main Dungiven–Derry road, the police warned them that there was a hostile crowd about three hundred yards ahead on high ground and that stones might be thrown. Although a number of alternative routes could have been taken, the police did not advise a re-route and the march proceeded, with a contingent of police wearing helmets and carrying shields at its head. Shortly afterwards they began to see people in the fields, which were banked up at some height above the road: first a single man wearing a white armband, then about fifty, standing in little knots. A little further on the march was bombarded with stones and bottles thrown from the fields. About 150 people could be seen, some of them wearing white armbands, and also groups of uniformed policemen, some of whom seemed to be engaged in amicable conversation with the attackers. When some marchers tried to escape by breaking through the hedges into the fields, these officers drew their batons and drove them back onto the road.

Worse was to come: a little further on two groups of attackers, armed with cudgels, lengths of lead piping, crowbars and iron bars, were concealed in and around Ardmore Road at its junction with the Derry–Claudy road, just before it reaches Burntollet Bridge. Since the police were grouped at the head of the march, they offered little or no protection when these attackers leaped out and assaulted the marchers. The attack was brutal and relentless;

the unresisting marchers were beaten, knocked down and kicked, prevented from seeking shelter, pursued and further assaulted. There was at least one near fatality when a girl was knocked unconscious and left lying face down in a stream. Several people were taken to hospital and although the police recorded only thirteen injured, the Cameron Report acknowledged that this was incomplete.

There was clear evidence of advance preparations for the attacks. Piles of newly quarried stones had been left in the fields. The previous evening, outside normal working hours, a group of workers arrived in a telephone engineering van and did some work on the telephone lines and next day local lines were dead. Bowes Egan and Vincent McCormack got an admission from the caretaker of a local Orange hall that it had been used to store and distribute cudgels. Many assailants wore white armbands which readily distinguished them from marchers. Egan and McCormack were able to identify a number of the attackers from photographs and these came from a wide area but not from districts outside the scope of the local farming and commercial community. Many were B Specials; this was a good propaganda point for the civil rights movement, but since membership of the B Specials in the area was roughly co-terminous with the status of adult, able-bodied male Protestant, this underlines the point that it was an attack by local people.[29]

The marchers were stoned again on their way into Derry and there was trouble at a DCAC rally and during the night. The most ominous feature of this was a breakdown in discipline by some policemen, who attacked shoppers in a city-centre supermarket and broke windows, kicked doors and sang sectarian songs in Catholic areas into the early hours of the morning. If the events at Burntollet had been shocking, those in Derry were menacing. As a result of clashes originating in communal tensions brought on by the PD march, the police had been more seriously compromised than ever before in the eyes of Derry Catholics and hostility between Protestants and Catholics was being superseded by hostility between the Catholic community and the forces of the state.

Terence O'Neill condemned the attempt to march to Derry as a 'foolhardy and irresponsible undertaking. At best those who planned it were careless of the effects it would have; at worst they

embraced with enthusiasm the prospect of adverse publicity causing further damage to the interests of Northern Ireland'.[30] Brian
Faulkner considered the march to be 'deliberately provocative . . .
Young people were used as bait in a hoped for and expected attack
which could be used to arouse community antagonisms'.[31] O'Neill
commended Eddie McAteer for his opposition to the march but the
Nationalist leader's interpretation of the motives of the PD was
more benign:

> God love them in their innocence, they thought that this thing could
> be conducted on an entirely civil rights plane without regard to
> sectarianism or nationalism or any of those other things which really
> move people . . . These dewy eyed innocents thought that in the
> sacred name of civil rights and democracy they could walk through
> . . . Orange areas without incurring Orange displeasure. As . . .
> anyone who had any knowledge of the terrain or knowledge of
> history could have told them . . . they were simply resented as
> people who were likely to disturb the established order.[32]

Frank Gogarty, chairman of NICRA, made a similar point: 'To me
they are the innocents, the wee folk out to slay the dragon. They at
times have the innocence of children and all their love. They are the
white in the Irish flag, martyred between the Orange and the
Green.'[33]

The 'innocence' thesis strains credulity, but O'Neill's and
Faulkner's analysis depended on the PD having calculated in
advance all of the consequences of its action. A passage from
Bernadette Devlin's autobiography explains the PD's motives:

> Our function in marching . . . was to break the truce, to relaunch
> the civil rights movement as a mass movement, and to show the
> people that O'Neill was, in fact, offering them nothing. We knew
> that we wouldn't finish the march without getting molested, and we
> were accused of looking for trouble. What we really wanted to do
> was pull the carpet off the floor to show the dirt that was under it.[34]

Paul Arthur quotes a PD militant who gave a similar interpretation:
'In marching we felt that we were pushing a structure . . . towards
a point where its internal proceedings would cause a snapping and
breaking to begin.' But he is too sweeping in his assertion that
'some PD members were now seeing their task as the destruction of
the State, no matter what the consequences'.[35] The PD's intentions

were radical but they were not revolutionary. Michael Farrell has recorded that the march was modelled on Martin Luther King's Selma–Montgomery march of 1966, 'which had exposed the racist thuggery of America's Deep South and forced the US government into major reforms'.[36]

Farrell explained the point further:[37] he had not been innocent; being from the south Derry area himself, he was well aware of the nature and depth of Protestant hostility. He had not, however, anticipated the full extent of the violence. He had thought that the march would force the Government either to confront the loyalists or to drop its pretensions about reform, but he had not been clear about the further consequences of forcing the Government to resist sections of its own supporters. The loyalists might back down, or the Government might fall, forcing the British government to intervene. The purpose of the march was to upset the status quo but it is going too far to say that it was an attempt to destroy the state – except in the very special sense that it might be supplanted by a stronger state. It was essentially an oppositional tactic, against what was seen as O'Neill's fake reformism, against the truce in civil rights activities, and against the leaderships of the civil rights movement and the Catholic community.

Almost on the heels of the Belfast–Derry march came the announcement of a march to be held in Newry on 12 January. This was billed as a PD march but in fact it was organised by the Newry PD, which had been set up following the PD visit on 9 November. It was not a student or an exclusively young body, but a group of local civil rights supporters who called themselves PD because that movement had been the first to evangelise them. Its first attempt to mount a demonstration, in December, had failed through lack of support but the traumatic events at Burntollet now ensured a big turnout. Its chosen route would have taken the march through part of the town's business centre. This was an area which did not have a resident population to be offended or inconvenienced but it was contained within a Unionist-held local government ward. Major Ronald Bunting threatened a counter-demonstration and the RUC imposed a change of route. This incensed the civil rights supporters, who saw it as a denial of their right to march through the centre of their Catholic-dominated town, when only people living outside the area would be offended. Police refused a compromise whereby the organisers would have accepted a change of route if there was evidence of a counter-demonstration, and even when Bunting called off his threatened rally, the ban remained. The march resulted in dramatic scenes as demonstrators broke through police barriers and attacked several police tenders, burning them, pushing them into the canal dock beside which they were parked, or driving them off to be vandalised elsewhere. The police lines were drawn up behind the tenders and many civil rights supporters alleged afterwards that this had been deliberate, to offer no deterrent to just such misbehaviour as had occurred. In any event it meant that there was no actual physical conflict until a baton charge drove the remnants of the crowd out of the area.[38]

The affair was intensely damaging to the civil rights movement. John Hume, Michael Farrell, Kevin Boyle and other civil rights leaders appealed for order and stewards attempted to restrain their supporters. But the local group lacked the experience and authority to keep control and it made serious blunders in its preparations for the march. The Cameron Report summed up the reasons for the débâcle as 'inefficient and inadequate arrangements', which included a lack of an effective loudspeaker and an adequate stewarding system. To this had been added an unworkable plan to occupy public buildings in order to divert attention away from trouble: 'In the event the organisers were confronted by an unorganised group which blocked their path . . . and by an extremist element . . . spoiling for an attack on the police . . . The march degenerated into a riot.'[39] As Kevin Boyle put it: 'The local organisation made a mess of it.'[40]

The Newry march led many people to conclude that civil rights marches could no longer be carried out peacefully and that the movement had lost control over the more hot-headed and extreme elements of its support. In fact, between the end of January and the end of July, there were ten occasions on which civil rights activities led to trouble and twenty-one on which they were carried out entirely peacefully, including a march in Newry on 28 June. But for the PD the issue of marching was thrust into the background when Terence O'Neill called a general election for 24 February. He was appealing over the heads of many in his own party for the support of all moderates, Catholic as well as Protestant. To the PD, however, his reformism was fake and it decided to

218

contest the election to challenge the idea that he had anything to offer.

The PD stood on a manifesto which encompassed the established civil rights demands on the franchise, state repression and housing allocation, but added other demands such as a crash housing programme, state investment and state-owned industries with workers' control, integrated comprehensive education and a break-up of large estates in the west to provide land for co-operative farms. No seats were won, but the PD candidates totted up 25,407 votes. Eamonn McCann stood as an NILP candidate in Foyle and if his 1,993 votes are added to those of the PD, this amounted to 29 per cent of the total poll in the seats contested. In South Down, Fergus Woods came within 220 votes of unseating the Nationalist MP. The PD saw this as a major triumph and an endorsement of their radical policies but a closer examination reveals the flaws in such an assumption. Overall the election weakened O'Neill's position, since he did not get the decisive endorsement across the sectarian divide for which he was looking, but the other significant aspect was the success of candidates with a record in the civil rights movement in challenging the Nationalist Party, of which John Hume's defeat of Eddie McAteer in Foyle was the best example. The events of the previous eighteen months had brought about a fundamental shift within the Catholic community for whom the civil rights movement was beginning to eclipse the Nationalist Party as a means of political expression.

The PD's vote has to be seen in this broader context of the performance of the civil rights candidates. The PD's support ranged widely, from 9.2 per cent of the poll in Belfast Cromac (the only lost deposit) to 48.8 per cent in South Down. The average over the nine constituencies was 26.4 per cent. This was not strikingly different from the performance of other unsuccessful candidates with a civil rights record. Erskine Holmes of the NILP got 29 per cent of the poll in Belfast Ballynafeigh, Sheelagh Murnaghan of the Liberal Party got 14.8 per cent in North Down and another Liberal, Claude Wilton, got 35.1 per cent in City of Londonderry. Paul Arthur comments: 'There is no strong evidence to suggest that [the PD] persuaded people to vote across the traditional divide.'[41] A more comprehensive analysis shows that in contests in Unionist-held seats they secured 'no more than a rather modest turn-out of voters'. In the Nationalist seat of South Fermanagh, PD got the support of 'dissident Catholics rather than Protestants'. Bernadette Devlin in South Londonderry achieved the best result in a Unionist-held seat, with 38.7 per cent of the poll, but this was almost the same as the Nationalist candidate who had fought the seat in the 1965 general election. In South Down, which included Newry, 'the performance can best be comprehended less as a People's Democracy achievement than as general Catholic support for a civil rights candidate'.[42]

On the day before the election Neil Blaney, Minister for Agriculture in the Dublin government, was presiding over a convention of the Fianna Fáil party in Cahir, County Tipperary. He departed from the prepared text of his speech in order to declare that the election in the north was about Irish unity and he urged 'Irish' voters not to support Unionist candidates. This was highly embarrassing for the Taoiseach, Jack Lynch, who was seated on the platform. It was part of an internecine war within the cabinet over northern policy which had begun in November 1968 when Blaney had made an uncompromising anti-partitionist speech, inspired by the events in Derry a month earlier. Together with statements by the Minister for Local Government, Kevin Boland, these constituted a challenge to Lynch's policy of not aggravating the situation in the north by public displays of traditional nationalist irredentism.

For the PD it was an opportunity to bring to the fore what they regarded as an important aspect of its policies. Its election manifesto had stated that the border was 'irrelevant' to the fight for civil rights: 'Our view of the Republic is that many of our demands . . . are equally relevant in the Republic and we support those who are working for full civil rights there as elsewhere.'[43] It announced a march from Belfast to Dublin, pointing out that the tactic used by Blaney and Boland of making intransigent statements just before an election was similar to the tactics of Unionists and Nationalists in the north:

> We are not opposed to people who believe in a united Ireland . . .
> But we are opposed to Southern politicians using the Northern situation to divert attention from the failings of their own state . . .
> Objections to the undemocratic laws that obtain in the Republic – such as the prohibition on divorce, the prevention of the sale of

contraceptives, the special constitutional position of the Catholic Church and the anti-strike legislation – does not come only from Unionists in the North but from an increasing number of all those interested in civil rights who are seeking a democratic society in their own situation.[44]

The march was a fiasco; the fact that the PD apparently could not distinguish between provisions of the Irish Republic's constitution and policies of the Fianna Fáil government was evidence of a rich potential for mutual misunderstanding. The most notorious incident was Cyril Toman's attempt to have two books seized by customs at the border. This was used by some newspapers to trivialise the whole event. Southern left-wingers saw it as a crude attempt to raise matters which they were obliged to treat with delicacy and the affair highlighted the PD's capacity to adopt simplistic solutions for complex political problems. By marching to Dublin it hoped to answer Unionist accusations that the civil rights movement was not concerned about the undue influence of the Catholic Church in the south and to show that the PD's commitment to radical change knew no boundaries. But co-ordination with its southern allies was poor and the demonstration in Dublin was marred by a very public split and by bitter recriminations afterwards. Instead of encouraging the emergence of a civil rights movement in the south and allaying the fears of northern Protestants, the PD blundered into a situation which it did not understand and was made to look foolish. Despite this, however, it had now established itself as an important component of the civil rights movement in the north and clearly was a third force, alongside NICRA and the DCAC.

The Belfast–Derry march had been undertaken against the wishes and advice of the two other main civil rights organisations but both had made gestures of sympathy. NICRA gave the PD £25 and the use of its banner and the DCAC organised a welcoming rally, meals and accommodation. After the attack at Burntollet they closed ranks in support of the PD and in genuine admiration of the physical and moral courage of the marchers. Patricia McCluskey, later to be a determined opponent of the PD's influence within NICRA, wrote to them on behalf of the CSJ congratulating them and telling them that 'your heroism and your bearing have added a new dimension to our considerable estimate of your qualities. I can tell you that we older people regard you with more admiration and respect than perhaps you think us capable of. We are all at one with you in your endeavours'.[45]

The march to Derry, at a time when NICRA had called a truce, did not imply as profound a difference between it and the PD as might be supposed. NICRA had come to a narrowly tactical decision, based on the situation in November and December 1968. One of its leading radicals, Frank Gogarty, made it clear that they had been 'blackmailed off the streets' by loyalist intimidation and police repression. But they 'would not remain off the streets forever'. The Government would have to give them a 'definite timetable of reform' or they would go back to the streets 'and protest louder than ever'.[46] NICRA was also being obliged to elaborate and extend its demands by changes in the political situation. O'Neill's promises of concessions on the franchise and housing, the abolition of Londonderry Corporation and his public-relations successes, together with the emergence of strong anti-O'Neill forces within the Unionist Party, created a more complex political situation. It was no longer a simple confrontation between the civil rights movement and an intransigent and insensitive government. NICRA was not prepared to accept O'Neill's promises and it wanted to keep up the momentum of its campaign. This made it necessary to make more radical demands and to enter qualifying clauses on its former simple and clear-cut aims. A NICRA circular pointed out that

the shortage of jobs and houses creates the situation that discrimination flourishes in, and we expect both the Stormont and Westminster Governments to make funds available for a crash house-building programme. In areas of high unemployment the Government should start local industries as they started the Forestry Commission.[47]

It also called for trade-union law to be brought into line with British law, for the disbandment of the B Specials and for the RUC to cease carrying revolvers. It had, in other words, adopted a number of demands which were also those of the PD. In addition both organisations were hostile to the proposed Public Order Bill. This made it necessary to give longer notice of parades and banned counter-demonstrations, sit-downs and the occupation of buildings. Since the focus of NICRA and the PD was swinging from marches to civil disobedience, they saw the bill as aimed directly at them. It became the central issue around which they agitated.

NICRA called a meeting in Toomebridge, County Antrim, on 16 January 1969 to discuss better co-ordination with the DCAC and the PD. It was not a great success; only one representative came from Derry and the PD delegates could not agree to anything, since they would have to report back to a mass meeting. A second meeting, ten days later, was more successful and it resulted in Michael Farrell and Kevin Boyle being co-opted onto the NICRA executive. Subsequently they were elected to that body at the association's annual general meeting in February, which was its first since becoming a mass movement, and it elected a decidedly more radical executive and adopted a more radical set of policies. In effect the PD and NICRA had reached a measure of political and strategic agreement.

The honeymoon did not last long; NICRA had caught up with the PD's shift to the left but the PD was racing leftwards faster than most people on the NICRA executive. The PD catalysed differences within the larger organisation and aroused suspicions of collusion and manipulation. Another irritant was the fact that the PD had ceased to be a mainly university-based body. During the election campaign many PD members had returned home and had found a new commitment to their local areas. Branches were set up in Newry, Armagh, Enniskillen and Cromac in Belfast.[48] This caused friction since it meant that the PD was organising in direct competition with NICRA and it also hastened the PD's leftward drift. Since it was no longer a purely student body and was competing for the same supporters as NICRA, it emphasised the characteristics which distinguished it most clearly from the association – its greater militancy and radicalism.

Kevin Boyle made the point, in a letter to Richard Rose in 1971, that

> those of us who had influence pushed the protest out of the University precincts. It was not difficult . . . because the students were so close to the society outside. Queen's is largely a dormitory university, the 'Revolution through the Vice Chancellor' theme appropriate to a student population isolated from society did not apply.[49]

However, it is not precisely true to say that the PD deserted the university. A group of PD activists continued as an active left-wing current within the Students' Union but during 1969 it tended to cut its links with the rest of the PD. Its experience, however, illustrates why the majority drifted away from student politics.

The SRC statutory meeting of 27 November 1969, at which various officers and sub-committees were elected, showed that the PD was the largest organised left force. When it gave its support to an independent left-winger for the post of international relations secretary, the candidate won with a handsome majority. Together with independent left-wingers, it took control of the disciplinary committee, which was important because of pending action against one of its members. But it failed by narrow margins to win three other key posts. The PD had submitted a petition calling for a ban on the holding of a closed meeting by the Conservative and Unionist Association; this was rejected by the executive's committee as unconstitutional. A motion calling for the dissolution of the SRC to make way for a smaller committee, with decisions taken by general meetings, was withdrawn. The PD was, therefore, an effective but far from dominant force and progress could only have been made through long-drawn-out, detailed work within the institutions of the Students' Union – not an attractive prospect when dramatic events were taking place outside. In any case the situation within the university was becoming more difficult and complex as the student body was polarised – the November 1969 meeting granted recognition to two new extreme right-wing societies, the Monday Club and The Honourable the Royalist Society, and a National Front supporter was elected to one of the committees.

The PD's increasing militancy was out of tune with the underlying attitudes of a majority of students. Up until October 1968 the moderate left had been on an ascending curve and students endorsed it because it advocated reconciliation and offered reasonableness and tolerance in place of intransigence. It was, in other words, at one end of a spectrum that ran from moderate to extreme, not one running from left to right. In the eyes of most students the PD was placing itself, along with Paisley and Craig, at the immoderate end of that spectrum. The PD was now becoming vulnerable to a challenge from any group which chose to try to mobilise the 'moderate' majority against the 'extremists'.

In November, after the events at the O'Neill prize-giving, the

SRC passed a resolution rapping the RSSF over the knuckles. This was probably unfair, since the RSSF was not alone in mobbing O'Neill's car, but it was an easy target. It testified to its own isolation in its news-sheet *Detonator*, with a spoof letter from 'about 5,000 slobbering students' complaining about 'troublemakers' who were giving students a bad name:

> We are at University because we are clever boys and girls who have passed EXAMINATIONS. We have done this because mummy and daddy and teacher and the church and the ministry of education said we should . . . Why don't you all get your hair cut or go to Russia with Red Ali and all your mates and let us get on with our vital studies?

This was a caricature of the attitude of a large proportion of QUB students but there was a core of truth to it. Although the first march, in October 1968, had mobilised an impressive number of students, Jeremy Comerford points out that 'probably as many as 2,000 to 3,000 students remained passive and kept well away from the Union on the Wednesday afternoon of the march'.[50]

At the beginning of the new academic year, 30 September 1969, Rory McShane, the Students' Union president, together with the vice-chancellor, Dr Arthur Vick, issued a joint statement. This referred to a resolution passed by a general meeting of some two thousand students on 22 April that year which had expressed concern at the growing civil unrest and went on: 'We hereby resolve never to allow religious differences to divide us. We call upon all students to refrain from any militant activity in the present situation.'[51] In the light of this, student and staff representatives, along with the university authorities, had agreed to restrict attendance at all political meetings in the Students' Union to enrolled students and staff. The Labour Group's news-sheet *Defamator* fulminated against McShane, one of its own members, as a 'spineless self-seeker', but the ban was never effectively challenged. Students were turning against militancy as something which challenged the delicate non-sectarian consensus within the university and were opting to shelter from the storm which was gathering outside.

The PD had broken its links with the majority of students because it had become radicalised through its experiences and no longer accepted the moderate consensus. It shifted to the left through the election campaign, through competition with other civil rights organisations, through moving out of the university, but also by losing members. Each of these phases saw a significant loss of support as groups and individuals who could not go along with the new departure ceased to be involved. There was a process of self-selection through which only those PD supporters who wanted to go on participated in the movement and force of circumstances made it necessary for them to become more militant and more explicitly left-wing. Also, as numbers fell, Michael Farrell's influence grew; his predominance was also reinforced by defections on the left, from those who disagreed with his fundamentally Leninist approach, and who

> were disaffected by the whole notion of fighting a parliamentary election . . . this faction consisted of . . . members from Republican backgrounds, together with a few Republicans with Anarchist leanings, whose natural sentiments, in accordance with Sinn Féin tradition, were to turn their backs . . . on the constitutional process.[52]

The decision to march to Derry illustrates another reason for the transition. It was taken by a smaller, less-publicised and less-representative meeting, following one at which the idea had been rejected. The PD radicals were accused of undemocratic obstructive tactics by the Conservative and Unionist Association. Given the open structure of the PD and the nature of its decision-making machinery, it was quite simple for any organised group to dominate particular meetings and entirely legitimate for them to do so. No rules would be broken because there were no rules. When serious differences arose, therefore, the result was paralysis and anyone who actually wanted to do something would have to indulge in manipulation. The consequence was that the mass movement evaporated and the name 'People's Democracy' became the property of whoever had the energy and commitment to sit it out until everyone else had departed, leaving them in possession.

The PD was one component of a broader movement and its political strategy was defined in relation to that broader movement, so that it cannot be treated as an entirely independent entity. By the spring of 1969 it was working within the civil rights movement as an *oppositional* grouping which, in some respects, was similar to a far-left entryist grouping within the British, Irish or Northern Ireland Labour parties. This trait can be seen at the very beginnings of the civil rights movement. It is well illustrated by Eamonn McCann's letter to Michael Farrell following the first meeting between the DHAC and NICRA to plan the 5 October march in Derry. Referring to the second meeting McCann said:

> The issue of bans and proscriptions should be pushed hard next Saturday . . . Moreover the police are more than likely to ban the march. [Betty] Sinclair adopted a 'cross that bridge when we come to it' attitude, which means she wants the back door left open for a sell out. I think one would have to push for a 'we are marching and that's that' position . . . It is necessary to introduce Socialist politics at the outset or we will be swamped by bums, opportunists and demagogues. The Labour right is 'walking into it' by so far saying that they will have nothing to do with the event, it being sectarian etc . . . I'm not going to push them very hard on this as I see no reason to enable them to avoid being exposed as the spineless bastards they are, and I'll do the exposing *after* the event.

There are two important points about this passage. First, it shows that McCann was far more concerned about a potential conflict with the right wing in the NILP and the moderates in NICRA than he was about a conflict with the state. Second, the term 'bans and proscriptions' was a ritual phrase used by Trotskyist entryists in the British Labour Party in the 1960s to refer to attempts by the party leadership to control far-left influence. These two points should be borne in mind when considering the influence of Trotskyism on some of the key leaders of the PD.

In 1939, at the outbreak of World War II, some British Trotskyists sought refuge from conscription in Ireland. Most settled in Dublin, where they achieved some influence within the Irish Labour Party and the republican movement. A group was started in Belfast, which had some success, but rapidly fell apart, although some former supporters joined Harry Diamond's Socialist Republicans which was later absorbed into Gerry Fitt's RLP.[53] There was a brief resurgence after the war but by the late 1950s Trotskyism in Ireland had died out. However, at the April 1965 conference of the NILP the guest speaker, Bessie Braddock MP, attacked Trotskyist influence on the NILP's youth organisation, the

Young Socialists. Following this, some supporters of the British Trotskyist group, the Socialist Labour League, were expelled and the Young Socialists were disbanded. Some of the left-wing members of the QUB Labour Group, who were later to be leaders of the PD, supported the Socialist Labour League against expulsion but they were not attracted to that particular brand of Trotskyism. By Easter 1965 they had made contact with another variety in the shape of the Irish Workers' Group (IWG).

William Craig referred to the IWG in his statement to the Stormont House of Commons on the events in Derry on 5 October 1968. He said that it was a 'revolutionary socialist group which aims to mobilise the Irish section of the international working class to overthrow the existing Irish bourgeois states, destroy all remaining imperialist organs of control and establish an all-Ireland Socialist Workers' Republic'.[54] This was a direct quotation from the statement of principles which appeared in the IWG's theoretical journal, the *Workers' Republic*, no. 20, Winter 1967/8. Craig's possession of a copy of this duplicated publication was a tribute to the diligence of the RUC Special Branch but more to the point, perhaps, might have been an investigation of whether the IWG was actually capable of achieving any of these grandiose aims. Craig named 'Gerard Richard Lawless . . . a former member of the IRA who was interned by the Government of the Irish Republic in 1957' as the leader of the IWG. Lawless, a Dublin-born electrician, had become involved in republicanism when very young and was one of the leaders of a Dublin faction of the IRA which broke away to join Saor Uladh (free Ulster), the group which initiated the 1956–62 IRA campaign. He was interned in the military prison at the Curragh, from which he was released following his appeal to the European Court of Human Rights – the first case ever considered by the organisation. He moved to London where he had a brief involvement with the Communist Party of Great Britain, then with the Socialist Labour League. In 1963 he helped to form the Irish Communist Group, an amalgam of Trotskyists and other left-wing Marxists. The organisation rapidly split and the Trotskyists around Lawless became the IWG. The IWG had groups of supporters in Ireland, mainly in Dublin, but was principally a London-based organisation.

Eamonn McCann first met Lawless on the 1965 Aldermaston

March. With the practical skills suitable to an IRA quartermaster, Lawless had known that an operation which involved marching over a weekend required material back-up. He appeared on the march not only with Marxist literature but also with sandwiches and an offer of accommodation in London after the march. As a result of this contact, Lawless visited Belfast and addressed a meeting at QUB. An IWG branch was set up, based in Queen's; according to a former member, Rory McShane, this never had more than seven members.[55]

McCann moved to London and became editor of the IWG newspaper, the *Irish Militant*.[56] Both he and Lawless had a natural flair for journalism and the paper was almost alone among extreme left-wing newspapers of the time in actually breaking stories rather than simply interpreting events from a 'correct' ideological standpoint. The first issue was brought out in April 1966 for the fiftieth anniversary of the Easter Rising and it is worth quoting from McCann's comments on the event, to give a flavour of the newspaper:

> Ireland is in an ecstasy of remembered glory. The hands of every poet, priest and politician are raised in valediction . . . Another whited sepulchre is being erected to the men of 1916. Presiding over it all will be the last surviving commander of the rising, Eamon de Valera, the old Fagin of the political pickpockets. But he will only be a decoration. Mr Lemass is the man who will lead the nation in its homage . . . He will tell of Ireland and its history and glory, of gentlemen and heroes; of Caitlin ni Houlihan Free and unfettered.
>
> But the beautiful legendary Caitlin ni Houlihan was a degenerated whore by the time political pimps like Sean Lemass had dragged her screaming into the murky territory where profit is the only law giver. The Republic of Pearse and Connolly does not exist. The miserable miscarriage of a republic which the back street abortionists in Leinster House have procured represents the triumph of Toryism, not the victory of the revolution.

The IWG was republican in the sense that it identified with the radical tradition of the United Irishmen, the Fenians and the Easter rising. Like the Communist Party in Ireland, it sought justification for a socialist revolution in the double failure of the national revolution of 1918–21 to achieve the full social emancipation for which James Connolly had stood and to wrest the whole of the island from British rule. But the IWG inserted a further layer of betrayal – that of the Communist Party which had participated in the 'degeneration' of the Comintern under Stalin and which wanted to limit the national revolution to those demands which were acceptable to the 'national bourgeoisie'. Since the shift to the left that was taking place within the republican movement was a result of influence by 'Stalinists', the IWG rejected this too, comparing it with earlier republican sorties into constitutional politics, such as Fianna Fáil and Clann na Poblachta.

The IWG had broken up by the end of 1968 as the result of a bitter factional dispute centred on London. But the Belfast members had already dropped out; in fact just a year after the establishment of the branch, Lawless was polemicising against his erstwhile disciples for their 'ultra-left . . . impetuous mistake' in thinking that the working class could 'by-pass the struggle against British imperialism in Ireland'.[57] This referred to IWG members in Belfast such as Cyril Toman, Tony McFarlane and Michael Farrell, who were opposed to giving much emphasis to the 'national question'. Of these, Farrell was to become the most important political thinker and strategist in the PD.

Farrell was from Magherafelt, County Derry. At Queen's he had become deeply involved in the Labour Group and the NILP and had successfully promoted the establishment of an Irish Association of Labour Students' Organisations. He also supported the establishment of a Council of Labour in Ireland, embracing the Irish Labour Party, the NILP and the RLP. Such links across the border were not so much an anti-partitionist gesture by Farrell as an assertion of the common interests of workers north and south against the Tories of the Orange and Green varieties. His position was encapsulated in a speech at James Connolly's grave in 1966: 'Fifty years after Connolly's death his dream of an Irish Workers' Republic has still to be achieved. Only the united action of working-class people North and South, Catholic and Protestant, in a single Labour and Trade Union Movement can achieve Connolly's aim.'[58]

Farrell saw Gerry Fitt's election to Westminster in 1966 as 'the most important development in Belfast for many years'. The working-class electors of 'Belfast's most sectarian constituency [west Belfast]' had 'at last realised that their Unionist masters are

the common enemy of Protestant and Catholic alike'. He emphasised the importance of the fact that nine thousand former NILP
votes had gone to Fitt, while RLP voters in Dock had supported the
NILP candidate:

> It now seems clear that the Labour unity which the left wing in the
> North has always urged will soon be forced upon a reluctant
> leadership by the superior consciousness of the working class . . .
> The lesson of the general election is clear; in the city Unionism is
> losing its grip . . . and soon Catholic and Protestant will unite to
> throw off their masters. In the country the discontent of the small
> farmers and the growth of the co-operative movement is sounding
> the death-knell of old-guard Nationalism and Republicanism.
> When city and country join hands together then Terence O'Neill
> will need more than public school liberalism to salvage his political
> career.[59]

The IWG was not the only influence on Farrell. At international
student conferences he came in contact with Maoists and he was
influenced by the radical wing of the Black civil rights movement in
the United States, especially the Student Non-Violent Co-
ordinating Committee. He was particularly impressed by a pamphlet written by an American Trotskyist, George Breitman, *How a
Minority Can Change Society*. Breitman was an important popula-
riser of the ideas of Malcolm X and of Black power. His pamphlet,
first published in 1964, contained much that was apposite to
Northern Ireland:

> What a minority can do depends on whether or not it is oppressed
> and exploited because of some minority trait or feature, is separated
> out by society for special inferior status, is denied equal treatment,
> opportunity and rights; whether or not it is at the bottom of the
> social ladder so that when it rises it shakes the whole structure;
> whether or not it is . . . part of the working class, and yet at the same
> time is denied the full benefits of membership in that class; . . .
> whether or not it realises that it has never made any gains except by
> fighting for them . . . whether or not it is developing a militant and
> radical consciousness that can motivate and spark sustained, auda-
> cious and independent struggle.[60]

Breitman went on to stress the possibility of independent action by
Blacks in the United States giving a lead to other oppressed groups,

dividing the majority and 'making the system so inconvenient and expensive that white people will be forced to ask themselves whether continued discrimination is worthwhile'. The key concept, one which was particularly stressed by the American Trotskyists, was of *mobilising* oppressed groups as a means of radicalising society and developing revolutionary consciousness not only among such minority groups but also within the working class as a whole.

Farrell and his associates took over the Young Socialists when the NILP reorganised them following the expulsion of the Socialist Labour League. However, they found that there were people with whom they could work who would not join a group linked to the NILP, so they organised an umbrella group called the Young Socialist Alliance (YSA)[61] which embraced the members of the Young Socialists and a handful of individuals from the Liberal Party, the NDP and the RLP, and this became the main vehicle through which they worked. Farrell was later to claim:

> The people who were batoned in Derry on October 5th and who were involved in the subsequent formation of the PD were mainly members of the Young Socialist Alliance. They travelled to Derry together as the Young Socialist Alliance, which at that time was about 30 or 40 strong and consisted of students and recent graduates of Queen's and they were responsible for the subsequent protest in Belfast. So right from the start the Young Socialist Alliance was the core of the People's Democracy.[62]

This claim should be treated with caution. It is clear from its context that Farrell made it at a time when he was trying to remould the PD into something which more closely resembled the YSA. The reference to the alliance as a 'core' of the PD was seized on by Unionist critics as evidence of far-left manipulation. But the most decisive shift to the left in the PD came *after* the YSA had been disbanded following the Belfast–Derry march and was produced very largely by circumstances. For 'YSA core' one should probably read 'Michael Farrell'. His political skills, his determination and the force of his personality and intellect made him the *de facto* leader of the PD. The role of the YSA, in comparison, was much less important. Bernadette Devlin testified that Farrell had 'a tremendous impact on the PD by his consistent explanations of the best method of attacking the evils of society'.[63] Kevin Boyle spoke of his 'range, his foresight, his capacity to anticipate results and to endure'.[64]

The YSA was not the only tendency or grouping within the early PD. There was also the RSSF, a British organisation set up in London in June 1968 in response to the May–June events in Paris. A group of QUB students went to London for the big Vietnam solidarity march of 27 October 1968; they visited the London School of Economics, which was occupied by students to provide a base to service the demonstration, and came in contact with the RSSF. On returning to Belfast they set up an RSSF group at Queen's. The RSSF was distinguished from the YSA by being younger and, as Farrell put it, 'even more ultra-left'. Only a small number of RSSF members took part in the early PD demonstrations and the group was criticised by PD leaders as 'armchair socialists' content to discuss revolutionary theory in the Students' Union coffee bar. The RSSF specialised in scandalising everyone else. Its news-sheet *Detonator* had headlines like 'Students Spit on Vick!' (a reference to the vice-chancellor) and 'Disembowel Enoch Powell!' This, of course, produced precisely the apoplectic rage among respectable citizens for which the federation had hoped, although behind its superficial irresponsibility the publication had serious points to make about academic freedom and student rights and conditions. But it did not succeed in getting these points across to its fellow students because its approach was so grossly ill-judged. The RSSF was not a serious threat to the stability of Northern Ireland.

Another tendency was the anarchists, which consisted of about two individuals whose contribution was to encourage the spontaneity and disorganised character of the early PD. They were less important than a fourth, more nebulous tendency around Kevin Boyle and Bernadette Devlin, who might be called, using Boyle's term, 'the innocents', meaning that they had no previously formed political commitment.

Boyle was a Newry Catholic who had studied law at Queen's and criminology at Cambridge. At Queen's he had come to know Farrell, Toman, McCann and some of the others, but he had not shared their interest in left-wing politics. He was a junior lecturer in law at Queen's when the Republican Club affair blew up. He and another lecturer had written a letter on the implications for civil liberties, which was published in the press, earning them a mild rap over the knuckles. He had not been in Derry on 5 October but his shock at what had happened led him to become involved in the PD, a little against his better judgement, and to get himself elected on to the Faceless Committee. He had no doctrinaire beliefs and had an instinct for public relations and for keeping the PD together; this made him a good foil for Farrell. As Boyle described it:

> Much of the time Bernadette and I tried to hold back the left from galloping, because we thought that they would lose too many of the students who didn't know where they were going . . . A dynamic policy was injected from Michael Farrell and was moderated by us, by being explained. And that relationship with Farrell was one I kept for a long time.[65]

Bernadette Devlin's role in the early PD tends to be obscured by her later career. It was, of course, a remarkable one and it was remarkable not only for the string of accidents which led to her becoming the extreme left MP for a rural constituency but also for her personal integrity and toughness of character, which meant that she was not overwhelmed or absorbed by the system she had gone to Westminster to fight. She personified an important aspect of the early PD; like the other 'innocents', she was swept along by events and had to construct a rough-and-ready ideological framework as she went. Like many of her generation and background, she combined a deep antipathy for unionism with a distaste for traditional nationalism. Her biases were towards a non-denominational republicanism and she was more influenced than she realised by the anti-partitionist propaganda which was part of her young environment. Farrell, McCann and Toman provided a set of explanations for what was happening and they had the ability to formulate and argue for a strategy. Devlin and the others seized on their ideas as fitting the needs of the moment but in her case she made no effort to grasp the underlying philosophical and methodological positions on which they were based. She spouted Marxist phrases but she was never a Marxist.

Discussing these tendencies as if they were separate groups is useful in identifying their distinctive characteristics, but it is somewhat artificial. They generally agreed about what was to be done and the more abstract points of political theory were matters for late-night discussion. An anarchist writer has provided what is probably the best description of how these left-wing influences worked:

> The chief architects of this politicising of the movement were Michael Farrell, Eamonn McCann and Cyril Toman, who were responsible for developing the lines of socialist thought à la Marx and Connolly, and John McGuffin who ensured that these lines should not be too narrowly drawn and that the libertarian idealism of the early PD should not be lost . . . Marx and Connolly were read and referred to, but not treated in the hushed reverence of holy icons . . . Even old 'Trotters' was spoken of with complete irreverence. Stalin occupied a place close to Sir Edward Carson, Sir James Craig, William of Orange and William Craig.[66]

All this was happening in a period when revolutionary student movements were appearing all over the world and an international network of revolutionary militants was exchanging ideas and information. It was natural for observers to see the PD as part of this movement. We have it on the authority of a writer in the prestigious French radical journal *Les Temps Modernes* that *'la PD d'alors ressemblait fort au Mouvement 22 Mars'*.[67] The 22 March Movement was a loose coalition of left-wing student groups which was at the centre of the events in Paris in May and June 1968. Like the PD, it was an alliance of Trotskyists, libertarians and independent leftists:

> The militants of the 22 March refused to be integrated into organisational structures, however informal or democratic. They wanted to exist only as an informal group, perpetually inventing forms of action . . . the group would meet only to decide on a course of action and only those in favour of these actions would attend. The actions were to be *exemplary*, that is, they were to have the character of political escalation designed to induce others to follow their example.[68]

The influence on the PD of revolutionary movements is evident but it is not difficult to account for. Unionists tended to suggest that it occurred because of some kind of conspiracy; such an assumption does not accord with the evidence. Belfast, after all, was one step beyond London, the farthest outreach of the revolutionary network. It was not until January 1969 that Tariq Ali arrived in Belfast for a brief visit to speak at a debate at Queen's. He bestowed his apostolic blessing on the civil rights movement on behalf of Marx, Engels, Lenin, Trotsky, Che Guevara and James Connolly, but he did not offer any tactical or strategic advice. Of more practical help was the single member of the London Poster Workshop who arrived in Derry in August 1969 with equipment and expertise which she put to good effect.

The fact that in August 1969 barricades were thrown up in Derry and Belfast and were defended with petrol bombs can give a misleading impression. In Northern Ireland, as in Paris, barricades and petrol bombs were used to repulse a police incursion into a particular area. But in Northern Ireland the social composition of those behind the barricades and their historical sense of territoriality were quite different. In any case it was not the PD which put up the barricades and its function in the barricaded areas was not to defend them – there were other, more experienced hands. The PD's role was as propagandists: writers, illegal broadcasters and leaflet distributors. If some of the methods used in Paris were also used in Belfast and Derry the explanation is not difficult to find – the source of information was sitting in the corner of every living room in the Bogside and the Falls. Some kinds of technical information were not available over television and Eamonn McCann notes that the Bogsiders were indebted to the students of Paris for methods of countering the effects of CS gas. The information, he says, came via the pages of Tariq Ali's newspaper the *Red Mole*.[69] This was merely a special case of the role of the media in transmitting information about revolutionary movements elsewhere. The movements themselves did very little to influence events in Northern Ireland. The most authoritative work on British Trotskyism notes that 'the far left was as unprepared as any other section of the British political spectrum for the eruption of generalised political struggles in Northern Ireland in 1969'[70] – a verdict which is borne out by the evidence of two far left writers, Tariq Ali and Teresa Hayter.[71]

The strategic and tactical problems confronting the PD in the second half of 1969 are dealt with in the only substantial piece of documentary evidence about the organisation in this period: the interview which appeared in *New Left Review*, no. 55, May–June 1969. This was quoted extensively by Unionists who wanted to present the PD as a ruthless revolutionary conspiracy. What the interview actually shows is the lack of coherence, realism, and above all unity, of the five participants. The interview took place in a hotel in Derry in the spring of 1969. It was conducted by Anthony Barnett of *New Left Review* and he stresses the difficulty he had in getting the PD members together for it. The published text does not make it clear that Bernadette Devlin was only there for part of the time and that people were constantly coming and going. The interview, he says, 'gives a sense of calm, strategic consideration which is due to good editing'.[72]

Barnett was struck by the fact that Farrell 'spoke in paragraphs', which made his contribution especially clear and authoritative. And it is Farrell's statements which require the closest scrutiny. Early in the interview he said:

> But the PD is not just part of the civil rights movement, it is a revolutionary assembly. Its formation was considerably influenced by the Sorbonne Assembly and by concepts of libertarianism as well as socialism. It has adopted a very democratic type of structure; there is no formal membership and all meetings are open. At the moment this structure is not working very satisfactorily, and I think it will be necessary . . . to find a way of introducing a little more co-ordination. I had hoped that the PD would realise the necessity of taking a stand on class issues and would therefore transform itself into a broadly socialist body . . . I no longer think that this will happen of its own accord. There have recently been some sharp disagreements within the PD and differences have arisen between socialists and an alliance of anarchists and right-wingers.[73]

Two Unionist critics of the PD, William Stratton Mills and Robin Bailie, quoted the first two sentences to prove that the PD was a revolutionary movement like that in Paris, but the full quote makes it clear that Farrell actually was critical of the Sorbonne aspects of the PD and had tolerated rather than encouraged them. He now wanted the PD to move towards a more formal type of structure and a politics which more closely resembled the old YSA. He proceeded to outline his strategic objectives. They had taken part in the civil rights movement in order to radicalise the Catholic working class and to radicalise the civil rights demands themselves (a clear reference to the strategy outlined in Breitman). They should now go on to 'complete the ideological development of the Catholic working class' and to 'develop concrete agitational work over housing and jobs to show the class interests of both Catholics and Protestants'. This was why it was necessary for the PD to become 'an organisation capable of carrying out this agitational work'.[74]

Eamonn McCann took a starkly different approach; they had failed to get their view across that Catholics were being exploited because they were workers, not because of their religion and this was because they had failed to fight within the civil rights movement. They had been scared of frightening off their mass audience: 'We thought we had to keep these people, bring them along, educate and radicalise them. It was a lot of pompous nonsense and we failed absolutely to change the consciousness of people. The consciousness of the people who are fighting in the streets at the moment is sectarian and bigoted.'[75] McCann, to all intents and purposes, had broken with the very idea of a civil rights movement. As early as November 1968, speaking at the New University of Ulster in Coleraine, he had pointed out the 'inherent disadvantages' of civil rights as a 'central co-ordinating issue for a political movement'.[76] It served as a cloak for 'reactionary movements' like the Nationalist Party and pitched demands for reform at the lowest common denominator. To maintain unity, socialists had to 'suspend any demands which would alienate [those] who are willing to campaign for social justice in electoral arrangements and housing and job allocation but are totally opposed to any meaningful redistribution of wealth and income'.[77]

Farrell and Toman thought that McCann was too much influenced by conditions in Derry. While they accepted that there was a good deal of sectarianism among Catholics who had been mobilised by the civil rights movement, they claimed that the PD had, to a certain extent, got across a realisation of their common interests with Protestant workers. But, Farrell said, 'there is now a more radicalised Catholic working class whilst the Protestant proletariat is still as remote and inert as ever'. Toman went somewhat further by suggesting that 'in future we must use the enthusiasm of the Catholic workers to get across to the Protestant working class as well'.

Bernadette Devlin, who had just been elected to Westminster, defended herself against accusations of having accommodated to traditional nationalism and of having given a platform to Nationalist MPs. She pointed out that in her victory speech she had told her supporters that they were wrong to think that she could do anything for them in the House of Commons. She anticipated a conflict with the middle-class nationalists among her supporters:

> I have no doubt that within a year these people will do their best to destroy me and may possibly succeed. Within a year we will have sorted out the Catholics who voted for us on a purely Catholic basis and we will still have the support of the Protestants who supported us on a socialist basis, therefore we will have established the normal situation of the socialists supporting us and the non-socialists pulling out.[78]

Far from being a united revolutionary force with a coherent strategy, the PD and the other extreme left leaders were just beginning to face up to the implications of the situation which they had helped to bring about. They had become more acutely aware of the reality of a divided working class and of the serious danger posed by the alienation and hostility of the Protestant workers. They agreed that a bridge had to be thrown across the sectarian chasm. They agreed that this bridge had to be constructed of agitation on social and economic issues. They agreed that communication with Protestant workers would be impossible if they were tainted by traditional middle-class nationalism. They were agreed, therefore, that there had to be a struggle against that wing of the civil rights movement. But they were divided over tactics. Farrell and Toman considered that they should work within NICRA to move it towards taking up the kind of social and economic issues which might win over Protestant workers. McCann, supported by the anarchists in the PD, wanted to break completely with NICRA. He was going to build up the left in the Derry branch of the NILP and use that as a base from which to launch attacks on the Government, the Unionist Party, the Nationalist Party, the DCAC and the middle-class elements of NICRA. He did not publicly attack his former comrades in the PD but he blocked their attempts to set up a branch in Derry and he set up a Young Socialists branch which fulfilled the functions of PD branches elsewhere. Bernadette Devlin was going to use her position as an MP to promote left-wing causes on both sides of the Irish Sea. She drifted apart from Farrell and the others because they thought that she should make the effort to seek advice from them, and she was alienated by their critical attitude and thought they should make the effort to come to her to give advice.

From the point of view of the rest of the civil rights movement, however, these tactical differences were of relatively minor significance. What all of the participants in the interview were agreed on was that they should go back to a more intensive and determined version of the oppositional politics which had characterised the Trotskyists in the IWG and the YSA. This meant launching a bitter, divisive struggle within and *against* the civil rights movement itself.

It was Eamonn McCann who made the running in developing the left-wing critique of the civil rights movement. Speaking to the Belfast Young Socialists in November 1968, he said: 'The struggle for civil rights has a clearly defined class content. Only workers have no local government vote. The upper classes of whatever religion do not suffer from bad housing, unemployment and low wages.' The aims of the civil rights movement, he claimed, could not be achieved 'without a change in the relationship between classes'. He rejected unity which involved subsuming different class interests under a slogan like 'one man, one vote', which served 'only to keep in check the demands and activities of those most denied social and civil rights'. He claimed that only an approach based on class demands could avoid sectarian conflict. The Protestants who had attacked the PD at Burntollet and in Derry 'are themselves deprived of the very things the marchers were demanding. Indeed I would argue that it is lack of privilege which underlies their viciousness'.[79] It was necessary for the civil rights movement to relate its activity to the 'day-to-day lives' of such workers. The PD argued along similar lines. The first issue of its paper *PD Voice*, published in June 1969, urged that civil rights activity be 'for demands and by methods which will unite the working people rather than divide them'. The PD's major emphasis, however, was on arguing that the civil rights movement had been mistaken in calling a truce in response to the concessions made by O'Neill and this it attributed to the influence of Green Tories within the movement. Its strategy was to push the movement to the left, attempting to open up class and political rifts within it in order to recompose it around a different leadership and strategy.

McCann was unwilling to wait for such an eventuality; by early

July 1969 he was prepared to make his differences with the civil rights movement public. He used the platform of a civil rights rally in Strabane in County Tyrone for an all-out attack. He claimed that the movement was 'making no meaningful efforts' to overcome religious differences and attacked Austin Currie's presence on the platform, criticising the anti-Unionist MPs at Stormont for accepting O'Neill's timetable for reform. Currie defended himself and his colleagues, and the chairman of the rally, Ivan Barr, dissociated the Strabane Civil Rights Committee from McCann's remarks. However, when Bernadette Devlin came to the microphone, they were subjected to an even fiercer attack. She said that she had never heard so many sectarian speeches from any platform. If the Nationalist Party was in charge at Stormont, 'the people standing here would not be the people of Strabane unemployed because they're Catholics, but the people of Strabane unemployed because they're Protestants'. If they were fighting for nothing more than equality for Catholics, the middle class would be equal and the working class would 'all be equal – at the bottom':

> I stand for honesty and this is what matters to me . . . I was elected . . . as a Unity candidate, but if you picked me for the same kind of unity as that Austin Currie stands for then I can't serve you and the sooner you get rid of me the better. I stand for Eamonn McCann's unity and let there be no mistake about it.[80]

The PD commented on the furore created by the Strabane speeches in a leaflet. It pointed out that the differences had existed for a long time and it refused to 'take sides between the personalities involved'. However, it endorsed the central critique made by McCann and Devlin:

> Those who put unity (in fact unity of all Catholics) before everything have tried to fix the civil rights demands at the lowest common denominator; the demands which pose the least threat to the status quo . . . Political differences within the movement have only been allowed to appear as a contrast between 'moderation' and 'militancy' . . . it is not as simple as that. Those who want to confine the civil rights demands to 'equal rights' for all ignore the fact that fair allocation of jobs and houses within the existing system . . . would simply mean equal shares of unemployment and bad housing for all.[81]

The leaflet proposed a programme of building government-owned factories, taking over factories closed by their owners, and control of profits and the export of capital – 'measures which cut sharply across the sanctity of private profit so dear to some civil rights supporters'. It attributed the reluctance of the civil rights movement to take up this programme to its desire for a united front between 'Green Tory slum landlord and the homeless and unemployed', which had resulted in a failure to attract Protestant support.

What was significant about this analysis was not that the PD had 'moved to the left' but that it had rejected the whole strategy of building a movement focused on the issue of discrimination against Catholics. By the end of 1969 it had reorganised itself into a small, quasi-Leninist revolutionary group with a card-carrying membership and formal organisational structures. But unlike McCann, whose break with the civil rights strategy led to a disengagement from the movement, the PD continued to work within NICRA and to try to influence it from outside. Only in early 1970, when it had completed its own transformation, did it turn outwards to direct socialist agitation. The activities of the PD helped to crystallise and to accelerate existing differences within the civil rights movement. But these divisions were not created by the PD, however much that organisation may have exacerbated them. The PD and its allies on the left had put their fingers on an important contradiction in the movement's perspectives. The mobilisation of Catholics was not leading to the emergence of a non-sectarian mass movement seeking advances for all the underprivileged in Northern Ireland; nor was it forcing reform from above through intervention by Westminster. As the events of August 1969 showed, it was leading to a re-emergence of the old animosities and the old violence. It was this which tore the civil rights movement apart.

The course of events from August 1969 has been recorded in detail in many histories of the Troubles and a recapitulation would be tedious and repetitive. There is still a gap in the literature, since no objective account has been given of the internal struggles in the civil rights movement. To have included this aspect in this book would, however, have required a major expansion in size and more time in order to elucidate all the complexities. So it will not be attempted, and we will leave the civil rights movement on the brink of its own internal crisis and caught up in the larger crisis which was sweeping away much of the superstructure of Northern Ireland. The government and parliament at Stormont, after ruling Northern Ireland for fifty years, proved incapable of withstanding the challenge of a movement which had never imagined the consequences of its actions.

CONCLUSION

In retrospect, the decision of the NICRA to turn to street demonstrations in the summer of 1968 was a fateful one. It is significant that the only member of the association's leadership to stand out vehemently against the strategy was Betty Sinclair. She was also the only one who had been continuously active in radical politics since the 1930s. She could remember when serious sectarian fighting had broken out in Belfast in the 1930s and was aware of the dangers of exacerbating communal animosities. Here the Black civil rights movement in the United States proved to be an inappropriate model. Street marches in Northern Ireland had a very definite historical and sectarian significance, with vast potential for upsetting the tacit understanding between the two communities about territorial divisions. The authorities, too, had a very strict definition, based on traditional marching routes, of what was, and was not, acceptable. The civil rights movement was perfectly sincere in its view of its marches as non-sectarian but it was a perception which was not widely shared. It was not just that many Protestants were upset and angered, but some less politically sophisticated Catholics interpreted the tactic as a signal to become more aggressive and combative towards the police and the Protestant community.

Although the Black civil rights movement in the United States had been an inspiration, strictly speaking it was not a model. There is no evidence that any of the founders or leaders of the Northern Ireland civil rights movement ever visited the Southern United States, consulted with any of the Black civil rights organisations, or even undertook a thorough study of that movement. Their information came from the media and, inevitably, their application of the lessons of the American movement was patchy and reflected their own preoccupations and experiences. There were two important parallels; the issue of discrimination itself and the resistance of a subordinate administration to principles and values long accepted by its superior government. But in a number of other ways the Black civil rights movement was an inappropriate model for Northern Ireland Catholics. The grievances of Southern Blacks were more intense and blatant than those in Northern Ireland. Adopting the style and rhetoric of the Black movement encouraged a natural tendency towards exaggeration and exacerbated communal polarisation. To outside observers it was clear that violence, and more especially the threat of violence, in the Deep South was almost entirely on the side of the white extremists and state administrations. In Northern Ireland there were fresh memories of the IRA border campaign and the possibility of renewed republican military activity had not been dispelled. Southern Blacks had important allies in liberal public opinion in the Northern states and internationally. Northern Ireland Catholics had few supporters outside the Irish Republic and the Irish diaspora. The United States Supreme Court gave Southern Blacks an effective legal channel for obtaining redress and the federal government was willing to give effect to its findings. In Northern Ireland an attempt to use the courts to enforce the anti-discrimination provisions of the Government of Ireland Act proved abortive and Westminster was unwilling to intervene in matters which had been devolved to Stormont. When legal and political channels were closed, the Northern Ireland civil rights movement took to the streets as a substitute for the constitutional battle. In the Deep South street demonstrations were used to reinforce the constitutional processes which were already moving through the courts. Another contrast was ironic – in Northern Ireland the most charismatic Christian preacher was on the opposite side. It was not just that Ian Paisley successfully mobilised Protestant resistance, but that the movement lacked a leader who combined spiritual and secular authority in the way that Paisley did. This meant that the movement could not have a leader who paralleled Martin Luther King's authority. This severely restrained the tactical flexibility of the inexperienced and divided civil rights leadership.

Why did the leadership of the civil rights movement not foresee the effects of its tactics? It did, after all, call off the demonstrations towards the end of 1968 when it was obvious that sectarianism was on the increase. Fred Heatley and Ann Hope both reveal that the tactic of marches arose out of a particular situation in Dungannon, when a local campaign for better housing linked up with a small civil liberties group looking for some way to make an impact. Bernadette Devlin's autobiography conveys something of the way in which the euphoria of that occasion gave way to righteous indignation when the marchers were excluded from the centre of town. The apparent success of the Dungannon march encouraged NICRA to agree to proposals from a group of militants in Derry that a march should be arranged for their town.

The events in Derry on 5 October 1968 boosted the movement to a new pitch. Seamus Heaney conveyed some of the feelings which prevailed among the civil rights supporters in his *Listener* article of 24 October 1968:

> The civil rights marchers who were banned from entering the walls and business centre of the city . . . represented after all the grievances of the Catholic majority; unemployment, lack of housing, discrimination of jobs and gerrymandering in electoral affairs. They were asking to be accepted as citizens of Derry also; they wanted at least the rights, too long the prerogative of the minority, to demonstrate and express themselves in public.

Heaney goes on to say that trust in O'Neill and in the new liberal spirit in Northern Ireland had been seriously threatened by Paisleyism, and that

> We were all afraid, and still are, of returning to the old Orange and Green polarisation of public life . . . But it seems now that the Catholic minority in Northern Ireland at large, if it is to retain any self-respect, will have to risk the charge of wrecking the new moderation and seek justice more vociferously. Since the cabinet have endorsed the actions of the police and still deny any notion of the injustice in a blatantly unjust situation, one can only conclude that their definition of 'improved relations' is 'the minority saying nothing to embarrass us'. 'The enemies of Ulster' – a favourite tag for extremists – must now embrace all those who march to complain about discrimination.

Heaney's mingled rage, sense of history and moral indignation evoke a special moment in the politics of Northern Ireland, when the old politics of the place had been sufficiently eroded to create hope among a new generation of self-confident young Catholics. At the same time they kept in their hearts a sense of the injustice to which their community believed it had been subjected, and a sense of history which enabled them to see the actions of the RUC, and the refusal of the Government to concede that something might be wrong, as a revival of past wrongs. But once the civil rights leadership went onto the streets at the head of a mass movement, it drew on support which was not necessarily committed to its world view. A PD supporter made a telling comment to a *Sunday Times* Insight Team reporter: 'Everyone applauds loudly when one says in a speech that we are not sectarian, but really that's because they see this as a new way of getting at the Protestants.' The civil rights leadership was not blind to the dangers but by the time they were apparent it was too late to turn back. The movement was already on the streets; the leaders were angry and their supporters were determined. They could not have turned back but they could hope to win enough concessions, quickly enough, to avoid a major confrontation. But, of course, if the grievances they were protesting about had been taken seriously by the Stormont and Westminster governments at a much earlier stage, there would have been no need to take to the streets at all.

After the events of August 1969 there was a hiatus in the development of the movement. In this period the Provisional republican movement emerged and NICRA, by now mainly influenced by Official republicans and Communists, sought to outflank it by reviving marches as a protest against internment. This strategy ended on 30 January 1972, with the deaths in Creggan on Bloody Sunday. Thereafter the Provisionals became the leaders of opposition on the streets as well as the promoters of urban guerrilla warfare. NICRA lapsed back into a role as a civil liberties body, much as its founders had originally intended. It propagandised for a Bill of Rights and took up individual cases of injustice. Its brief moment at the centre of the political stage was over and it stood on the sidelines, wringing its hands and condemning both the Provisionals and the security forces for the violence.

The civil rights movement failed as a collective, but so also did its individual components. The CSJ and the CDU succeeded in stirring much greater interest in Northern Ireland among British

Labour MPs and in giving the impression that Harold Wilson's government might intervene. This simply created hopes which could not be fulfilled on one side and fears which could not be assuaged on the other. NICRA underestimated the problems which its slight republican taint would cause and overestimated the extent to which the grievances of some disfranchised Protestants would overcome their hostility to a movement which mobilised Catholics in street demonstrations. The DCAC overestimated the time span during which it could keep control over what was, essentially, a communal upsurge of Catholics in Derry. Like NICRA, it also overestimated the likelihood of the movement succeeding quickly enough in wresting sufficient concessions from the Stormont government, or intervention from Westminster, to satisfy the appetite for change which had been aroused among Catholics. The PD underestimated the ferocity of the violence which its Belfast–Derry march would provoke and it failed to realise the extent to which the march would exacerbate communal hostilities.

So the civil rights movement failed, and even with greater tactical sophistication and better luck it is hard to see how the outcome could have been different. Nevertheless, the crisis which it precipitated transformed the context within which the grievances of Northern Ireland Catholics could be considered. The Unionist Party could never have responded adequately because, quite apart from its sheer lack of political and administrative competence, it was too close to the community which voted for it and too susceptible to communalist pressures. But when Westminster took over in 1972 it became possible to tackle the problem of discrimination through the more detached processes of bureaucratic social engineering.

In attempting to resolve the Irish land question in the 1870s and 1880s, the British government produced what Gladstone referred to as 'a litter of reports'. The same term might be applied to governmental attempts to deal with the problem of discrimination a century later. There have been ten official and officially commissioned reports since 1978, and in addition there have been regular reports by the Fair Employment Agency, the Equal Opportunities Commission, the Police Authority, and the Police Complaints Board. These official efforts have been supplemented by a mass of academic research and by investigative journalism. Much more information is now available, and more sophisticated techniques have been applied to interpreting it than was the case in the 1960s.

In response to the crisis brought on by the civil rights movement, the Northern Ireland and United Kingdom governments implemented a series of reforms. These introduced universal adult suffrage for local council elections in 1969 and proportional representation for local and European elections in 1972. A Parliamentary Commissioner for Complaints (ombudsman) was appointed in 1969 and in the same year a Commissioner for Complaints was appointed to deal with local government. The Prevention of Incitement to Hatred Act (1970) made it a criminal offence to stir up hatred on grounds of religion or race, and the act was strengthened in 1980 and 1987. A Police Authority was set up in 1970, an independent Director of Public Prosecutions in 1972 and a Police Complaints Board in 1977. The Northern Ireland Housing Executive was set up in 1971; it took responsibility for all former local authority and NIHT housing, establishing a uniform points system for housing allocation and removing the location of housing from local authority control. In 1972 local government was comprehensively reorganised, wiping away many of the small authorities which had been most associated with sectarianism and, at the same time, significantly narrowing the range of issues within the remit of elected local councils. The Fair Employment Act was passed in 1976; this outlawed discrimination on grounds of religion or politics in job allocation and it set up the Fair Employment Agency to monitor compliance with the act. The Sex Discrimination Order of 1976 prohibited discrimination on grounds of gender and set up the Equal Opportunities Commission. In 1981 the Government announced that tenders for government contracts would be dependent on possession of an Equal Opportunity Employer certificate issued under the Fair Employment Act.

These massive efforts have not succeeded in stilling complaints about discrimination, or even in clarifying completely its origins, causes and extent. They have certainly not succeeded in eliminating it, as the Standing Advisory Commission on Human Rights made clear in its 1987 report. But since 1968 the context of the discrimination problem has changed in four ways. First, there is now broad agreement within Northern Ireland that discrimination ought to be eliminated. It is worth noting that all the main political parties have endorsed the demand, first put forward by NICRA in 1970, for a Bill of Rights for Northern Ireland citizens. However, this unanimity breaks down when they are asked to endorse specific measures to deal with discrimination.

Second, it has become clear that Northern Ireland is not unique within the United Kingdom in facing a problem of inequality of opportunity. Many of the problems faced by Blacks and Asians in Britain do not differ in kind from those experienced by Northern Ireland Catholics. In both societies discrimination on grounds of race or religion is crosscut and intensified by discrimination on grounds of gender. In Britain, as in Northern Ireland, every attempt to deal with these problems reveals a further layer of complexity.

Third, the Northern Ireland problem has been internationalised. The early civil rights activists wanted to get Britain involved because they believed that Westminster would impose British standards of impartiality and fairness. This was a somewhat naïve view but, in any case, by the time Britain did intervene it was in circumstances which they had not envisaged. The intervention was not primarily in order to bring about equality of rights, but to contain civil unrest. Such measures as were taken were introduced in a situation already poisoned by violence and suspicion. It was almost inevitable that they would be too little and too late to quench the anger of Catholics. To the caution of all governments responding to popular demands was added a fear of provoking Protestant opposition and a deep-seated reluctance to get entangled in Irish affairs at all. By the time Westminster took over full control of Northern Ireland in March 1972, the British presence itself had become a problem, and the Provisional IRA had changed the terms of the debate. Discrimination shrank back in importance when compared with the problem of political violence.

Commenting on the report of the Standing Advisory Commission on Human Rights, David Richmond, writing in *Fortnight*, the Belfast monthly political periodical, in December 1987, pointed to the paradox that while the Westminster government was resisting any strengthening of the Race Relations Act for Britain, it was at the same time pursuing rigorous new measures for Northern Ireland. He suggested that the explanation lies in the success of the proponents of the MacBride Principles in the United States. These

Principles, sponsored by Irish statesman Sean MacBride, seek to bring pressure to bear on American investors in Northern Ireland not to support or trade with firms which are guilty of anti-Catholic discrimination; they are based on well-established measures to counter racial discrimination in the United States. Richmond comments:

> The critical problem for the [British] Government is that it needs to convince an American audience that it is serious about change. It is arguable that . . . earlier proposals . . . were more concerned with creating the impression of change, rather than actually bringing change about. However, politicians in the United States have first-hand experience of the problems of providing equality of opportunity. Discussions now taking place in Northern Ireland about why and how change should be brought about raise issues debated in the US for decades.

The fourth change is that since the early 1970s the civil right to life itself has been threatened by terrorist organisations. The Protestant community can, with justice, point to the way in which the activities of the IRA and the Irish National Liberation Army usurp its basic right to personal security. The fact that the Catholic community has suffered from the activities of loyalist terrorists and questionable actions by the security forces underlines, but does not weaken, the point that injustices are being perpetrated by more than one agency. (To its credit, NICRA consistently opposed republican military actions as vigorously as it did the excesses of the security forces.) This is the context which explains the British government's intensive diplomatic efforts in the United States; it is another front in the battle against republican terrorism. The other front is in the Irish Republic and it provides a further reason for taking vigorous action to deal with the problem of discrimination. Action on this issue has the added advantage that it presents fewer problems than tackling the Irish government's worries about violations of human rights by the security forces and defects in the British system of justice.

As yet there is no evidence that by internationalising the Northern Ireland problem the British government will solve it. There is not even any proof that it will be successful in its attempts to overcome discrimination. But the fact that the problem of discrimination in Northern Ireland is now seen as a crucial issue by three governments is vindication, of a sort, for the civil rights movement. The movement's vision was broader and more generous than any seen in Northern Ireland before. It inspired people who had lost faith in the possibilities of change, although it did not succeed in finding a way to bring change about. The civil rights movement is dead. It was torn apart by violence and sectarian polarisation. It cannot be revived, but it can be learned from.

While this book was being prepared for publication, Europe lurched, unexpectedly, into a new era, as country after country in Eastern Europe shook free of the ossified and repressive regimes which had been stifling them for decades. Northern Ireland is part of Europe and it will be affected by the changes now taking place throughout the Continent. This does not mean that it will be changed by some disembodied abstract force. As in Eastern Europe, it will be changed by its people. Most of the problems now coming to the fore in Europe concern precisely the issues of civil liberties and of relations between ethnic and religious communities which Northern Ireland has been trying to solve in the last twenty years. The fundamental decency of the Northern Ireland people and their great common sense will enable them to learn from the experiences of the new Europe – and also to contribute to creating that new Europe by helping others to learn from their experiences.

NOTES

Where the title of a book, article or pamphlet is not given fully, the complete reference will be found in the bibliography. In some cases collections of papers in the Public Record Office of Northern Ireland had not been fully catalogued when I consulted them and it has not been possible, therefore, to give a fuller reference than the general accession number.

ABBREVIATIONS

HC Deb.	Westminster House of Commons *Debates* (Hansard)
NIHCD	Northern Ireland House of Commons Debates
PRONI	Public Record Office of Northern Ireland
UCD	University College Dublin Archives Department

CHAPTER I

1 *Belfast Telegraph*, 31 October 1962
2 For this debate *see* NIHC 52: 702–16, 30 October 1962
3 *See* Bew, Gibbon and Patterson, 1979, pp. 63–128, for a discussion of Unionist 'populism'.
4 *Irish Weekly*, 17 February 1962
5 *Ibid.*, 29 May 1965
6 O'Neill, 1969, p. 42
7 *Irish Weekly*, 5 September 1964
8 Rea, 1966, pp. 7–8
9 Bailie, 1964, p. 15
10 McCafferty, Niall, 1966, p. 30
11 Bleakley, 1964, p. 104
12 Boulton, 1973, p. 53
13 Smethwick was a parliamentary constituency in the English Midlands made (in)famous by the victory of the Conservative candidate in the 1964 general election, after what was widely interpreted as a racialist campaign.
14 However, members of the UVF may have been partly the victims of political manipulation. Many years later, UVF leader Gusty Spence told a journalist of how 'frightening' had been reports of an IRA plot in 1966. This referred to a ludicrous scare story of the time about a planned 1916-style takeover of the main Belfast post office, combined with infiltration by republicans of, among other bodies, the Protestant churches, the Salvation Army and the Freemasons. The reports seem to have been a highly coloured interpretation of the rather more modest plans which the republicans did have, and which will be outlined in Chapter 3. Since the Ministry of Home Affairs had copies of the relevant documents, suspicion about the source of the reports must fall on it; *see* Belfrage, 1988, p. 265, for Spence's statement.
15 Nelson, 1984, p. 72
16 PRONI D 3342/A/3
17 The Matthew Plan, or the *Belfast Regional Survey and Plan* of 1963 was drawn up for the

253

Brookeborough government by Professor Sir Robert Matthew of the University of Edinburgh. It established a 'stop-line' to limit the growth of Belfast and introduced the first comprehensive urban planning seen in Northern Ireland. The Wilson Plan was commissioned by the O'Neill government and was published in 1965. Drawn up by Thomas Wilson, a distinguished economist of Northern Ireland origins, and Adam Smith, Professor of Political Economy at the University of Glasgow, it introduced regional planning and was designed to encourage growth outside the Belfast area, including the new university and the new town of Craigavon.

18 The Larne gun-running took place in February 1914, when Major Fred Crawford, aboard the *Clyde Valley*, landed 35,000 Mauser rifles and 2,500,000 rounds of ammunition obtained from Germany to arm the UVF to resist Home Rule for Ireland. The incident holds a place in Unionist and loyalist mythology somewhat parallel to that which the landing of guns for the Irish Volunteers by Erskine Childers in July 1914 has for nationalists.

CHAPTER 2

1 For a discussion of the APL, *see* Purdie, 1986.
2 *See* Purdie, 1983
3 *Irish Weekly*, 28 April 1962
4 Thayer, 1965, p. 204
5 Ó hÁgáin et al., 1975, p. 3
6 Bell, 1970, p. 341
7 Rooney, 1984, p. 80
8 *Ibid.*, p. 81
9 Not to be confused with the *An Phoblacht* published by

Provisional Sinn Féin after the republican split in 1970.
10 McAllister, 1977, pp. 13–15
11 Quoted in Van Voris, 1975, p. 14
12 *See* Thayer, 1965, pp. 215–16
13 Quoted in White, 1984, pp. 43–4
14 Johnson, 1964, p. 3
15 O'Brien, 1972, p. 141
16 McAllister, 1975, p. 358
17 Duffy, 'Cross Roads'. *New Nation*, July 1964, p. 11
18 Duffy, 'A Reviving Proposal . . . Should the Northern Ireland Parliament Have More Powers?', *New Ireland*, March 1963
19 Thayer, 1965, p. 216
20 White, 1984, pp. 53 *and* 56
21 McKeown, Ciaran, 1984, p. 24
22 *Ibid.*, p. 29
23 *Irish Weekly*, 12 August 1967
24 McKeown, Ciaran, 1984, pp. 30–1
25 *Irish Weekly*, 4 March 1967
26 Harkness, 1983, p. 185
27 *See* Elliott, 1973, pp. 93–4
28 Brett, 1963, p. 19
29 Nelson, 1984, pp. 46–7
30 Long, 1963, p. 19
31 The Mater Hospital was a Catholic voluntary hospital on Belfast's Crumlin Road which received no financial assistance from the Government.
32 Brett, 1978, p. 62
33 PRONI D 3026/1
34 *Ibid.*
35 *Ibid.*
36 Wright, 1973, p. 267
37 *Ibid.*, p. 268
38 Brett, 1978, p. 131
39 McAughtry, 1981
40 Gillespie, 1985, p. 11
41 *Belfast Telegraph*, 14 December 1962
42 McElroy, 1964, p. 22
43 PRONI D 3342/A/7
44 PRONI D 3342/A/2
45 Gillespie, 1985, p. 26
46 PRONI D 3342/A/2

CHAPTER 3

1 *Ulster Year Book 1963–5*
2 Birrell et al., 1971, pp. 125–6
3 Rose, Richard, 1971, p. 294
4 Whyte, 1983 *and* Brett, 1986
5 *Irish Weekly*, 14 November 1963
6 *See* Tomlinson, 1980, pp. 128–9
7 *Dungannon Observer*, 21 September 1963
8 *Ibid.*
9 *Ibid.*, 18 May 1963
10 *Ibid.*, 15 June 1963
11 *Ibid.*, 31 August 1963
12 Quoted in Van Voris, 1975, p. 50
13 Feeney, 1976, pp. 4–5
14 Quoted in Van Voris, 1975, p. 50
15 Interview, 26 August 1981
16 *Irish News*, 18 January 1964
17 Quoted in Van Voris, 1975, p. 53
18 Interview, 26 August 1981
19 CSJ *Campaign Newsletter*, no. 10, 28 December 1969
20 PRONI D 2993
21 At this time the franchise in Northern Ireland was different for Westminster, Stormont and local government elections:

a. For Westminster it was the same as in the rest of the United Kingdom, that is, all adults who had reached the age of twenty-one and whose names were on the register were entitled to vote, except that there was a qualifying period of three months' residence in Northern Ireland.

b. For Stormont it required electors to have been born in Northern Ireland or to have been resident in the United Kingdom for seven years (a provision mainly intended to exclude citizens of the Irish Republic). There were also additional votes for the occupiers of business premises in the constituency, with a value of at least £10 per annum (electors with premises in several constituencies could only use one extra vote in a constituency of their choice). Graduates of QUB resident in Northern Ireland could vote both in their constituency of residence and for the three Stormont MPs elected to represent the university. (Graduates entitled to a business vote could not use that *and* the University vote.)

c. For local government the franchise was restricted to householders and their spouses who were on the Stormont register. This excluded tenants and other adults living in only part of a house. There were additional votes for businesses, which could nominate up to six electors to use one extra vote each.

R. J. Lawrence (1965, p. 26) found that more than a quarter of the parliamentary electors had no local government vote. It should also be noted that the local government electoral boundaries were drawn up in such a way as to ensure greater representation for those paying the greatest amount in rates. This, for example, was the reason given to two Quakers, Denis Barritt and Charles Carter, for the apparently anomalous division of the wards in Derry, when they investigated allegations of discrimination (1962, pp. 121–5). It is not easy, therefore, to decide exactly how far the electoral laws discriminated against Catholics. They were not the only ones to be disqualified from the local government franchise but they were disproportionately affected by the ward boundaries which delivered into Unionist control some local authorities which might otherwise have been controlled by Nationalists. However, Unionist defences of the system have the unmistakable ring of special pleading, and there seems to be no common-sense reason to doubt that there was discrimination against Catholics and that it was deliberate.

22 Charles Brett, in a commentary on the Legal Aid and Advice Bill, noted that one of the few unanimous recommendations of the Steele Committee, which had been responsible for drawing up its main proposals, had been the provision of a special form of legal aid, without financial limit, for cases involving matters of public interest, brought before the Court of Appeal and the House of Lords. This had been ignored when the legislation was drafted; *see* Brett, 1964.

23 Boyle, Hadden and Hillyard, 1975, p. 12

24 Quoted in Van Voris, 1975, p. 53

25 Rose, Richard, 1976, p. 251

26 Greaves, 1963, p. 518

27 Interview given to Ken Pringle, January 1984, and kindly made available to the author

28 HC Deb. 736:225, 15 November 1966

29 Quoted in *The Plain Truth*, 2nd ed.

30 *Irish News*, 3 October 1964

31 Interview given to Ken Pringle, January 1984

32 *Irish Weekly*, 4 August 1962

33 *Ibid.*, 10 November 1962

34 *Civil Liberties*, January 1948

35 Connolly Association, *Our Plan to End Partition*, p. 9

36 Introduction to CDU Papers, PRONI D 3026/1

37 PRONI D 3026/3

38 PRONI D 3026/1

39 Rose, Paul, 1981, p. 178

40 PRONI D 3026/1

41 PRONI D 3026/2

42 Rose, Paul, 1981, p. 194

43 *Ibid.*, p. 180

44 *Ibid.*, pp. 197–8

45 PRONI D 3026/1

46 Government of Ireland Act, 1969

47 Quoted in Van Voris, 1975, p. 53

48 Wallace, 1967, pp. 168–9

49 Mackintosh, 1968, p. 173

50 Wallace, 1967, p. 161

51 For this debate *see* HC Deb. 733:1296, 8 August 1966

52 Wilson, 1971, p. 270

53 O'Neill, 1972, p. 83

54 Brett, 1978, pp. 134–5

55 *Irish Weekly*, 9 December 1967

56 PRONI D 3026/1

57 *Ibid.*

58 At that time Gerald Kaufman was Harold Wilson's personal press officer.

59 PRONI D 3026/2

60 *Ibid.*

CHAPTER 4

1 *Irish Weekly*, 22 September 1962

2 Johnston, 1966, p. 1

3 Johnston, 1968, p. 30

4 The Scarman Tribunal, presided over by Mr Justice (now Lord) Scarman, was an inquiry into the riots and shootings in the summer of 1969. Its report was published in April 1972.

5 Scarman Report, vol. II, p. 48

6 *See* NIHCD 70:191–4, 13 June 1968. Van Voris wrongly identifies this document as the one which was annexed to the Scarman Report. For a description of the incident referred to, which took place in Derry, *see* Chapter 5.

7 Irish Universities Press, *Northern*

256

Ireland Political Literature
(microfiche collection), fiche 42
8 *Ibid.*
9 Johnston, 1972, p. 17
10 *Ibid.*
11 Anthony Coughlan has informed
the author that this was, in fact,
the *Tuairisc* document already
referred to, and that he was its
author although he was not
present at the Maghera meeting
(letter, 12 August 1988).
12 Interview, 6 April 1986
13 NICRA, 1978, p. 20
14 Heatley, *Fortnight*, 22 March
1974, p. 11
15 Hope, 1976, p. 33
16 NICRA, 1978, p. 11
17 *Irish News*, 26 August 1968
18 *Irish Times*, 26 August 1968
19 Cameron Report, para. 35. The
Cameron Commission was a three-
man commission of inquiry,
presided over by Lord Cameron,
set up by Terence O'Neill in
January 1969 to investigate the
violence since 5 October 1968. Its
report was published in
September 1969.
20 Devlin, 1969, p. 92
21 McCann, 1974, p. 37
22 Copy of undated letter written by
Eamonn McCann and sent to
Michael Farrell before 5 October
1968. Permission to quote from
the letter kindly given by Eamonn
McCann.
23 Unless otherwise stated, the
information given here about these
events, and the quotes, are taken
from Fergus Pyle's superb report
in the *Irish Times* of 7 October
1968, or from the *Irish News*
report of the same date.
24 At the time the Fianna Fáil
government was proposing to
abolish proportional representation
for elections in the Irish Republic.

This would probably have
guaranteed Fianna Fáil a
permanent Dáil majority and
opponents saw this as a civil
liberties issue parallel to those
raised by the civil rights
movement in the north.
25 *Sunday News*, 13 October 1968
26 NIHCD 70:108–9, 16 October 1968
27 *Derry Journal*, 10 December 1968
28 *Irish News*, 7 October 1968;
Goulding proved that he was
actually in Dublin at the time.
Fred Heatley recalls that Goulding
had originally intended to take
part but that his car had broken
down.
29 NIHCD 70:1014, 16 October 1968;
in fact no members of the DHAC or
the Young Socialists were involved
in NICRA at this time, nor was the
Connolly Association, which has
never been organised in Ireland.
Craig meant the Connolly Society
of Derry, which was a purely
nominal body used by the left
republicans to get extra
representation on the organising
committee for the march. Craig
had a habit of quoting politically
inept police reports as if they were
matters of indisputable fact.
30 Riddell, 1970, p. 139
31 Mac Stíofáin, 1975, p. 108
32 *See* Stewart, James, *The Struggle
in the North*
33 NIHCD 70:1008, 15 October 1968
34 Morrissey, 1983, p. 129
35 BBC Radio 4, 'Ireland: the Spark
that Lit the Flame', presented by
Mary Holland and broadcast on
28 February 1988.
36 Wright, 1988, p. 165
37 Bruce, 1986, p. 266

CHAPTER 5
1 Nairn, 1967, p. 115

2 Robinson, 1970, pp. 217–18
3 McCafferty, Nell, 1979, p. 157
4 *Irish Militant*, April 1967
5 Quoted in Van Voris, 1975, p. 38
6 UCD P29a/158(3)
7 McGonagle was to become Northern Ireland's first ombudsman and later a member of the Irish Senate.
8 *Derry Journal*, 3 May 1968
9 *Irish Militant*, June 1968
10 Mitchel McLaughlin in the BBC Radio 4 programme, 'Ireland: the Spark that Lit the Flame', presented by Mary Holland and broadcast on 28 February 1988.
11 McCann, 1974, p. 29
12 It was on this occasion that links were first established between McCann and the Derry republican militants. He was living in London at the time and helped them to organise their campaign.
13 Workers' Research Unit, 1978, p. 16
14 *Derry Journal*, 2 February 1962
15 *Ibid.*, 23 November 1962
16 *Ibid.*, 19 May 1967
17 *Ibid.*, 19 November 1968. O'Leary was not a member of the CPNI, which had no members in Derry at this time.
18 *Ibid.*, 2 April 1968
19 *Ibid.*, 31 May 1968
20 McCann, 1974, p. 33
21 *Derry Journal*, 5 July 1968
22 McCann, 1974, pp. 34–5
23 *Ibid.*, p. 35
24 *Derry Journal*, 19 July 1968
25 *Ibid.*, 23 July 1968
26 *Ibid.*, 10 September 1968
27 *Ibid.*, 1 November 1968
28 McCann, 1974, p. 33
29 *Ibid.*
30 Curran, 1986, p. 85
31 McCann, 1974, p. 32
32 *Ibid.*
33 McClean, 1983, pp. 47–8

34 This provoked the resignation of the DCAC's first press officer, the independent liberal Unionist and department store owner, Major Campbell Austin. He could not associate himself with what was, technically, an illegal protest.
35 *Derry Journal*, 22 October 1968
36 *Ibid.*

CHAPTER 6

1 Arthur, 1974, p. 23
2 *Varsity*, 1969/70, p. 14
3 Devlin, 1969, p. 74
4 *Ibid.*
5 *New Ireland*, 1966, p. 7
6 McKeown, Ciaran, 1984, p. 20
7 *Belfast Telegraph*, 5 April 1967
8 *Irish Militant*, April 1967
9 Quoted in Van Voris, 1975, pp. 60–1
10 It is a measure of his anonymity that NICRA's official history (NICRA, 1978) published a photograph in which he was identified merely as a 'bespectacled megaphone carrier'.
11 *Impact*, Spring 1964
12 NIHCD 66:1063, 9 May 1967
13 NIHCD 67:1794, 14 November 1967
14 NIHCD 67:1796, 14 November 1967
15 *Belfast Telegraph*, 6 November 1967
16 McKeown, Ciaran, 1984, p. 50
17 Heaney, 1968, p. 522
18 Devlin, 1969, pp. 100–1
19 McKeown, Michael, 1986, p. 47
20 Cameron Report, para. 195
21 PRONI D 3297
22 *Irish Times*, 10 October 1968
23 *Irish News*, 11 October 1968
24 *See* Farrell (ed.), 1988, pp. 26–8 *and* 90–3
25 PRONI D 3297
26 *See* Farrell (ed.), 1988, pp. 124–5

27 Paul Arthur noted the conflicting accounts of the origins of the name but accepted the statement of the PD printer, John D. Murphy, that he had thought of the name when he had to put out a printed announcement (1974, p. 37). This version was supported by Bernadette Devlin in her autobiography (p. 102), and in a slightly different form by Ciaran McKeown (p. 47).

28 O'Neill, 1969, pp. 143–4

29 This account of the march is largely based on that in Egan and McCormack, 1969.

30 *Irish News*, 6 January 1969

31 Faulkner, 1978, p. 50

32 Quoted in Van Voris, 1975, p. 90

33 PRONI D 3253

34 Devlin, 1969, p. 120

35 Arthur, 1974, p. 41

36 Farrell, 1976, p. 249

37 Interview, 4 July 1987

38 Five years later there was a macabre footnote to the events in Newry. The body of Kenneth Lennon, a Newry-born Luton car worker, was found in a Surrey ditch. He had been murdered by the Provisional IRA after having been exposed as an informer. A police photograph submitted to the Cameron Commission showed him attacking police barriers in Newry, raising the possibility that he may have been acting as an *agent provocateur*; *see* Robertson, 1976, p. 18.

39 Cameron Report, para. 118

40 Quoted in Van Voris, 1975, pp. 97–8

41 Arthur, 1974, p. 47

42 Rumpf and Hepburn, 1977, p. 193

43 Quoted in Arthur, 1974, p. 119

44 *Irish Weekly*, 8 March 1969

45 PRONI D 3297

46 PRONI D 3253

47 *Ibid*.

48 A London branch and later a Dublin branch were also set up. These were composed mainly of northern exiles and concentrated on publishing information and statements on behalf of the PD.

49 PRONI D 3297

50 Comerford, 1982, p. 41n.

51 PRONI D 3297

52 Comerford, 1982, p. 74

53 *See* Milotte, 1984, pp. 189–215

54 NIHCD 70:1022, 16 October 1968

55 *Irish News*, 18 October 1968

56 The name did not signify any affiliation with what has since become known as the 'Militant Tendency'. Both the British *Militant* and the *Irish Militant* took their names from the American publication of the same name, the oldest English-language Trotskyist newspaper in the world, published in New York since 1928.

57 Lawless, 1966

58 *Irish News*, 21 May 1966

59 *Campus*, 3 May 1966

60 Breitman, 1981, p. 16

61 The name was adopted from an American Trotskyist youth movement which was prominent in student radicalism and protests against American intervention in Vietnam.

62 Baxter, et al., 1969, p. 118

63 Quoted in Van Voris, 1975, p. 61

64 *Ibid*., p. 81

65 *Ibid*.

66 Quinn, 1971, p. 18

67 'The PD of that time was strongly reminiscent of the 22 March Movement'; Levy, 1972, p. 2011.

68 Gombin, 1970, p. 420

69 He meant the *Black Dwarf*; the *Red Mole* was not published until 1970.

70 Callaghan, 1984, p. 137

71 Ali, 1972, p. 229 *and* Hayter, 1971, p. 105
72 Interview, June 1988
73 Baxter et al., 1969, p. 4
74 *Ibid.*, p. 5
75 *Ibid.*
76 *Derry Journal*, 8 November 1968
77 *Ibid.*
78 Baxter et al., 1969 p. 6
79 *Derry Journal*, 29 November 1968
80 *Irish Weekly*, 5 July 1969
81 McGuffin Papers

BIBLIOGRAPHY

BOOKS, PAMPHLETS AND ARTICLES

Ali, Tariq. *The Coming British Revolution*, London, Jonathan Cape, 1972

Arthur, Paul. *The People's Democracy 1968–73*, Belfast, Blackstaff Press, 1974

   Government and Politics of Northern Ireland, Harlow, Longman, 1980

Arthur, Paul and Keith Jeffrey. *Northern Ireland Since 1968*, Oxford, Basil Blackwell, 1988

Bailie, Robin. 'Finding a Basis for North–South Co-operation', *New Ireland* (March 1964), pp. 15–19

Barritt, Denis P. and Charles F. Carter. *The Northern Ireland Problem: A Study in Group Relations*, Oxford, Oxford University Press, 1962

Baxter, Liam, Bernadette Devlin, Michael Farrell, Eamonn McCann and Cyril Toman. 'People's Democracy: a Discussion on Strategy', *New Left Review*, no. 55 (May–June 1969), pp. 3–19

Belfrage, Sally. *The Crack: A Belfast Year*, London, Grafton Books, 1988

Bell, Geoffrey. *The Protestants of Ulster*, London, Pluto, 1976

Bell, J. Bowyer. *The Secret Army: A History of the IRA 1916–1970*, London, Anthony Blond, 1970

Bew, Paul, Peter Gibbon and Henry Patterson. *The State in Northern Ireland 1921–72: Political Forces and Social Classes*, Manchester, Manchester University Press, 1979

Bew, Paul and Henry Patterson. *The British State and the Ulster Crisis*, London, Verso, 1985

Bing, Geoffrey. *John Bull's Other Ireland*, London, *Tribune*, 1950

Birrell, W. D., P. A. R. Hillyard, A. Murie and D. J. D. Roche. *Housing in Northern Ireland*, University Working Paper 12, London, Centre for Environmental Studies, 1971

Bleakley, David. *Young Ulster and Religion in the Sixties*, Belfast, a group of Church of Ireland members, 1964

Boulton, David. *The UVF 1966–73: An Anatomy of a Loyalist Rebellion*, Dublin, Torc, 1973

Boyd, Andrew. *Holy War in Belfast*, Tralee, Anvil Books, 1969

Boyle, Kevin, Tom Hadden and Paddy Hillyard. *Law and State: The Case of Northern Ireland*, London, Martin Robertson, 1975

Breitman, George. *How a Minority Can Change Society: The Real Potential of the Afro-American Struggle*, 2nd ed., New York, Pathfinder Press, 1981

Brett, C. E. B. 'Northern Ireland Labour: the Last Election and the Next', *New Ireland*, vol. 1, no. 1 (March 1963), pp. 19–21

'The Legal Aid and Advice Bill (Northern Ireland)', *Northern Ireland Legal Quarterly*, vol. 5, no. 3 (September 1964), pp. 352–70

Long Shadows Cast Before: Nine Lives in Ulster, 1625–1977, Edinburgh, John Bartholomew, 1978

Housing in a Divided Community, Dublin, Institute of Public Administration in association with the Institute of Irish Studies, Queen's University Belfast, 1986

Bruce, Steve. *God Save Ulster: The Religion and Politics of Paisleyism*, Oxford, Clarendon Press, 1986

Buckland, Patrick. *The Factory of Grievances: Devolved Government in Northern Ireland 1921–39*, Dublin, Gill and Macmillan, 1978

A History of Northern Ireland, Dublin, Gill and Macmillan, 1981

Callaghan, John. *British Trotskyism: Theory and Practice*, Oxford, Basil Blackwell, 1984

Calvert, H. 'Human Rights in Northern Ireland', *Review of the International Commission of Jurists* (2 June 1969), pp. 14–19

Campaign for Social Justice in Northern Ireland. *Londonderry. One Man, No Vote*, Dungannon, Campaign for Social Justice in Northern Ireland, 1965

Northern Ireland. The Plain Truth, 2nd ed., Dungannon, Campaign for Social Justice in Northern Ireland, 1969

Why Justice Cannot Be Done, Dungannon, Campaign for Social Justice in Northern Ireland, n.d.

Northern Ireland. The Plain Truth, Dungannon, Campaign for Social Justice in Northern Ireland, n.d.

Legal Aid to Oppose Discrimination – Not Likely!, Dungannon, Campaign for Social Justice in Northern Ireland, n.d.

Communist Party of Northern Ireland. *Ireland's Path to Socialism*, Belfast, Communist Party of Northern Ireland, 1962

Connolly Association. *Our Plan to End Partition*, London, Connolly Association, n.d.

What is the Connolly Association? Constitution and Explanation, London, Connolly Association, n.d.

Coogan, Tim Pat. *The IRA*, London, Fontana, 1970

Craig, F. W. S. *Minor Parties at British Elections*, London, Macmillan, 1975

Craig, William. *Irish Times*, interview with Olivia O'Leary, 9 and 10 December 1980

Curran, Frank. *Derry: Countdown to Disaster*, Dublin, Gill and Macmillan, 1986

De Paor, Liam. *Divided Ulster*, Harmondsworth, Penguin, 1970

Devlin, Bernadette. *The Price of My Soul*, London, André Deutsch, 1969

Devlin, Paddy. 'The "*Over The Bridge* Controversy"', *Linen Hall Review*, vol. 2, no. 3 (1985), pp. 4–6

Duffy, John C. 'A Reviving Proposal. The Powers That Be. Should the Northern Ireland Parliament Have More Powers?', *New Ireland*, vol. 1, no. 1 (March 1963), pp. 25–35

  'Cross-Roads', *New Nation*, vol. 1, no. 6 (July 1964), pp. 11–14

Edwards, J. LL. J. 'Special Powers in Northern Ireland', *Criminal Law Review* (1956), pp. 7–18

Edwards, Owen Dudley. *The Sins of Our Fathers: Roots of Conflict in Northern Ireland*, Dublin, Gill and Macmillan, 1970

Egan, Bowes and Vincent McCormack. *Burntollet*, London, LRS Publishers, 1969

Elliott, Sydney. *Northern Ireland Parliamentary Election Results 1921–1972*, Chichester, Political Reference Publications, 1973

Farrell, Michael. *The Struggle in the North*, London, Pluto, 1969

  Northern Ireland: The Orange State, London, Pluto, 1976

Farrell, Michael (ed.). *Twenty Years On*, Dingle, Brandon, 1988

Faulkner, Brian. *Memoirs of a Statesmen*, London, Weidenfield and Nicholson, 1978

Feeney, Vincent E. 'The Civil Rights Movement in Northern Ireland', *Éire-Ireland*, vol. 9, no. 2 (1974), pp. 30–40

  'Westminster and the Early Civil Rights Struggle in Northern Ireland', *Éire-Ireland*, vol. 11, no. 4 (1976), pp. 3–13

Gallagher, Frank. *The Indivisible Island: The History of the Partition of Ireland*, London, Gollancz, 1957

Gallagher, Tom. 'Religion, Reaction and Revolt in Northern Ireland: the Impact of Paisleyism in Ulster', *Journal of Church and State*, vol. 23, no. 3 (1981), pp. 423–44

Gardiner, Louis. *Resurgence of the Majority*, n.p., Monday Club Ulster Committee, n.d.

Gillespie, Gordon. *Albert H. McElroy: The Radical Minister 1915–1975. A Memorial Volume*, Dunmurry, Albert McElroy Memorial Fund, 1985

Gombin, Richard. 'The Ideology and Practice of Contestation Seen Through Recent Events in France', *Government and Opposition*, vol. 5, no. 4 (Autumn 1970), pp. 410–29

Goulding, Cathal. 'The Present Course of the IRA', *New Left Review*, no. 64 (November–December 1970), pp. 50–61

Greaves, C. Desmond. 'A Programme For Ireland', *Labour Monthly*, vol. 14, no. 11 (November 1963), pp. 518–23

Reminiscences of the Connolly Association, London, Connolly Association, 1978

Harbinson, John F. *The Ulster Unionist Party, 1882–1973: Its Development and Organisation*, Belfast, Blackstaff Press, 1973

Harkness, David. *Northern Ireland Since 1920*, Dublin, Helicon, 1983

Hastings, Max. *Ulster 1969: The Fight for Civil Rights in Northern Ireland*, London, Gollancz, 1970

Hayter, Teresa. *Hayter of the Bourgeoisie*, London, Sidgwick and Jackson, 1971

Healy, Cahir. *The Mutilation of a Nation: The Story of the Partition of Ireland*, Derry, *Derry Journal*, 1945

Heaney, Seamus. 'Old Derry's Walls', *Listener*, vol. 80, no. 2065 (24 October 1968)

Heatley, Fred. 'Civil Rights in the Six Counties', *Celtic League Annual* (1969), pp. 77–80

'The Beginning, 1964 – February 1968', *Fortnight* (22 March 1974), pp. 10–11

'The Early Marches', *Fortnight* (5 April 1974), pp. 9–11

'The PD and Burntollet', *Fortnight* (26 April 1974), pp. 8–9

'The NICRA Split', *Fortnight* (10 May 1974), pp. 13–14

Hewitt, Christopher. 'Catholic Grievances, Catholic Nationalism and Violence During the Civil Rights Period: a Reconsideration', *British Journal of Sociology*, vol. 32, no. 3 (September 1981), pp. 362–80

Hillan, J. J. *A Real Constitution: A Suggested Framework for Nationalist Government*, Belfast, National Democratic Group of Queen's University, n.d.

Johnson, Hilary. 'Convention Time – Tyrone Style', *New Nation*, vol. 1, no. 6 (July 1964), pp. 3–4

Johnston, Roy. '1916 and After', *Torch*, vol. 2, no. 2 (1966)

'The Lessons of the Irish Question', *Catalyst*, vol. 2, no. 1 (Winter 1968), pp. 28–30

'Roy Johnston's Apologia', *Hibernia* (31 March 1972), pp. 16–17

Kane, J. J. 'Civil Rights in Northern Ireland', *Review of Politics*, vol. 33 (1970), pp. 54–77

Keenan, Joe. *An Argument on Behalf of the Catholics of Northern Ireland*, Belfast, Athol Books, 1987

Kelleher, Terry. 'The Civil Rights Takeover', *Hibernia* (3 March 1972), pp. 16–17

Kelly, James. 'Whither Northern Nationalism', *Christus Rex*, vol. 13, part 4 (1959), pp. 269–83

Orders for the Captain, Dublin, Author, 1971

Lane, Jim. 'On the IRA Belfast Brigade Area', Cork, Cork Branch Irish
    Communist Organisation, 1970, photocopy
Lavin, Deborah. 'Politics in Ulster, 1968', *The World Today*, vol. 24, no.
    12 (1968), pp. 530–6
Lawless, Gery. Introduction to Sean Murray, *The Irish Revolt: 1916 and
    After*, London, Irish Workers' Group, 1966
    'Where the Hillside Men Have Sown – 40 Years of the IRA', *Workers
    Republic*, no. 17 (Spring 1967), pp. 26–40
Lawrence, R. J. *The Government of Northern Ireland: Public Finance and
    Public Services 1921–1964*, Oxford, Clarendon Press, 1965
Levy, Jean-François. 'La People's Democracy', *Les Temps Modernes*, vol.
    20, no. 311 (1972), pp. 2009–47
Long, S. E. *Belfast County Grand Orange Lodge Centenary Official History
    1863–1963*, Newtownabbey, Universal Publishing Company, 1963
Long, S. Ernest and W. Martin Smyth (eds.). *The Twelfth*, Belfast,
    County Grand Orange Lodge, 1968
Lysaght, D. R. O'Connor. *The Making of Northern Ireland (and the Basis of
    its Undoing)*, Dublin, Citizens' Committee, 1970
McAllister, Ian. 'Political Opposition in Northern Ireland: the National
    Democratic Party, 1965–1970', *Economic and Social Review*, vol. 6
    (1975), pp. 353–66
    *The Northern Ireland Social Democratic and Labour Party: Political
    Opposition in a Divided Society*, London, Macmillan, 1977
McAteer, Eddie. *Irish Action*, Belfast, Athol Books, 1979
McAughtry, Sam. 'The Fall of the NILP', *Irish Times*, 19 May 1981
    'Northern Ireland Labour Lives On', *Irish Times*, 19 May 1981
MacBride, Sean. 'The "Special Powers" Act of Northern Ireland', *Quis
    Custodiet*, vol. 24 (1969), pp. 106–12
McCafferty, Nell. 'The 1950s and 1960s in Derry', in *Irish Life*, edited by
    Sharon Gmelch, Dublin, O'Brien Press, 1979
McCafferty, Niall. 'The New Spirit in Northern Ireland', *Focus*, vol. 9,
    no. 2 (February 1966), pp. 30–1
McCann, Eamonn. *War and an Irish Town*, Harmondsworth, Penguin,
    1974
    '1968: an Activist Recalls', *Workers' Research Bulletin*, no. 4 (1978), pp.
    3–4
McClean, Raymond. *The Road to Bloody Sunday*. Swords, Ward River
    Press, 1983
McElroy, Albert. 'Liberalism and the Ulster Past', *New Ireland* (March
    1964), pp. 21–3

McGurk, Tom. 'Civil Rights and the Decline of the Nationalists', *Irish Times*, 11 September 1980

McKeown, Ciaran. *The Passion of Peace*, Belfast, Blackstaff Press, 1984

McKeown, Michael. *The Greening of a Nationalist*, Lucan, Marlough Press, 1986

Mackintosh, J. P. *The Devolution of Power, Local Democracy, Regionalism and Nationalism*, Harmondsworth, Penguin, 1968

Mac Stíofáin, Seán. *Memoirs of a Revolutionary*, Edinburgh, Gordon Cremonisi, 1975

Marrinan, Patrick. *Paisley: Man of Wrath*, Tralee, Anvil Books, 1973

Martens, C. 'Report on Civil and Social Rights in Northern Ireland', *Human Rights Journal*, vol. 2, part 3 (1969), pp. 507–45

Mills, William Stratton and Robin Bailie. *The Manipulators: The Revolutionary Strategy for an Explosion in Ulster*, Belfast, Ulster Unionist Party, 1969

Milotte, Mike. *Communism in Modern Ireland: The Pursuit of the Workers' Republic Since 1916*, Dublin/New York, Gill and Macmillan/Holmes and Meier, 1984

Moloney, Ed and Andy Pollak. *Paisley*, Swords, Poolbeg Press, 1986

Moody, T. W. *The Ulster Question 1603–1973*, Dublin and Cork, Mercier Press, 1974

Morgan, Austen. 'Discrimination and the Fair Employment Agency in Northern Ireland', privately circulated paper, 1980

Morrissey, Hazel. 'Betty Sinclair: a Woman's Fight for Socialism, 1910–1981', *Saothar 9* (1983, Journal of the Irish Labour History Society), pp. 121–32

Nairn, Ian. *Britain's Changing Towns*. London, British Broadcasting Corporation, 1967

National Council for Civil Liberties. *Report of a Commission of Inquiry Appointed to Examine the Purpose and Effect of the Civil Authorities (Special Powers) Acts (Northern Ireland) 1922 and 1935*, London, National Council for Civil Liberties, 1936

Nelson, Sarah. *Ulster's Uncertain Defenders: Protestant Political, Paramilitary and Community Groups and the Northern Ireland Conflict*, Belfast, Appletree Press, 1984

Northern Ireland Civil Rights Association. *We Shall Overcome . . . The History of the Struggle for Civil Rights in Northern Ireland 1968–78*, Belfast, Northern Ireland Civil Rights Association, 1978

Northern Ireland Labour Party. *Signposts to the New Ulster*, Belfast, Northern Ireland Labour Party, 1964

O'Brien, Conor Cruise. *States of Ireland*, London, Hutchinson, 1972

Ó Cuinneagháin, Míceál. *Monaghan: County of Intrigue*, Cavan, Abbey Printers, 1978

Ó hÁgáin, Deasun, et al. *Liam McMillen: Separatist, Socialist, Republican*, Dublin, Repsol, 1975

Oliver, John A. *Working at Stormont*, Dublin, Institute of Public Administration, 1978

O'Neill, Terence. *Ulster at the Crossroads*, London, Faber and Faber, 1969
    The Autobiography of Terence O'Neill, London, Hart-Davis, 1972

Paisley, Ian R. K., Peter D. Robinson and John D. Taylor. *Ulster: The Facts*, Belfast, Crown Publications, 1982

Patterson, Henry. *Class Consciousness and Sectarianism*, Belfast, Blackstaff Press, 1980

Policy Studies Institute. *Equality and Inequality in Northern Ireland: Part I, Employment and Unemployment; Part II, The Work Place; Part III, Perceptions and Views*, London, Policy Studies Institute, 1987

Power, Paul F. 'Civil Protest in Northern Ireland', *Journal of Peace Research*, vol. 9, no. 3 (1972), pp. 223–36

Provisional IRA. *Freedom Struggle by the Provisional IRA*, n.p., Provisional IRA, 1972

Purdie, Bob. 'The Friends of Ireland: British Labour and Irish Nationalism 1945–49', in *Contemporary Irish Studies*, edited by Tom Gallagher and James O'Connell, Manchester, Manchester University Press, 1983
    'The Irish Anti-Partition League, South Armagh and the Abstentionist Tactic 1945–58', *Irish Political Studies*, I (1986), pp. 67–77
    'Was the Civil Rights Movement a Republican/Communist Conspiracy?', *Irish Political Studies*, 3 (1988), pp. 33–41

Quinn, J. 'No Surrender. History of the Early PD', *Anarchy*, 2nd series, vol. I, no. 6 (1971), pp. 14–21

Rea, Desmond. 'Goodbye to 1690?' *Focus* (January 1966) pp. 7–9

Republican Education Department. *Ireland Today*, n.p., Republican Education Department, 1969
    Ways and Means, n.p., Republican Education Department, 1970

Richmond, David. 'Discrimination: the Politics', *Fortnight*, no. 257 (December 1987), pp. 15–16

Riddell, Patrick. *Fire Over Ulster*, London, Hamish Hamilton, 1970

Roberts, David A. 'The Orange Order in Ireland: a Religious Institution?', *British Journal of Sociology*, vol. 22 (1971), pp. 269–82

Robertson, Geoff. *Reluctant Judas: The Life and Death of the Special Branch Informer Kenneth Lennon*, London, Temple Smith, 1976

Robinson, Alan. 'Londonderry, Northern Ireland: a Border Study', *Scottish Geographical Magazine*, vol. 86 (1970), pp. 209–21

Rooney, Eddie. 'From Republican Movement to Workers' Party: an Ideological Analysis', in *Culture and Ideology in Ireland*, edited by Chris Curtin, Mary Kelly and Liam O'Dowd, Galway, Galway University Press, 1984

Rose, Paul. *Backbencher's Dilemma*, London, Frederick Muller, 1981

Rose, Richard. *Governing Without Consensus: An Irish Perspective*, London, Faber and Faber, 1971

  'On the Priorities of Citizenship in the Deep South and Northern Ireland', *Journal of Politics.*, vol. 38, no. 2 (1976), pp. 247–91

Rumpf, E. and A. C. Hepburn. *Nationalism and Socialism in Twentieth-Century Ireland*, Liverpool, Liverpool University Press, 1977

Shea, Patrick. *Voices and the Sound of Drums: An Irish Autobiography*, Belfast, Blackstaff Press, 1981

Shearman, Hugh. 'Conflict in Northern Ireland', *Year Book of World Affairs* (1982), pp. 182–96

Smyth, Clifford. *Ulster Assailed*, n.p., 1971

  Ian Paisley: Voice of Protestant Ulster, Edinburgh, Scottish Academy Press, 1987

'Special Powers Extraordinary. The Court of Appeal in Forde v. McEldowney', *Northern Ireland Legal Quarterly*, vol. 20 (1969), pp. 1–18

Stetler, Russell. *The Battle of Bogside*, London and Sydney, Sheed and Ward, 1970

  Northern Ireland: From Civil Rights to Armed Struggle, Somerville, Massachusetts, New England Free Press, 1970

Stewart, A. T. Q. *The Narrow Ground: Aspects of Ulster 1609–1969*, London, Faber and Faber, 1977

Stewart, James. *The Struggle in the North*, edited by Michael Fox, 2nd ed., Belfast, Communist Party of Ireland, n.d.

Sunday Times Insight team. *Ulster*, Harmondsworth, Penguin, 1972

Targett, G. W. *Bernadette: The Story of Bernadette Devlin*, London, Hodder and Stoughton, 1975

Thayer, George. *The British Political Fringe: A Profile*, London, Anthony Blond, 1965

Tomlinson, Mike. 'Housing, the State and the Politics of Segregation', in *Northern Ireland: Between Civil Rights and Civil War*, edited by Liam O'Dowd, Bill Rolston and Mike Tomlinson, London, CSE Books, 1980

Van Voris, W. H. *Violence in Ulster: An Oral Documentary*, Amherst, University of Massachusetts Press, 1975

Wallace, Martin. 'Home Rule in Northern Ireland – Anomalies of Devolution', *Northern Ireland Legal Quarterly*, vol. 18, no. 1 (June 1967), pp. 159–76

'What of the North?', *Éire–Ireland*, vol. 4, no. 3 (1969), pp. 130–4

Drums and Guns: Revolution in Ulster, London, Geoffrey Chapman, 1970

White, Barry. *John Hume: Statesman of the Troubles*, Belfast, Blackstaff Press, 1984

Whyte, John. 'How much Discrimination was there Under the Unionist Regime, 1921–68?', in *Contemporary Irish Studies*, edited by Tom Gallagher and James O'Connell, Manchester, Manchester University Press, 1983

Wilson, Harold. *The Labour Government 1964–70: A Personal Record*, London, Weidenfeld and Nicolson/Michael Joseph, 1971

Winchester, Simon. *In Holy Terror: Reporting the Ulster Troubles*, London, Faber and Faber, 1974

Workers' Research Unit. *Derry Ten Years After*, Bulletin 4, Belfast, Workers' Research Unit, 1978

Wright, Frank. 'Protestant Ideology and Politics in Ulster', *European Journal of Sociology*, vol. 14 (1973), pp. 213–80

Northern Ireland: A Comparative Analysis, Dublin, Gill and Macmillan, 1988

GOVERNMENT PUBLICATIONS

Aunger, E. A. *Industrial and Occupational Profile of the Two Sections of the Community in Northern Ireland*, Belfast, Fair Employment Agency, 1978

Cameron Report. *Disturbances in Northern Ireland: Report of the Commission Appointed by the Governor of Northern Ireland*, Belfast, HMSO, Cmd 532, 1969

Government of Ireland Act. The Constitution of Northern Ireland being the Government of Ireland Act 1920 as amended to 31st December 1968, Belfast, HMSO, 1969

Scarman Report. *Violence and Civil Disturbances in Northern Ireland in 1969: Report of Tribunal of Inquiry*, Belfast, HMSO, Cmd 566, 1972

Shearman, Hugh. *Northern Ireland*, Belfast, HMSO, 1968

Standing Advisory Committee on Human Rights. *Religious and Political Discrimination and Equality of Opportunity in Northern Ireland: Report on Fair Employment*, London, HMSO, Cmnd 237, 1987

Ulster Year Book. Belfast, HMSO (1962–70)

DISSERTATIONS AND THESES

Comerford, Jeremy. 'The Dynamics of a Radical Movement in Northern Ireland Politics – the People's Democracy', M.Sc. dissertation, University of Strathclyde, 1982

Graham, J. A. V. 'The Consensus-forming Strategy of the NILP', M.Sc. thesis, Queen's University Belfast, 1982

Hope, Ann. 'From Civil Rights to Guerrilla War: the Northern Ireland Civil Rights Association's Struggle for Democracy 1969–1972', Labour Studies Diploma thesis, Ruskin College, Oxford, 1976

Purdie, Bob. 'The Irish Anti-Partition League 1945–49: Irish Nationalism and British Labour', M.Sc. dissertation, University of Strathclyde, 1980

Robinson, Alan. 'A Social Geography of the City of Londonderry', MA thesis, Queen's University Belfast, 1967

Thompson, James. 'The Civil Rights Movement in Northern Ireland', MA thesis, Queen's University Belfast, 1973

DOCUMENTS

Kevin Boyle Papers, PRONI D 3297

Campaign for Democracy in Ulster Papers: PRONI D 3026

Campaign for Social Justice in Northern Ireland Papers: PRONI D 2993

Frank Gogarty Papers: PRONI D 3253

Irish Universities Press. *Northern Ireland Political Literature* (microfiche collection)

John Johnston Papers: PRONI D 3219

Albert McElroy Papers: PRONI D 3342

John McGuffin Papers: Belfast Central Library

Northern Ireland Civil Rights Association Papers: Linen Hall Library, Belfast

INTERVIEWS

Anthony Barnett: Oxford, 30 June 1988

Michael Farrell: Dublin, 4 July 1987

Brian Gregory and Conor Gilligan: Belfast, 26 August 1981

Fred Heatley: Belfast, 6 April 1986

Eamonn McCann: Derry, 25 June 1987

Kevin McNamara: interview given to Ken Pringle, London, January 1984

NEWSPAPERS AND PERIODICALS

Anarchy, British anarchist journal

Billy Liar, People's Democracy newspaper

Campus, University College Dublin student newspaper
Catalyst, journal of the 1320 (Scottish Nationalist) Club
Civil Liberties, National Council for Civil Liberties
Defamator, Queen's University Belfast Labour Group paper
Derry Journal
Detonator, Queen's University Belfast Revolutionary Socialist Students'
    Federation paper
Focus, ecumenical Protestant magazine
Fortnight, an independent review for Northern Ireland
Gown, Queen's University Belfast student paper
Hibernia
Impact, Queen's University Belfast left review
Impartial Reporter
Irish Independent
Irish Militant
Irish News
Irish Press
Irish Times
Irish Weekly
Listener
Londonderry Sentinel
New Ireland, journal of the Queen's University Belfast New Ireland Society
New Nation, journal of National Unity
PD Voice
Qubist, Queen's University Belfast student magazine
Sunday News
Sunday Press
This Week, Dublin news magazine
Torch, republican theoretical journal
Tuairisc, Wolfe Tone Societies journal
Varsity, yearbook of the Queen's University Conservative and Unionist
    Association
Workers' Republic (formerly *An Solas*), Irish Workers' Group theoretical
    journal, London

WORKS OF REFERENCE

Deutsch, Richard and Vivien Magowan (eds). *Northern Ireland 1968–73: A Chronology of Events*, vol. 1 (1968–71), Belfast, Blackstaff Press, 1973
Flackes, W.D. *Northern Ireland: A Political Directory 1968–79*, Dublin, Gill and Macmillan, 1980

INDEX

Action Committee for a Peaceful Protest (QUB), 208
Agnew, Kevin, 135
Aiken, Frank, 53
Ali, Tariq, 235–6
Allen, Cecil, 67–8
Alliance Party, 58
Amalgamated Engineering Union, 167
Amalgamated Union of Engineering Workers Technical and Administrative Staffs Section (AUEW TASS), 133, 152
An Phoblacht, 47–8
An tÓglach, 125–7
anarchists, 233
Ancient Order of Hibernians (AOH), 17–18, 43, 50–1, 135
Anderson, Albert, 162, 187
Andrews, J.L.O., 86
Anglo-Irish Free Trade Agreement (1965), 124, 127
Anti-Internment League, 200
Anti-Partition League, 38–9, 40, 41
Anti-Partition of Ireland League (GB), 105–6
Antrim Unionist Association, 35
Apprentice Boys of Derry, 139–40, 148
Ardill, Austin, 29
Ardoyne Tenants' Association, 133
Armour, Rev. J.B., 75
Arthur, Paul, 198, 216–17, 219–20
Asmal, Kadar, 132

B Specials, 101, 215, 222
Bacon, Alice, 103, 113, 116
Bailie, Robin, 16, 66, 237
Banks, Ken, 152
Barnett, Anthony, 237
Barr, Ivan, 241
Beattie, Jack, 39–40
Behal, Richard, 45, 46
Belfast
  sectarian violence, 10, 26–7, 31–2, 197
  Labour vote, 10
  ecumenism, 21

tricolour demonstration, 30
  Wolfe Tone Society, 130–1
  Connolly commemoration, 131
  population, 162
  barricades, 236
Belfast and District Trades Union Council, 79–80, 133
Belfast City Council, 61–2
  elections, 60, 62
  'Sunday swings' scandal, 72
Belfast Corporation, 27
Belfast County Grand Orange Lodge, 10, 22, 23–4, 66
Belfast Telegraph, 46, 63, 88–9, 140, 149–50
Bell, Geoffrey, 209
Bell, J. Bowyer, 46
Bennett, Jack, 122, 130, 132
Bing, Geoffrey, 40
Blaney, Neil, 220
Bleakley, David, 18, 69, 72, 168
Bloody Sunday, Derry, 4, 247
Blythe, Ernest, 54, 76
Boal, Desmond, 13
Boland, Kevin, 220
Bose, Mr Justice, 121
Boyd, Tom, 69, 70
Boyd, William, 62, 72
Boyle, Kevin, 99, 200, 209
  and PD, 201, 207, 233–4
  and Newry march, 218
  NICRA executive, 223
  on Farrell, 233, 234
Boyle, Louis, 201, 203
Braddock, Bessie, 227–8
Bradley, J. Conor, 15–16
Breaky, Rev. J.C., 19
Breitman, George, 231–2, 237
Brennan, John, 60
Brett, Charles, 65, 84
  and NILP, 68–9, 72, 73, 117–18, 168
Brick, Ian, 204, 208
British Army, 3, 4, 197
Brockway, Lord Fenner, 105, 109
Brookeborough, Lord, 9–13, 37, 65, 73, 79, 107
Brooks, Edwin, 115

275

Republican Clubs, 76, 131, 133
  banned, 134, 202
  and protest marches, 137, 138,
    139
  and NICRA, 155
Republican Congress, 109
Republican Education Department,
  128–30
Republican Labour Party (RLP), 39,
  77, 94, 133, 230–2
  and Fitt, 59–60, 61, 62, 227
  and protest marches, 135
Republican News, 122
republicans, 76
  electoral tactics, 41–2
  commemorations, 42–4, 185
  violent tradition, 44–7
  and Nationalist Party, 48–9
  share of vote, 62–3
  and civil rights movement, 127–30
  and NICRA, 135, 148–52
  in Derry, 171–3
Revolutionary Socialist Students'
  Federation (RSSF), 211–12, 225,
  233
Richardson, Eddie, 79
Richmond, David, 250
Riddell, Patrick, 149
Ripon, Bishop of, 21, 133
Robinson, Alan, 160–1
Rose, Paul, 71, 108–9, 110, 111
Rose, Richard, 84, 102, 223
Round Table, 15, 16, 65
Rowan, Peter, 201, 206
Royal Belfast Academical Institution,
  209
Royal Ulster Constabulary (RUC), 28,
  228
  and Derry march, 3, 140–9, 155,
    192
  and Paisleyite march, 26
  opposed to sectarianism, 26
  and Belfast riots, 30–1
  flags and emblems, 41, 44
  and IRA, 46–7
  religious divisions, 101
  and NICRA, 134
  and Coalisland–Dungannon march,
    135–8
  reports, 154

and nationalist commemorations,
  185
and student demonstrations, 204,
  205–6, 208
and PD demonstrations, 210–11,
  213–15, 217–18
call to disarm, 222
Catholic distrust of, 247
Royalist Society, The Honourable the
  (QUB), 224
Ryan, John, 140, 143

Saor Uladh, 228
Scarman Report, 124
Scots-Irish Association of
  Philadelphia, 35
Sean McCaughey Club, Belfast, 46
sectarianism, 238
  violence, 26–8, 31–2, 212
  flags and emblems, 28–31
  increasing, 31–2, 246
  elections, 65
  and NILP, 65–70, 72–3
  and unemployment protests, 79
Sex Discrimination Order (1976), 249
Shankill Defence Association, 131
Sharkey, John, 166
Shearman, Hugh, 83
Shepherd, James, 132–3
Sheridan, Anthony, 99
Signposts to the New Ulster (NILP), 69
Silent Valley reservoir, 32
Simpson, Dr Robert, 22
Simpson, Vivian, 11–12, 69, 168
Sinclair, Betty, 80, 136, 140
  opposed to demonstrations, 135,
    139, 185, 244
  Derry march, 141–2
  and NICRA, 152–4
Sinn Féin, 41–2, 43, 122
Smyth, W. Martin, 21
Smythe, Tony, 132–3
Social Democratic and Labour Party
  (SDLP), 52, 60, 62, 201
socialism
  in Northern Ireland, 39, 58, 65, 66,
    152, 228–30, 232
Socialist Labour League, 228, 232
Socialist Republican Party, 39, 227
Spanish Civil War, 70, 109

284

and labour movement, 80
and housing, 86, 174, 175–7
possible coalition against, 102
and NICRA, 133
Derry university question, 165
attitude to Derry, 179, 195–6
HQ picketed, 210
and PD, 232, 236–7
Unionist Trade Unionist Association, 204
United Ireland Association, 105–6
United Irishman, 45
United Irishmen commemoration, 41
United States; *see also* civil rights movement (USA)
Irish-American lobby, 38, 40
Universal Declaration of Human Rights, 196
University College Dublin, 204
University for Derry Action Committee, 5, 165, 189

Vatican II, 19, 24
Vick, Dr Arthur, 203, 225

Wallace, Martin, 113, 114
Ward, Margaret, 209
Warnock, Edmond, 12
Westminster, 11, 43, 103, 245; *see also* Campaign for Democracy in Ulster (CDU) *and* elections
subsidies for NI, 14
Labour government and NI, 38, 62, 248
Unionist representation in, 38, 40, 103–4
Friends of Ireland, 39–40
support for civil rights, 40, 69–71
National Unity contests election, 57
NDP contests election, 59–60
Fitt in, 63–4
and Ulster Liberals, 77–8

powers over Northern Ireland, 107, 112–18
Section 75 debated, 114–16
MPs on Derry march, 140, 146
reports, 248
What the Papers Say (CSJ), 96, 98
White, John, 172, 183
Why Justice Cannot Be Done (CSJ), 96–7
Whyte, John, 84
Willcock, Janet, 169–70, 182, 185
Wilson, Harold, 62, 73, 116, 117–18, 195, 248
and CSJ, 100, 104–5
and CDU, 118–19
Wilson, Paddy, 62
Wilson family, 182
Wilson Plan, 34
Wilton, Claude, 78, 169, 170, 189, 219
Wolfe Tone commemorations, 30, 43, 44
Wolfe Tone Societies, 122, 123–4, 130, 132, 133, 149
protest marches, 135
and NICRA, 151, 155
Wolseley, Raymond, 166
Woods, Fergus, 219
Workers' Republic, 228
Working Committee on Civil Rights in Northern Ireland (QUB), 199–200
Wright, Frank, 67, 72, 156–7
Wylie, Rev. John, 208

Young Socialist Alliance (YSA), 232, 237, 240
Young Socialists, 81, 110, 131, 228, 232, 239
protest marches, 137, 139, 141, 146, 148, 153
Young Unionists, 13, 133

OTHER TITLES

from

BLACKSTAFF PRESS

DESPATCHES FROM BELFAST

DAVID MCKITTRICK

The events of 1985 to 1989 – the signing of the Anglo-Irish agreement, Unionist attempts to wreck it, police clashes with extreme loyalists, the increased ferocity of the IRA's campaign, the Enniskillen bombing – are now seen by many as a significant watershed in Northern Ireland politics.

From the pages of the *Independent* and other papers, *Despatches from Belfast* presents the best of David McKittrick's courageous and vivid reports during that time – providing an invaluable insight into a crucial period of recent history.

'. . . discerning and balanced writing . . . essential reading for anyone with the remotest interest in journalism'
Birmingham Daily News

'succinct and penetrating . . . he reminds us of events and victims most of us have shamefully forgotten'
Irish News

'. . . a prose style which is economical, lucid and free of the ambiguity and cliché which characterise much coverage of the north. Overlay it all with a hint of black humour and you have the McKittrick combination . . . splendid reportage.'
Fortnight

234 × 153mm; 232pp; illus; 0 85640 427 6; pb

£8.95

NORTHERN IRELAND

A POLITICAL DIRECTORY 1968–88

W. D. FLACKES
SYDNEY ELLIOTT

First published in 1980, *Northern Ireland: A Political Directory* has established itself as the foremost reference book in its field. This third edition, completely revised and updated, covers in detail the twenty years since the onset of the current troubles.

With an Introduction and Chronology of Events, Alphabetical Dictionary of people, parties, organisations and key places, and sections on Election Results, Systems of Government in Northern Ireland and the Security System, this is an indispensable guide for anyone with a serious interest in Irish politics.

'No better man to compile a political directory of Northern Ireland . . . impeccably precise in defining political positions of all colours and degrees of stubbornness.'
Sunday Independent

'Immensely useful work by one of the foremost authorities on Northern Ireland and the politics of the region.'
Cork Examiner

198 × 129mm; 448pp; 0 85640 418 7; pb
£9.95

KINGS IN CONFLICT

THE REVOLUTIONARY WAR IN IRELAND AND ITS AFTERMATH 1689–1750
edited by
W. A. MAGUIRE

The tempestuous events of the late seventeenth century – at Derry, Enniskillen, the Boyne, Aughrim, Limerick – and their consequences have had a fundamental and lasting impact on Irish history and politics. Exploited as powerful and emotive symbols of triumph and disaster by successive generations of Irish people, they have become difficult to appreciate as historical events in their own right.

Marking the tercentenary of the battle of the Boyne, *Kings in Conflict* is an innovative collection of recent work by scholars of the period, studying the dramatic conflicts of the time in a wider European context – examining the role of France's Louis XIV in what was effectively a 'war of three kings' rather than the 'war of two kings' of popular mythology. Unravelling the tangle of personal, religious, political and economic motives for William's intervention in English and Irish affairs, this is a timely reassessment of a crucial watershed in Irish and European history.

245 × 182mm; 236pp; illus (b & w and colour); 0 85640 435 7; hb
£14.95

THE BOYNE WATER

THE BATTLE OF THE BOYNE 1690

PETER BERRESFORD ELLIS

In the year 1690 Ireland, still suffering from the effects of Cromwell's colonisation, found itself the pivot of a wider European crisis, with the battle eventually fought at the River Boyne proving decisive of both international and Irish issues. Peter Berresford Ellis's masterly account of the battle and of its causes and consequences makes it plain why, after almost three hundred years, the Boyne remains one of the most potent symbols in Irish politics.

'It throws new light on that encounter and on the men who fought on either side on that scorching July day . . . Well told, the account is enlivened by vivid eye-witness descriptions of the battle and its aftermath.'
Evening Herald

'an admirably impartial account'
Sunday Telegraph

'Although this is a history, it has the readability of a well-written suspense novel, without losing any of the complexity of life.'
Irish Democrat

'Thoroughly researched, competently put together and fluently written. It can be recommended without reserve.'
British Book News

First paperback edition

198 × 129mm; 176pp; illus; 0 85640 419 5; pb
£5.95

ORDERING BLACKSTAFF BOOKS

All Blackstaff Press books are available through
bookshops. In the case of difficulty, however, orders
can be made directly to the publisher. Indicate clearly
the title and number of copies required and send
order with your name and address to:

CASH SALES

**Blackstaff Press Limited
3 Galway Park
Dundonald
Belfast BT16 0AN
Northern Ireland**

Please enclose a remittance to the value of the cover
price plus: £1.00 for the first book plus 60p per copy
for each additional book ordered to cover postage and
packing. Payment should be made in sterling by UK
personal cheque, postal order, sterling draft or international money order, made payable to
Blackstaff Press Limited.

Applicable only in the UK and Republic of Ireland
Full catalogue available on request